Deliciously FoxTrot

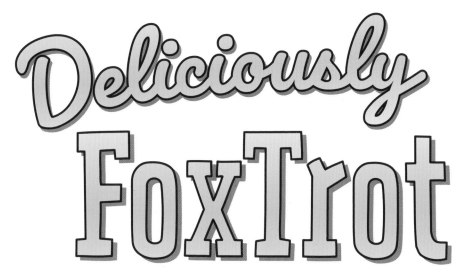

Other FoxTrot Books by Bill Amend

FoxTrot
Pass the Loot
Black Bart Says Draw
Eight Yards, Down and Out
Bury My Heart at Fun-Fun Mountain
Say Hello to Cactus Flats
May the Force Be with Us, Please
Take Us to Your Mall
The Return of the Lone Iguana
At Least This Place Sells T-shirts
Come Closer, Roger, There's a Mosquito on Your Nose
Welcome to Jasorassic Park
I'm Flying, Jack . . . I Mean, Roger
Think iFruity
Death by Field Trip
Encyclopedias Brown and White
His Code Name Was The Fox
Your Momma Thinks Square Roots Are Vegetables
Who's Up for Some Bonding?
Am I a Mutant or What!
Orlando Bloom Has Ruined Everything
My Hot Dog Went Out, Can I Have Another?
How Come I'm Always Luigi?
Houston, You Have a Problem
And When She Opened the Closet, All the Clothes Were Polyester
Math, Science, and Unix Underpants
FoxTrot Sundaes
Jasotron: 2012
AAAA! A FoxTrot Kids Collection
Some Clever Title
Mother Is Coming

Anthologies

FoxTrot: The Works
FoxTrot en masse
Enormously FoxTrot
Wildly FoxTrot
FoxTrot Beyond a Doubt
Camp FoxTrot
Assorted FoxTrot
FoxTrot: Assembled with Care
FoxTrotius Maximus
Jam-Packed FoxTrot
Wrapped-Up FoxTrot
The Best of FoxTrot

A Comic Collection by Bill Amend

Andrews McMeel
PUBLISHING®

Not That Bad

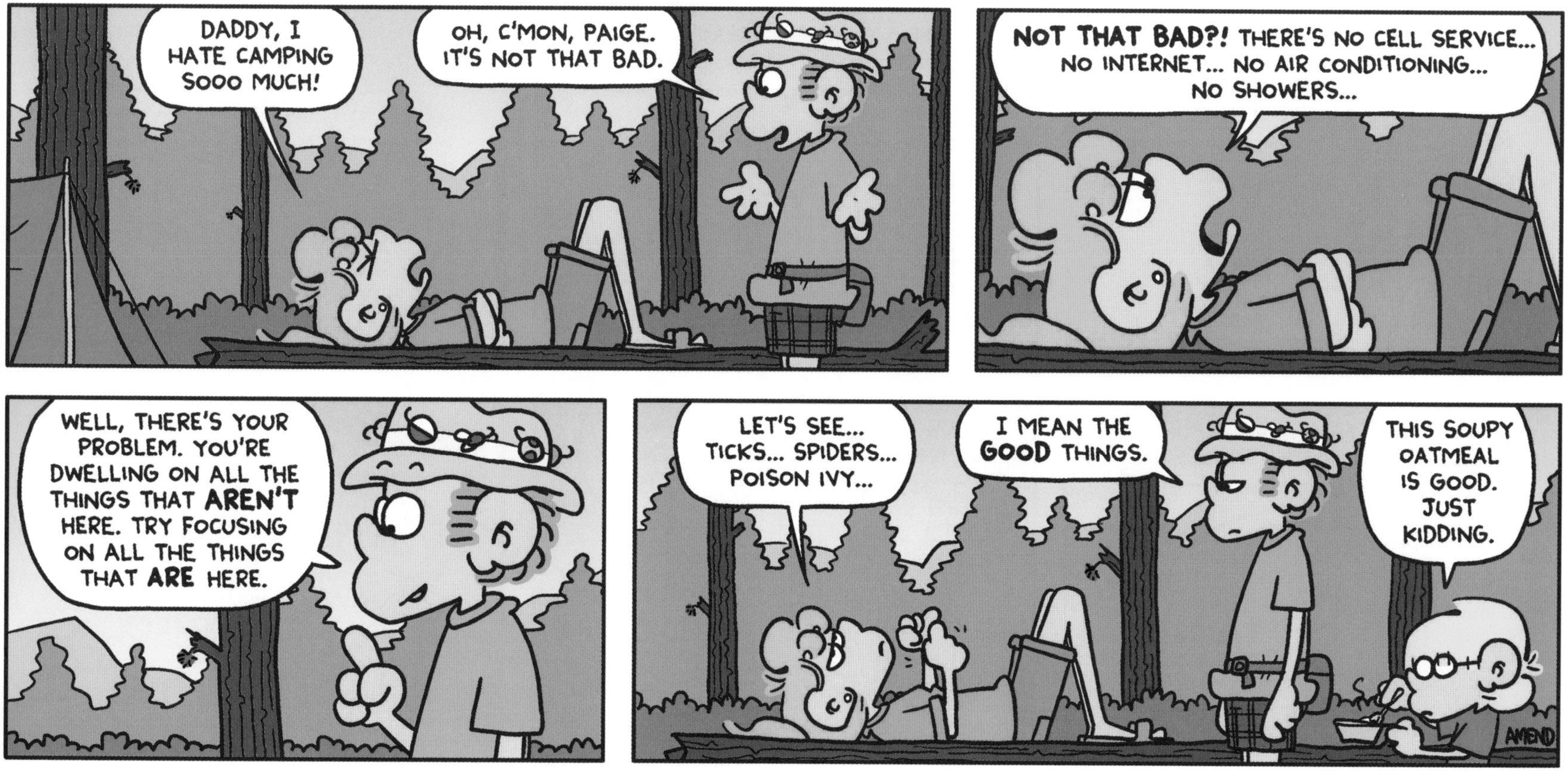
DADDY, I HATE CAMPING SOOO MUCH!
OH, C'MON, PAIGE. IT'S NOT THAT BAD.
NOT THAT BAD?! THERE'S NO CELL SERVICE... NO INTERNET... NO AIR CONDITIONING... NO SHOWERS...
WELL, THERE'S YOUR PROBLEM. YOU'RE DWELLING ON ALL THE THINGS THAT AREN'T HERE. TRY FOCUSING ON ALL THE THINGS THAT ARE HERE.
LET'S SEE... TICKS... SPIDERS... POISON IVY...
I MEAN THE GOOD THINGS.
THIS SOUPY OATMEAL IS GOOD. JUST KIDDING.
AMEND

Writing Supplies

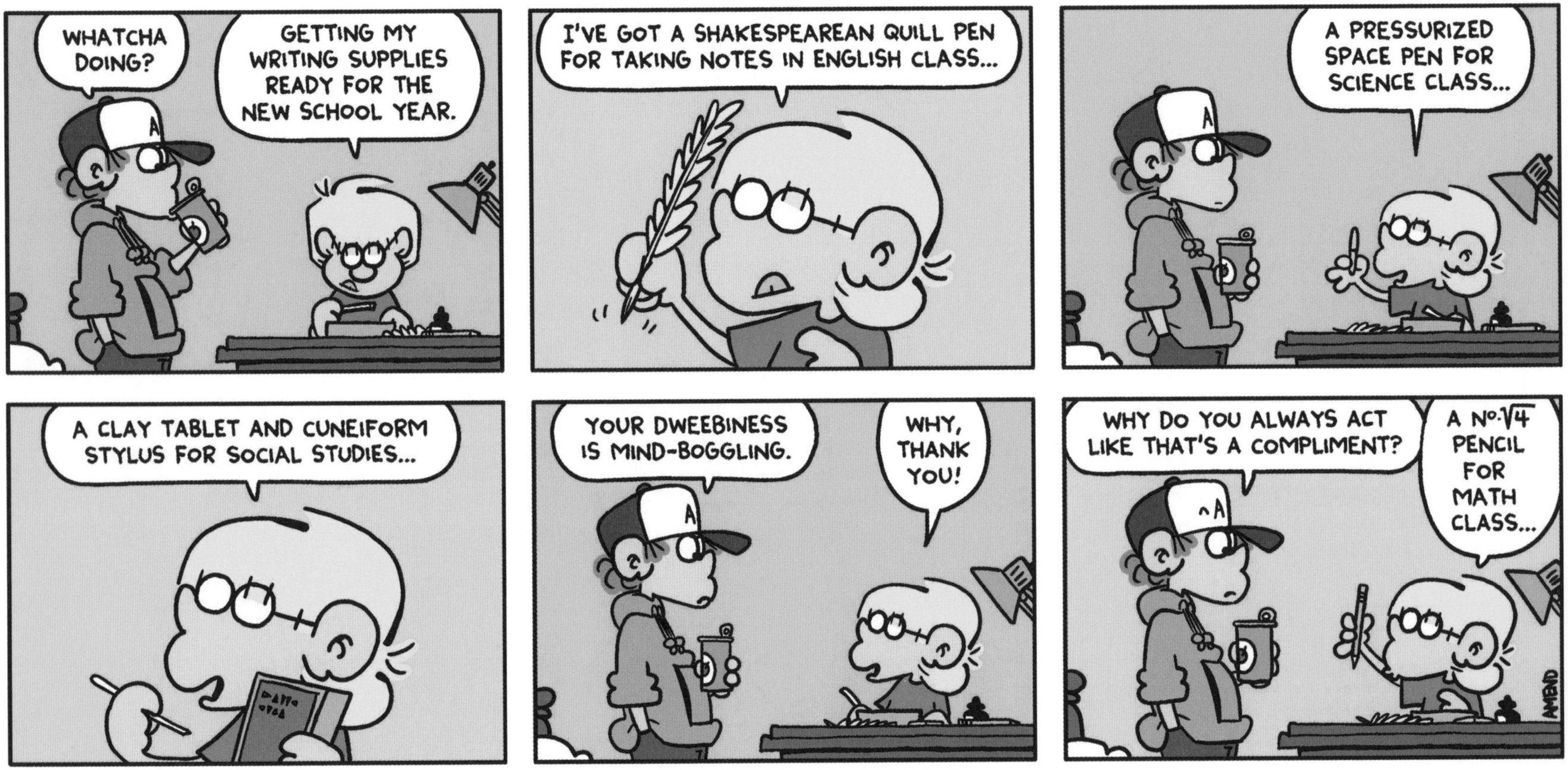

WHATCHA DOING?
GETTING MY WRITING SUPPLIES READY FOR THE NEW SCHOOL YEAR.
I'VE GOT A SHAKESPEAREAN QUILL PEN FOR TAKING NOTES IN ENGLISH CLASS...
A PRESSURIZED SPACE PEN FOR SCIENCE CLASS...
A CLAY TABLET AND CUNEIFORM STYLUS FOR SOCIAL STUDIES...
YOUR DWEEBINESS IS MIND-BOGGLING.
WHY, THANK YOU!
A Nº √4 PENCIL FOR MATH CLASS...
WHY DO YOU ALWAYS ACT LIKE THAT'S A COMPLIMENT?
AMEND

Head Protection

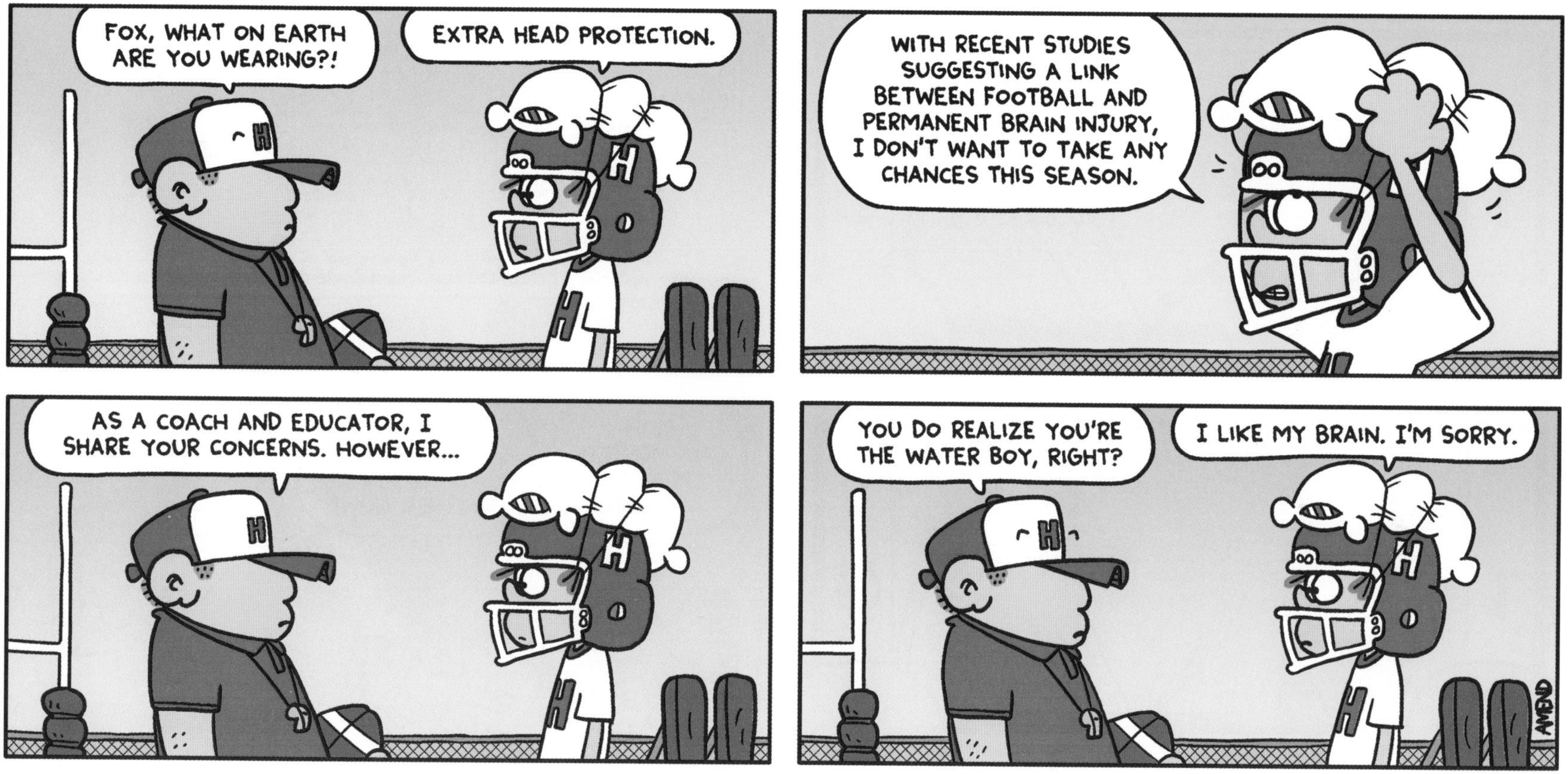
FOX, WHAT ON EARTH ARE YOU WEARING?!
EXTRA HEAD PROTECTION.
WITH RECENT STUDIES SUGGESTING A LINK BETWEEN FOOTBALL AND PERMANENT BRAIN INJURY, I DON'T WANT TO TAKE ANY CHANCES THIS SEASON.
AS A COACH AND EDUCATOR, I SHARE YOUR CONCERNS. HOWEVER...
YOU DO REALIZE YOU'RE THE WATER BOY, RIGHT?
I LIKE MY BRAIN. I'M SORRY.
AMEND

Sib-Away

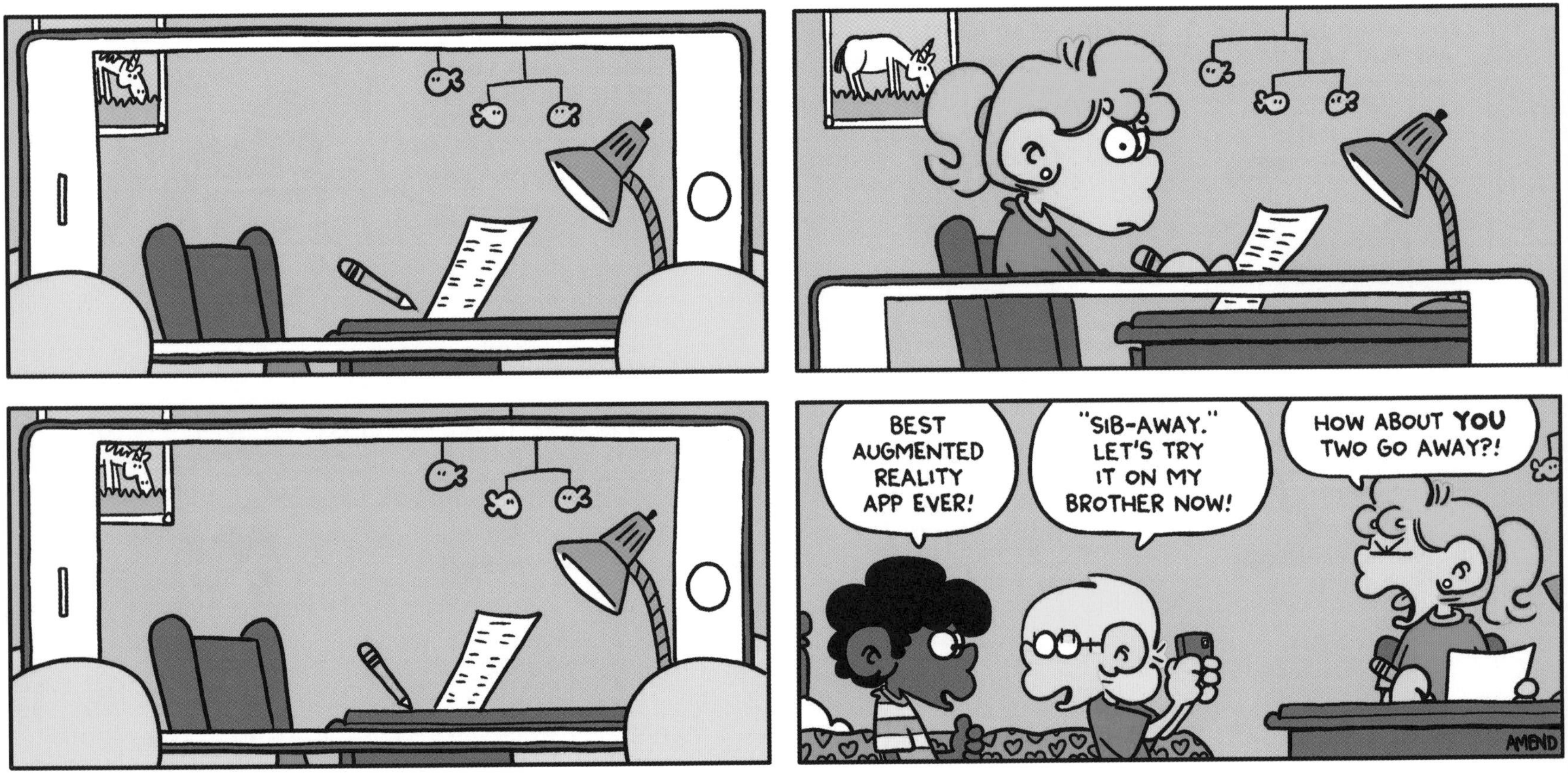
BEST AUGMENTED REALITY APP EVER!
"SIB-AWAY." LET'S TRY IT ON MY BROTHER NOW!
HOW ABOUT YOU TWO GO AWAY?!
AMEND

Finishing His Run

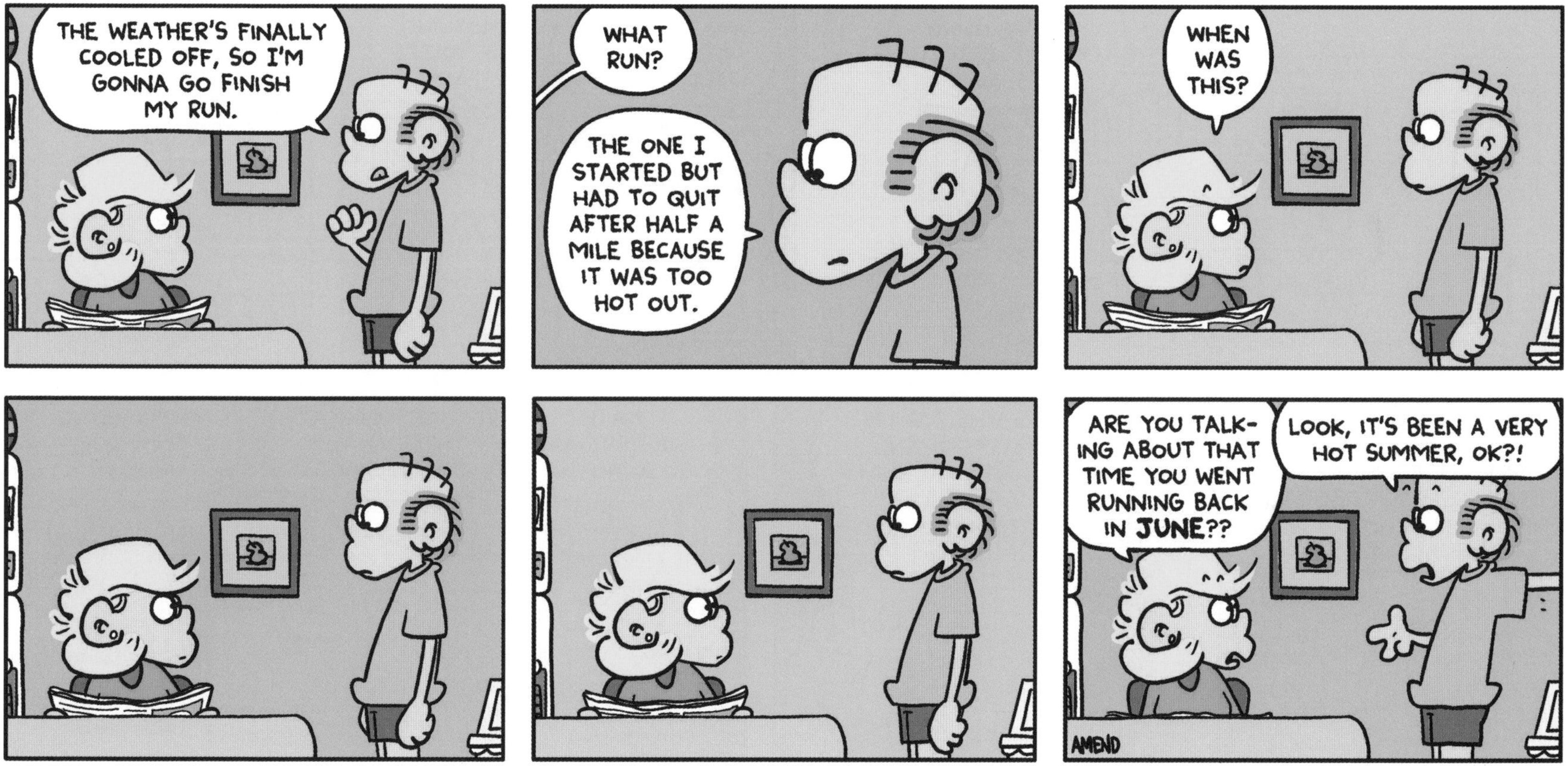

THE WEATHER'S FINALLY COOLED OFF, SO I'M GONNA GO FINISH MY RUN.
WHAT RUN?
THE ONE I STARTED BUT HAD TO QUIT AFTER HALF A MILE BECAUSE IT WAS TOO HOT OUT.
WHEN WAS THIS?
ARE YOU TALKING ABOUT THAT TIME YOU WENT RUNNING BACK IN **JUNE**??
LOOK, IT'S BEEN A VERY HOT SUMMER, OK?!
AMEND

Math Hipsters

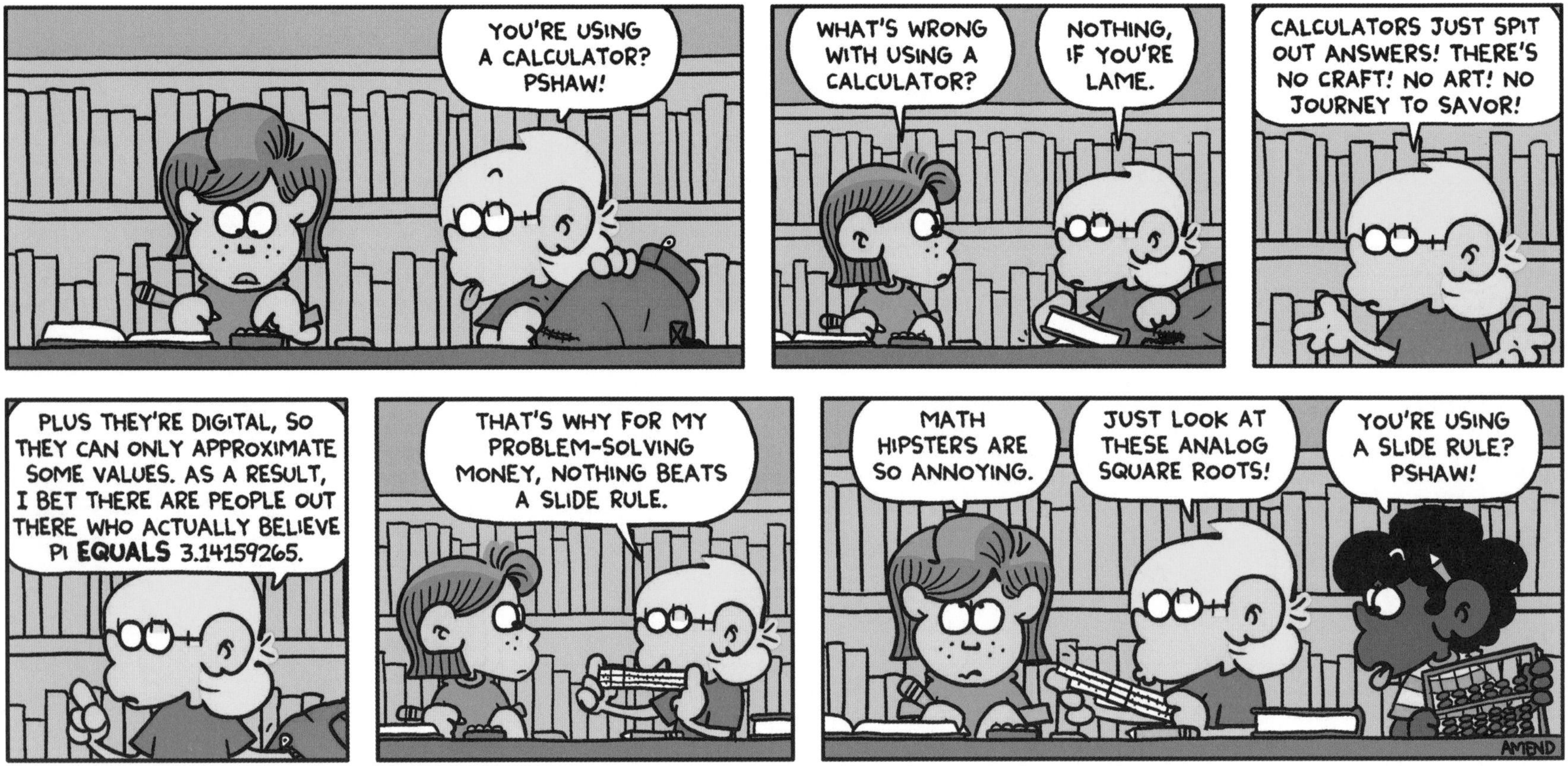
YOU'RE USING A CALCULATOR? PSHAW!
WHAT'S WRONG WITH USING A CALCULATOR?
NOTHING, IF YOU'RE LAME.
CALCULATORS JUST SPIT OUT ANSWERS! THERE'S NO CRAFT! NO ART! NO JOURNEY TO SAVOR!
PLUS THEY'RE DIGITAL, SO THEY CAN ONLY APPROXIMATE SOME VALUES. AS A RESULT, I BET THERE ARE PEOPLE OUT THERE WHO ACTUALLY BELIEVE PI **EQUALS** 3.14159265.
THAT'S WHY FOR MY PROBLEM-SOLVING MONEY, NOTHING BEATS A SLIDE RULE.
MATH HIPSTERS ARE SO ANNOYING.
JUST LOOK AT THESE ANALOG SQUARE ROOTS!
YOU'RE USING A SLIDE RULE? PSHAW!
AMEND

P.I.Z.Z.A.

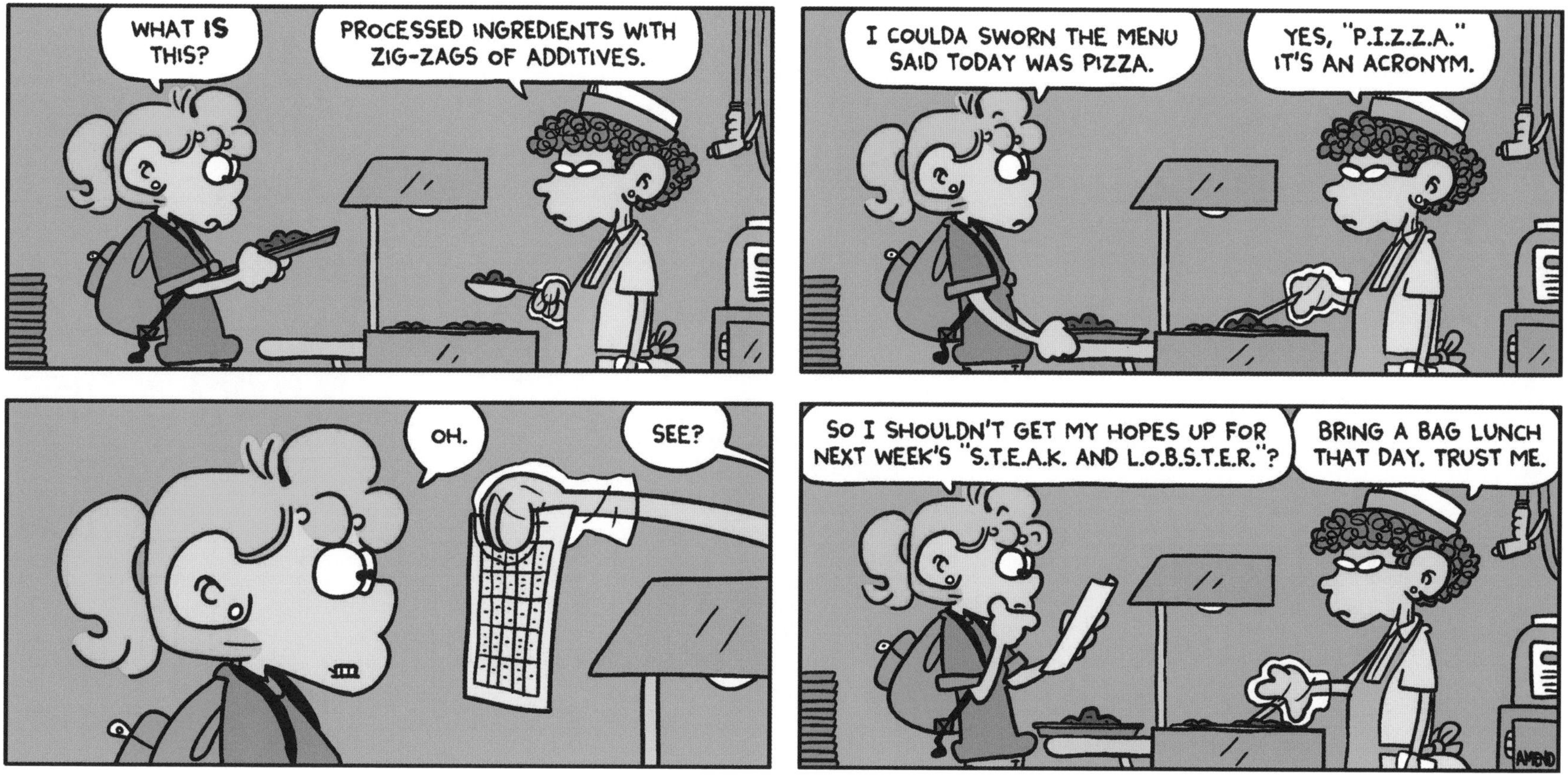
WHAT **IS** THIS?
PROCESSED INGREDIENTS WITH ZIG-ZAGS OF ADDITIVES.
I COULDA SWORN THE MENU SAID TODAY WAS PIZZA.
YES, "P.I.Z.Z.A." IT'S AN ACRONYM.
OH.
SEE?
SO I SHOULDN'T GET MY HOPES UP FOR NEXT WEEK'S "S.T.E.A.K. AND L.O.B.S.T.E.R."?
BRING A BAG LUNCH THAT DAY. TRUST ME.
AMEND

RC Raker

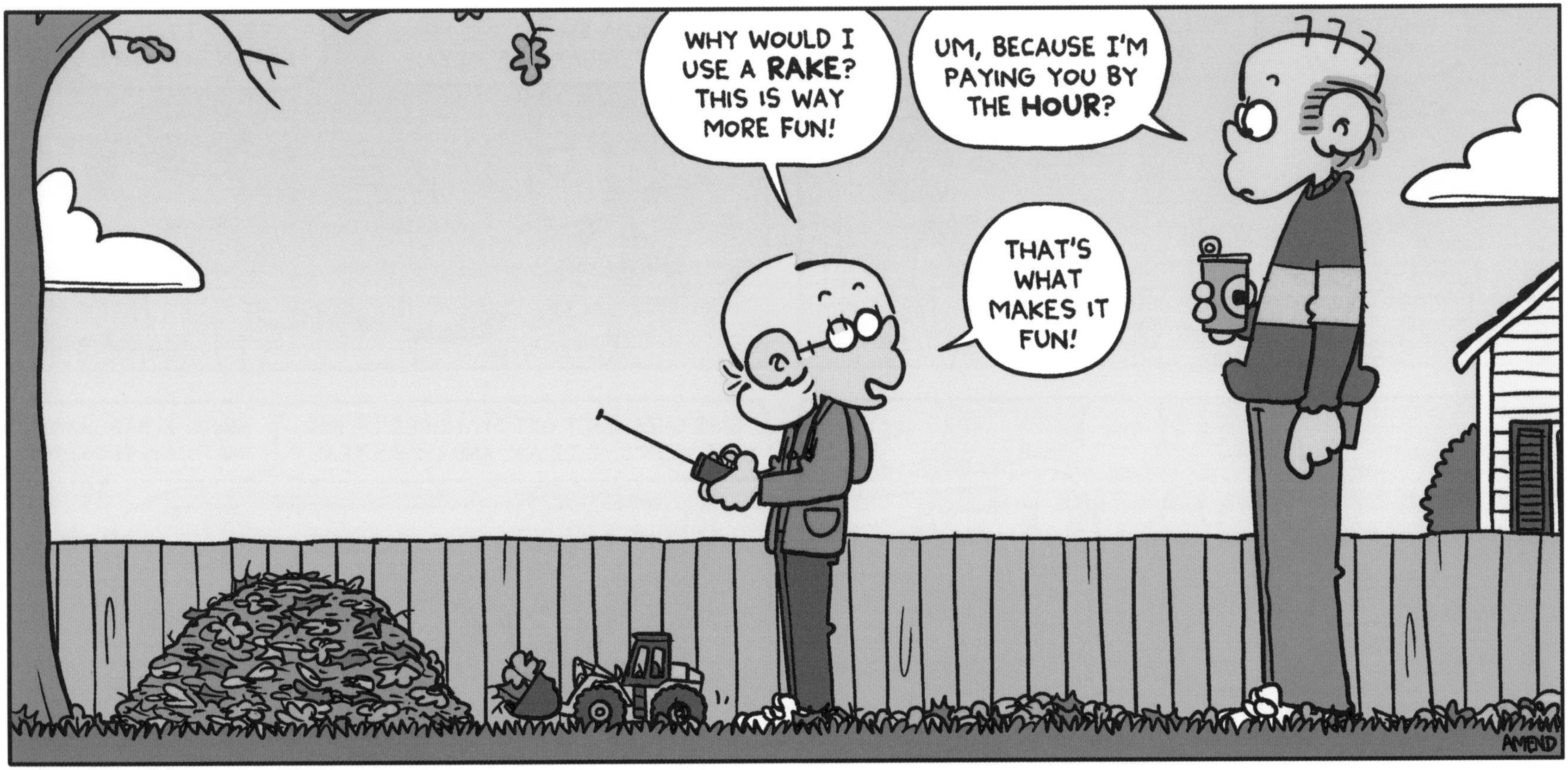
WHY WOULD I USE A **RAKE**? THIS IS WAY MORE FUN!
UM, BECAUSE I'M PAYING YOU BY THE **HOUR**?
THAT'S WHAT MAKES IT FUN!
AMEND

Studying Time

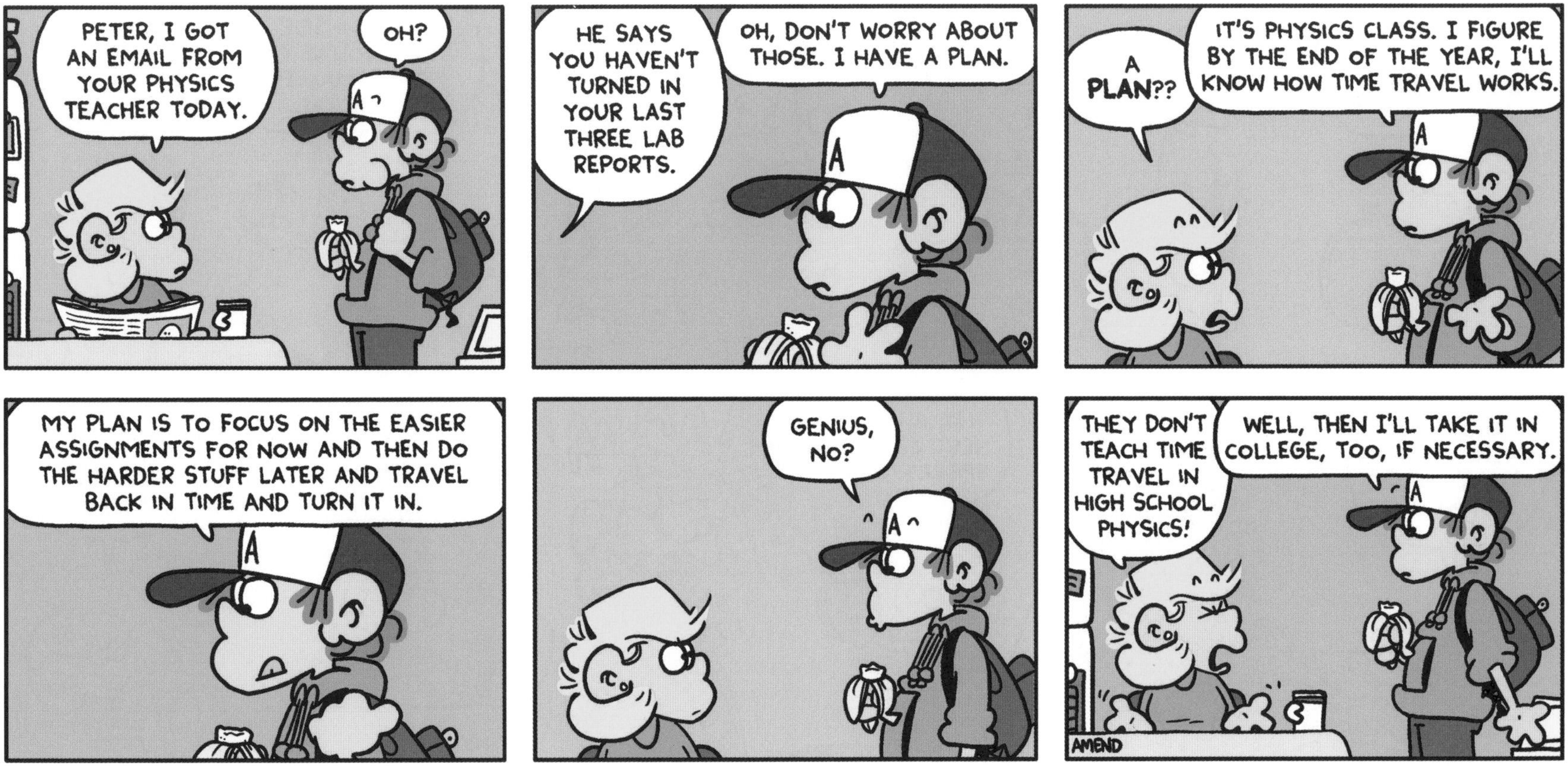
PETER, I GOT AN EMAIL FROM YOUR PHYSICS TEACHER TODAY.
OH?
HE SAYS YOU HAVEN'T TURNED IN YOUR LAST THREE LAB REPORTS.
OH, DON'T WORRY ABOUT THOSE. I HAVE A PLAN.
A **PLAN**??
IT'S PHYSICS CLASS. I FIGURE BY THE END OF THE YEAR, I'LL KNOW HOW TIME TRAVEL WORKS.
MY PLAN IS TO FOCUS ON THE EASIER ASSIGNMENTS FOR NOW AND THEN DO THE HARDER STUFF LATER AND TRAVEL BACK IN TIME AND TURN IT IN.
GENIUS, NO?
THEY DON'T TEACH TIME TRAVEL IN HIGH SCHOOL PHYSICS!
WELL, THEN I'LL TAKE IT IN COLLEGE, TOO, IF NECESSARY.
AMEND

Nested Pumpkins

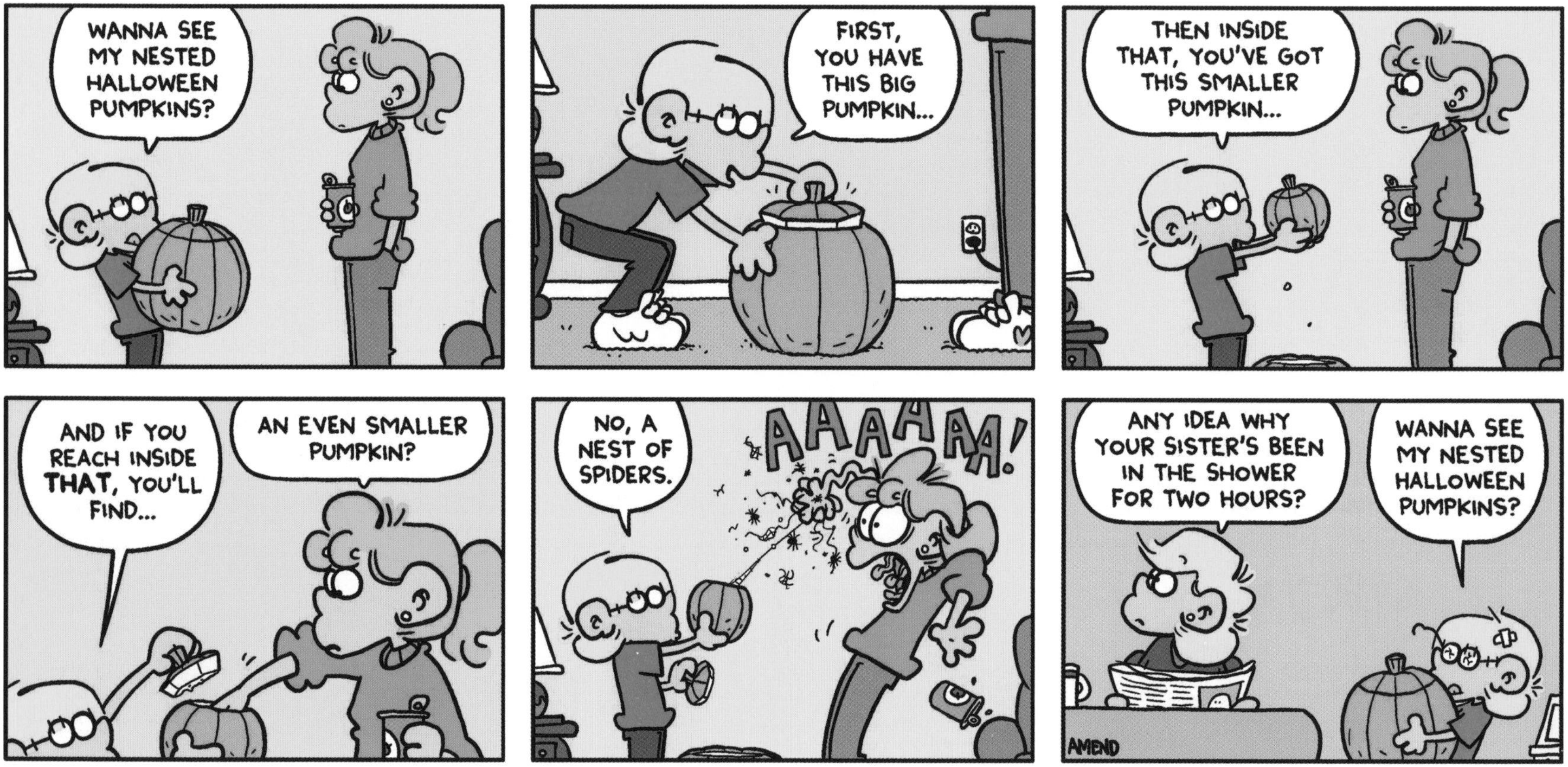
WANNA SEE MY NESTED HALLOWEEN PUMPKINS?
FIRST, YOU HAVE THIS BIG PUMPKIN...
THEN INSIDE THAT, YOU'VE GOT THIS SMALLER PUMPKIN...
AND IF YOU REACH INSIDE THAT, YOU'LL FIND...
AN EVEN SMALLER PUMPKIN?
NO, A NEST OF SPIDERS.
AAAAAA!
ANY IDEA WHY YOUR SISTER'S BEEN IN THE SHOWER FOR TWO HOURS?
WANNA SEE MY NESTED HALLOWEEN PUMPKINS?
AMEND

Brains

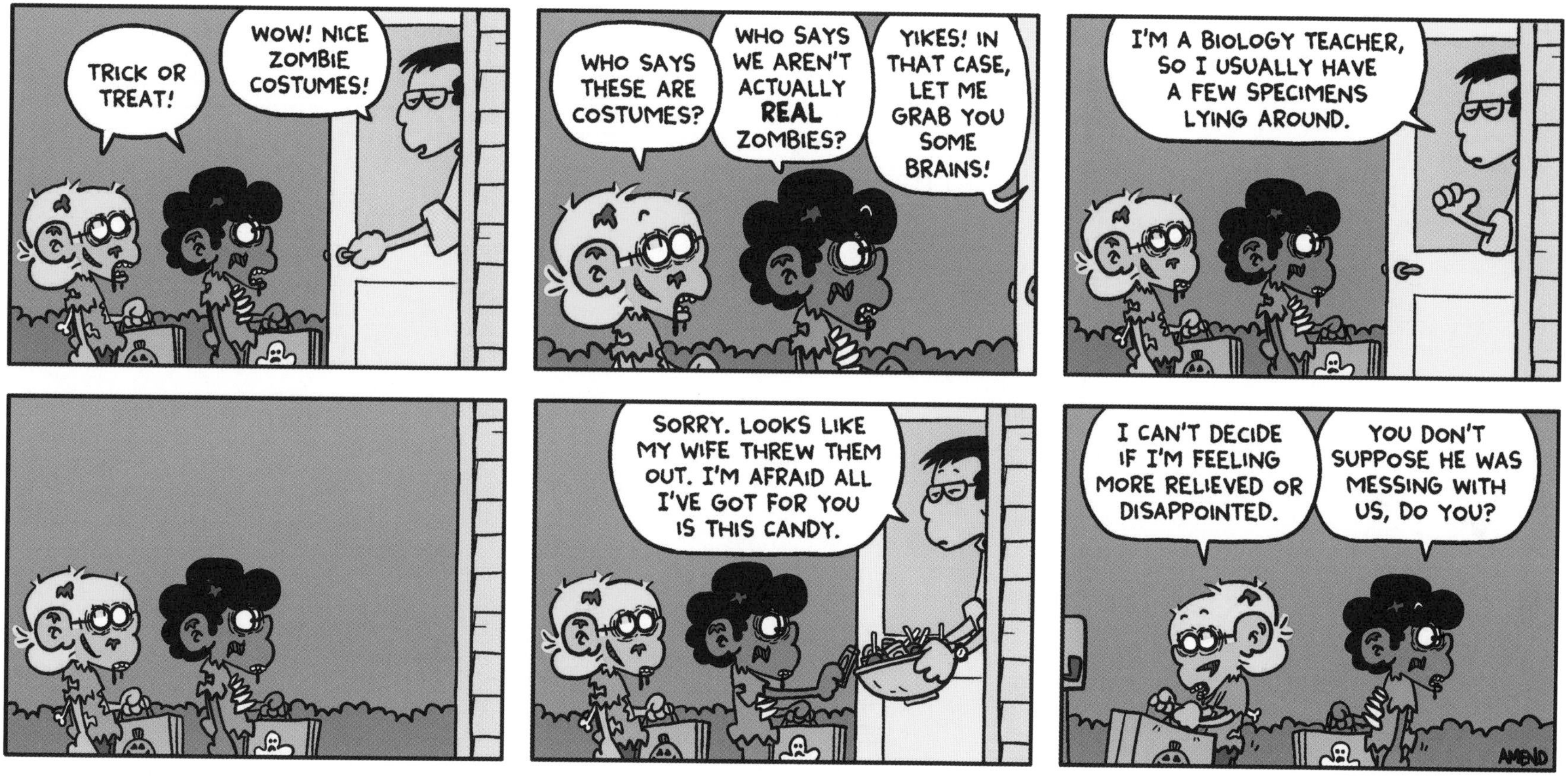
TRICK OR TREAT!
WOW! NICE ZOMBIE COSTUMES!
WHO SAYS THESE ARE COSTUMES?
WHO SAYS WE AREN'T ACTUALLY **REAL** ZOMBIES?
YIKES! IN THAT CASE, LET ME GRAB YOU SOME BRAINS!
I'M A BIOLOGY TEACHER, SO I USUALLY HAVE A FEW SPECIMENS LYING AROUND.
SORRY. LOOKS LIKE MY WIFE THREW THEM OUT. I'M AFRAID ALL I'VE GOT FOR YOU IS THIS CANDY.
I CAN'T DECIDE IF I'M FEELING MORE RELIEVED OR DISAPPOINTED.
YOU DON'T SUPPOSE HE WAS MESSING WITH US, DO YOU?
AMEND

Brilliant

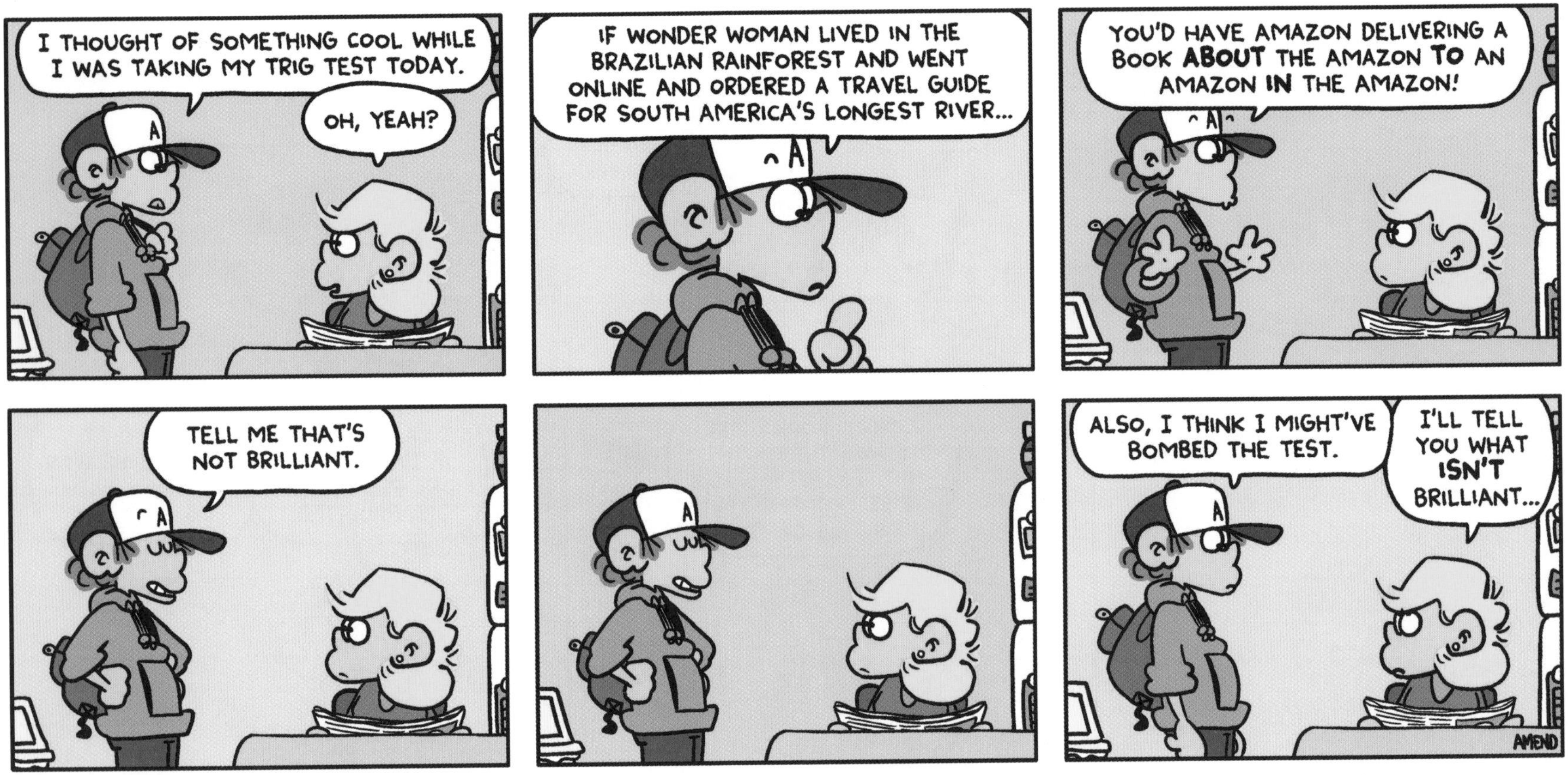
I THOUGHT OF SOMETHING COOL WHILE I WAS TAKING MY TRIG TEST TODAY.
OH, YEAH?
IF WONDER WOMAN LIVED IN THE BRAZILIAN RAINFOREST AND WENT ONLINE AND ORDERED A TRAVEL GUIDE FOR SOUTH AMERICA'S LONGEST RIVER...
YOU'D HAVE AMAZON DELIVERING A BOOK **ABOUT** THE AMAZON **TO** AN AMAZON **IN** THE AMAZON!
TELL ME THAT'S NOT BRILLIANT.
ALSO, I THINK I MIGHT'VE BOMBED THE TEST.
I'LL TELL YOU WHAT **ISN'T** BRILLIANT...
AMEND

Smarta

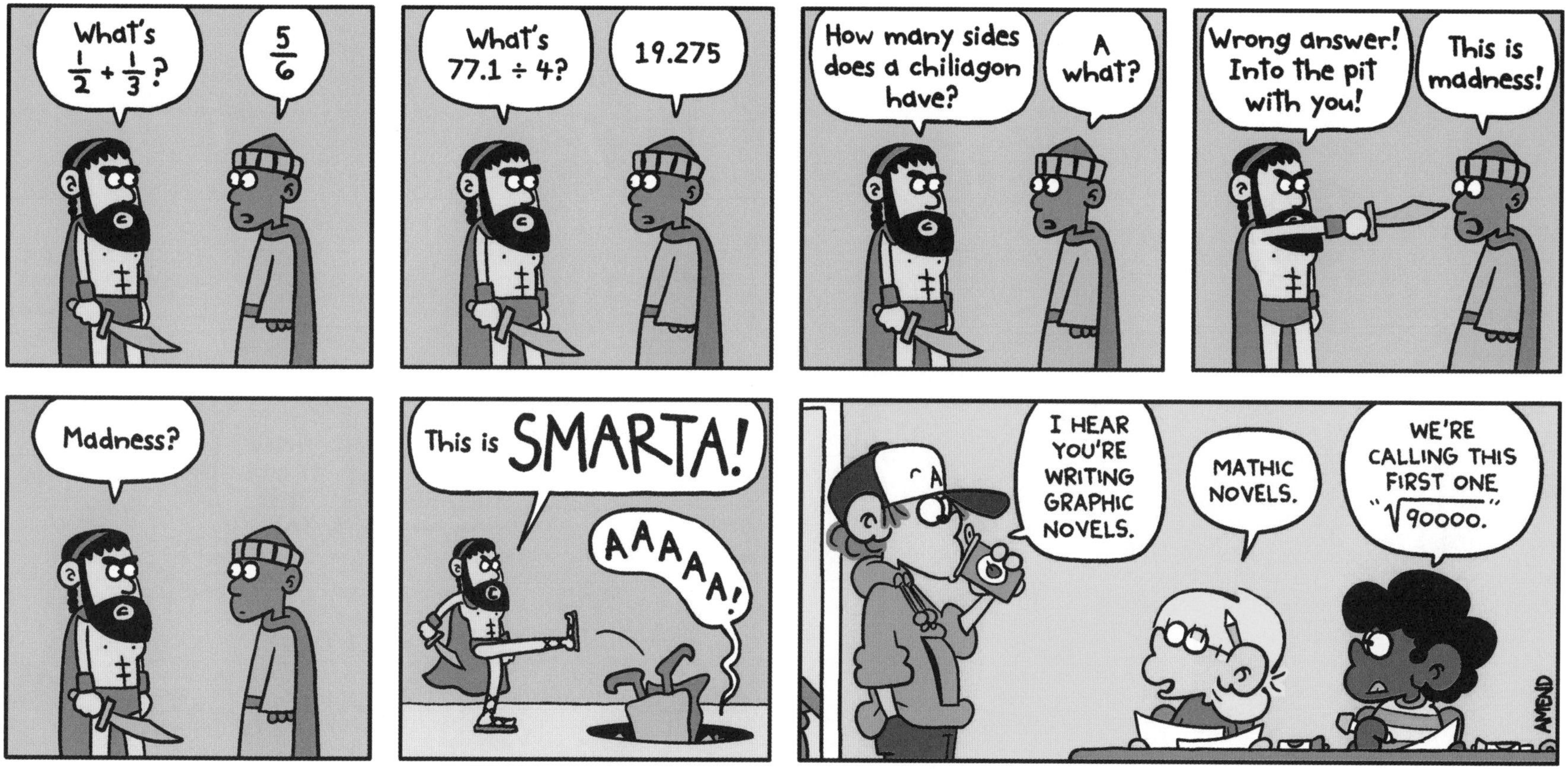

What's $\frac{1}{2} + \frac{1}{3}$?
$\frac{5}{6}$
What's 77.1 ÷ 4?
19.275
How many sides does a chiliagon have?
A what?
Wrong answer! Into the pit with you!
This is madness!
Madness?
This is SMARTA!
AAAAAA!
I HEAR YOU'RE WRITING GRAPHIC NOVELS.
MATHIC NOVELS.
WE'RE CALLING THIS FIRST ONE "$\sqrt{90000}$."
AMEND

Fantasticy Football

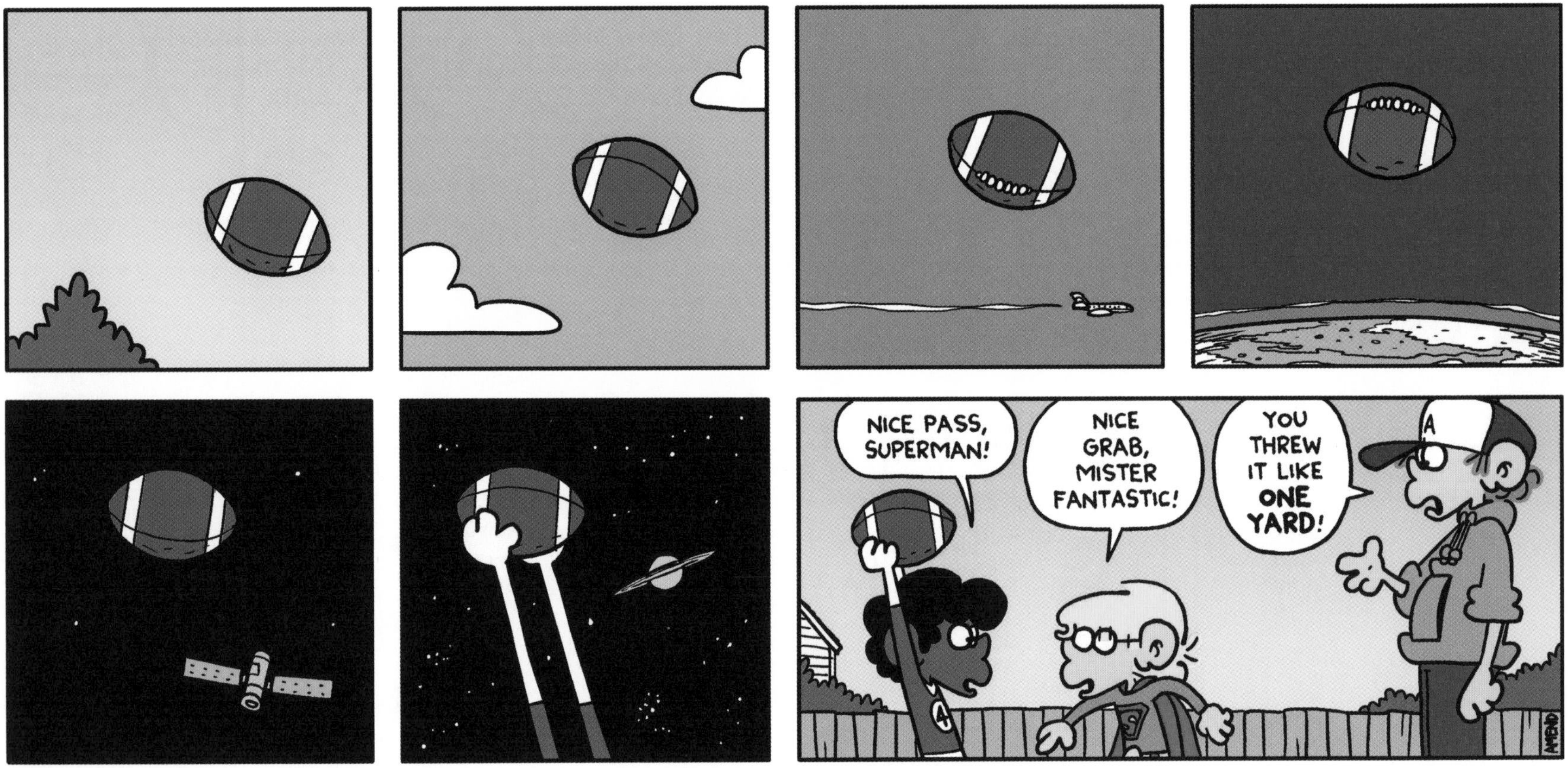
NICE PASS, SUPERMAN!
NICE GRAB, MISTER FANTASTIC!
YOU THREW IT LIKE ONE YARD!
AMEND

Impossible

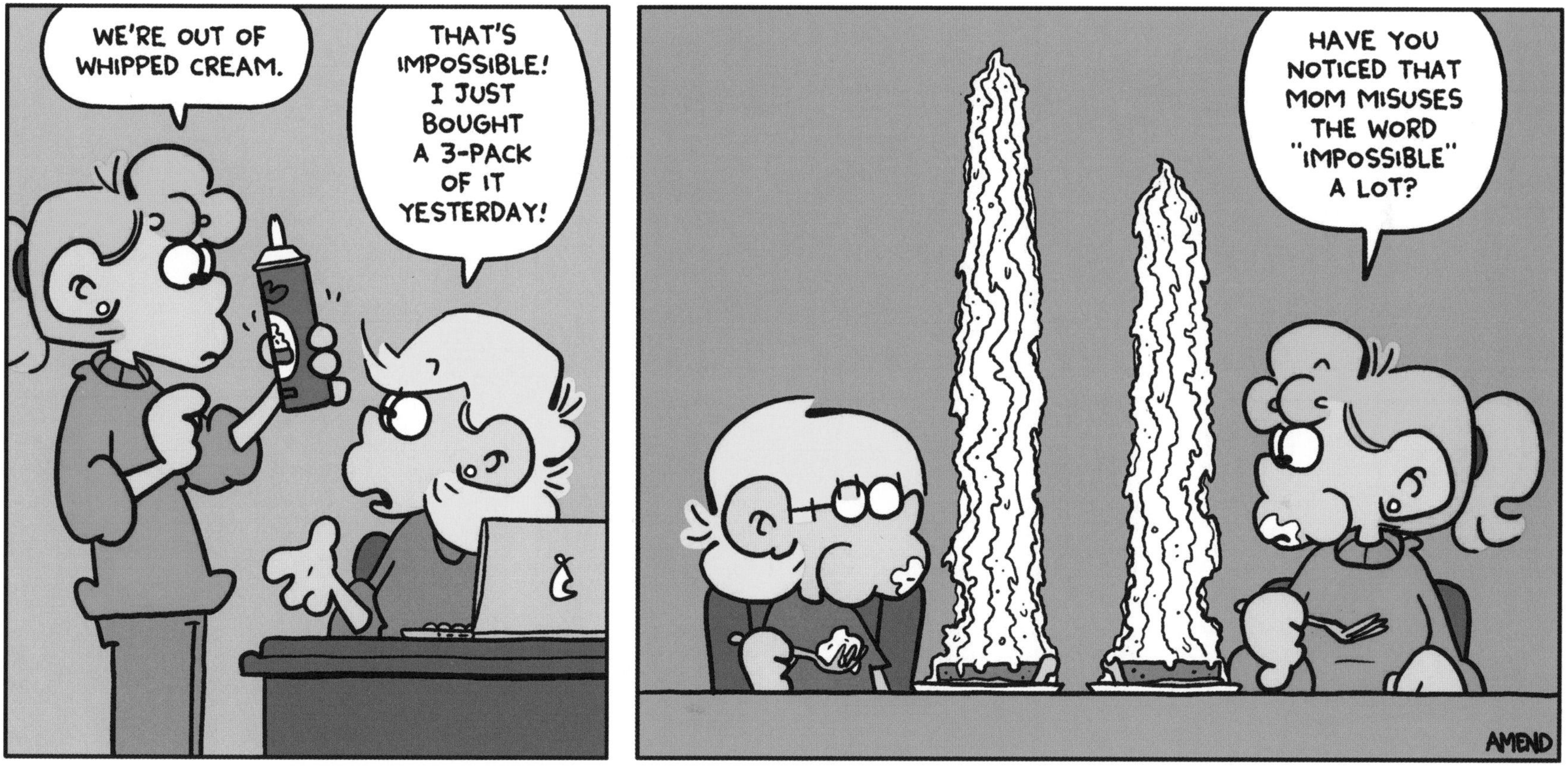
WE'RE OUT OF WHIPPED CREAM.
THAT'S IMPOSSIBLE! I JUST BOUGHT A 3-PACK OF IT YESTERDAY!
HAVE YOU NOTICED THAT MOM MISUSES THE WORD "IMPOSSIBLE" A LOT?
AMEND

#YOYO

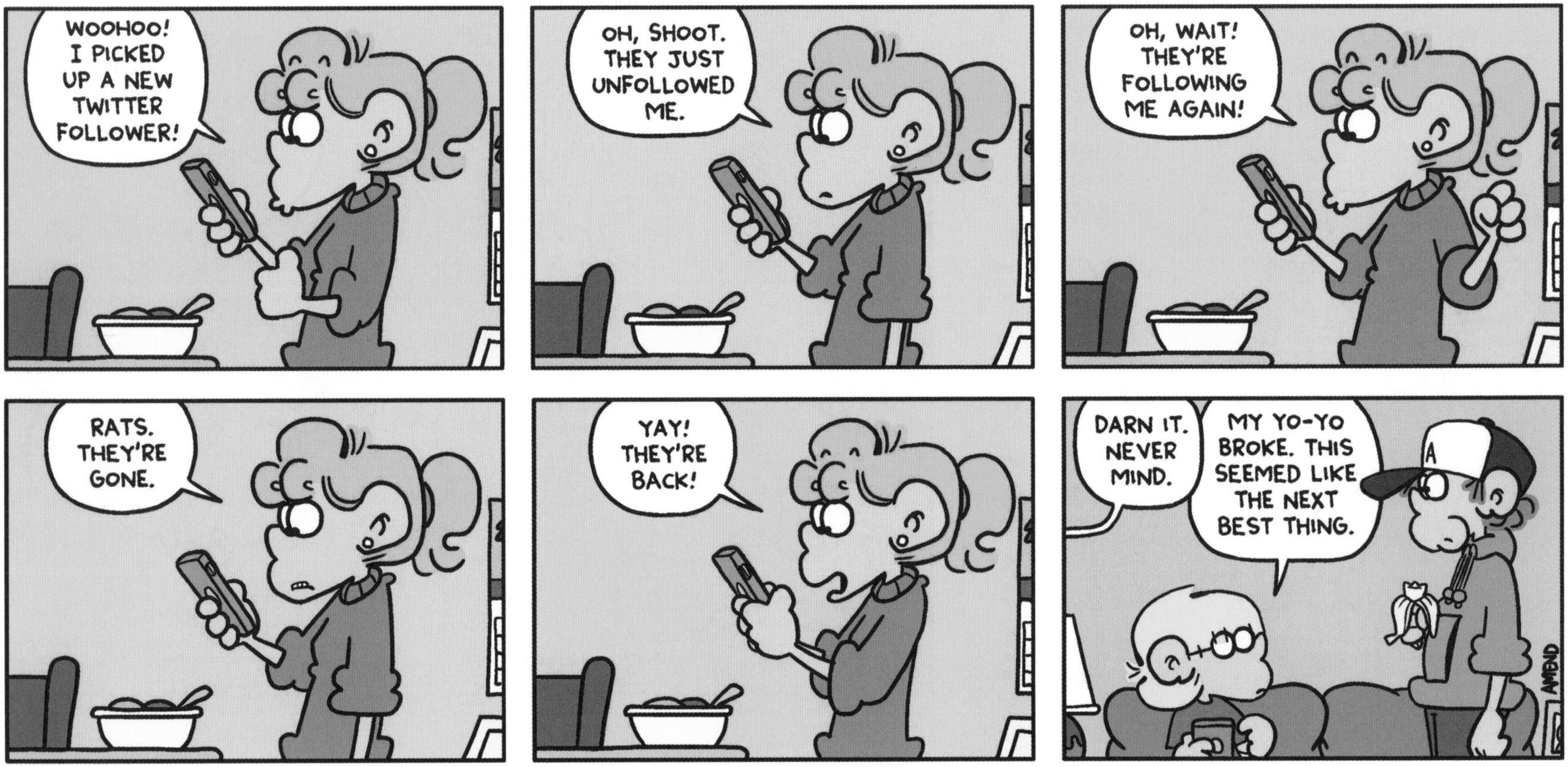
WOOHOO! I PICKED UP A NEW TWITTER FOLLOWER!
OH, SHOOT. THEY JUST UNFOLLOWED ME.
OH, WAIT! THEY'RE FOLLOWING ME AGAIN!
RATS. THEY'RE GONE.
YAY! THEY'RE BACK!
DARN IT. NEVER MIND.
MY YO-YO BROKE. THIS SEEMED LIKE THE NEXT BEST THING.
A
AMEND

Probably Fake

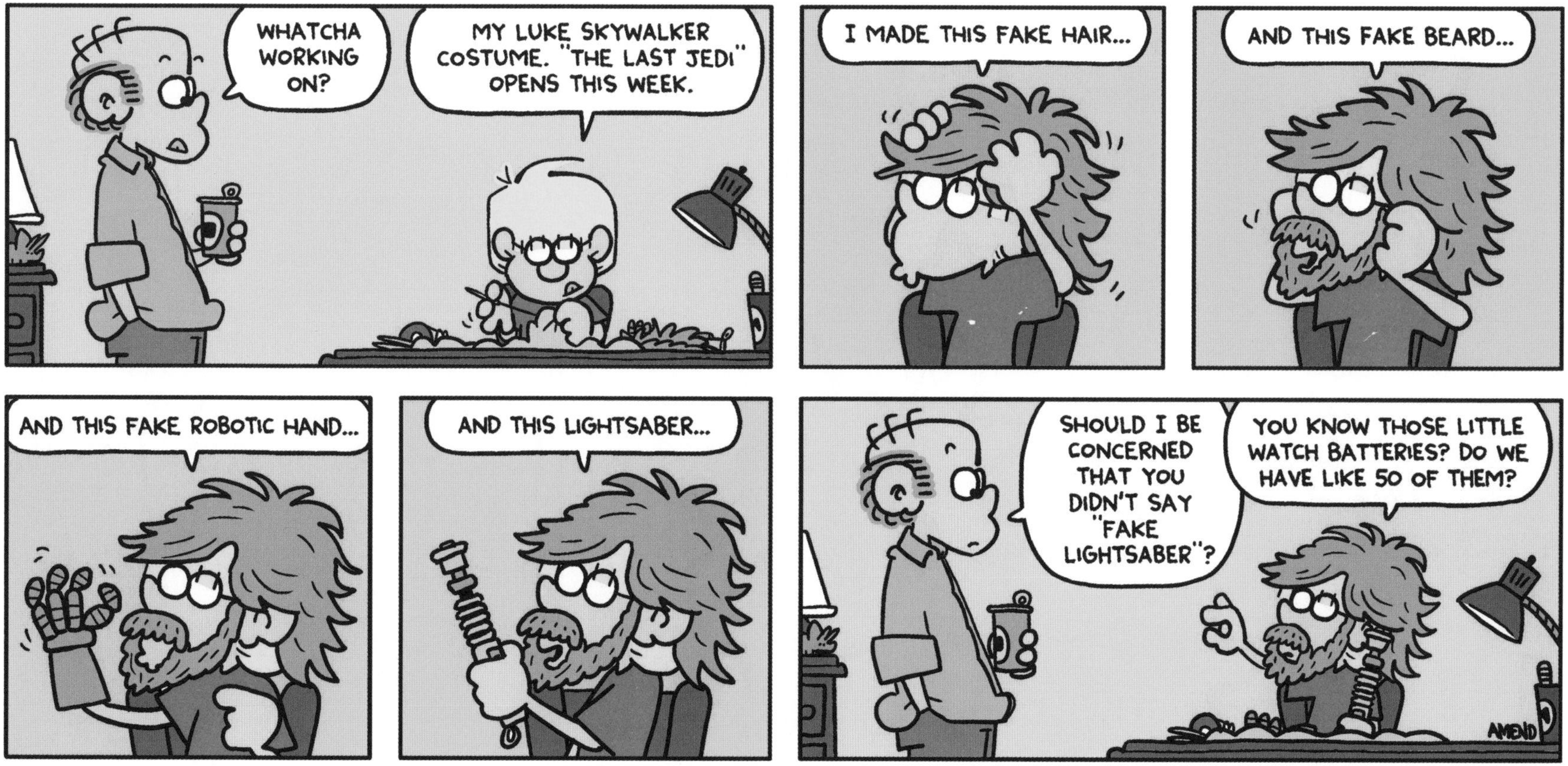
WHATCHA WORKING ON?
MY LUKE SKYWALKER COSTUME. "THE LAST JEDI" OPENS THIS WEEK.
I MADE THIS FAKE HAIR...
AND THIS FAKE BEARD...
AND THIS FAKE ROBOTIC HAND...
AND THIS LIGHTSABER...
SHOULD I BE CONCERNED THAT YOU DIDN'T SAY "FAKE LIGHTSABER"?
YOU KNOW THOSE LITTLE WATCH BATTERIES? DO WE HAVE LIKE 50 OF THEM?
AMEND

Freeze Before Serving

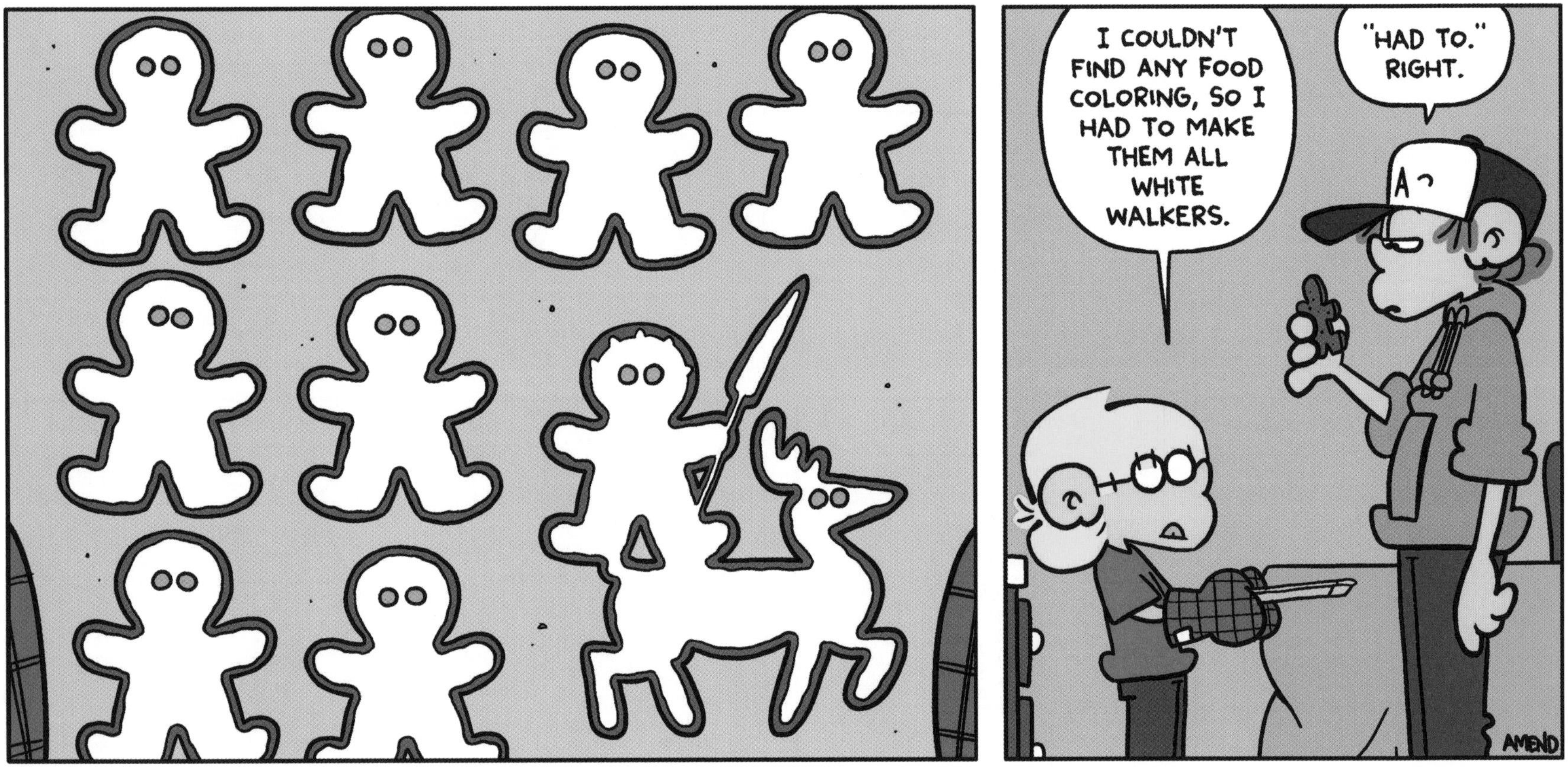

I COULDN'T FIND ANY FOOD COLORING, SO I HAD TO MAKE THEM ALL WHITE WALKERS.
"HAD TO." RIGHT.
AMEND

Quince Quingle

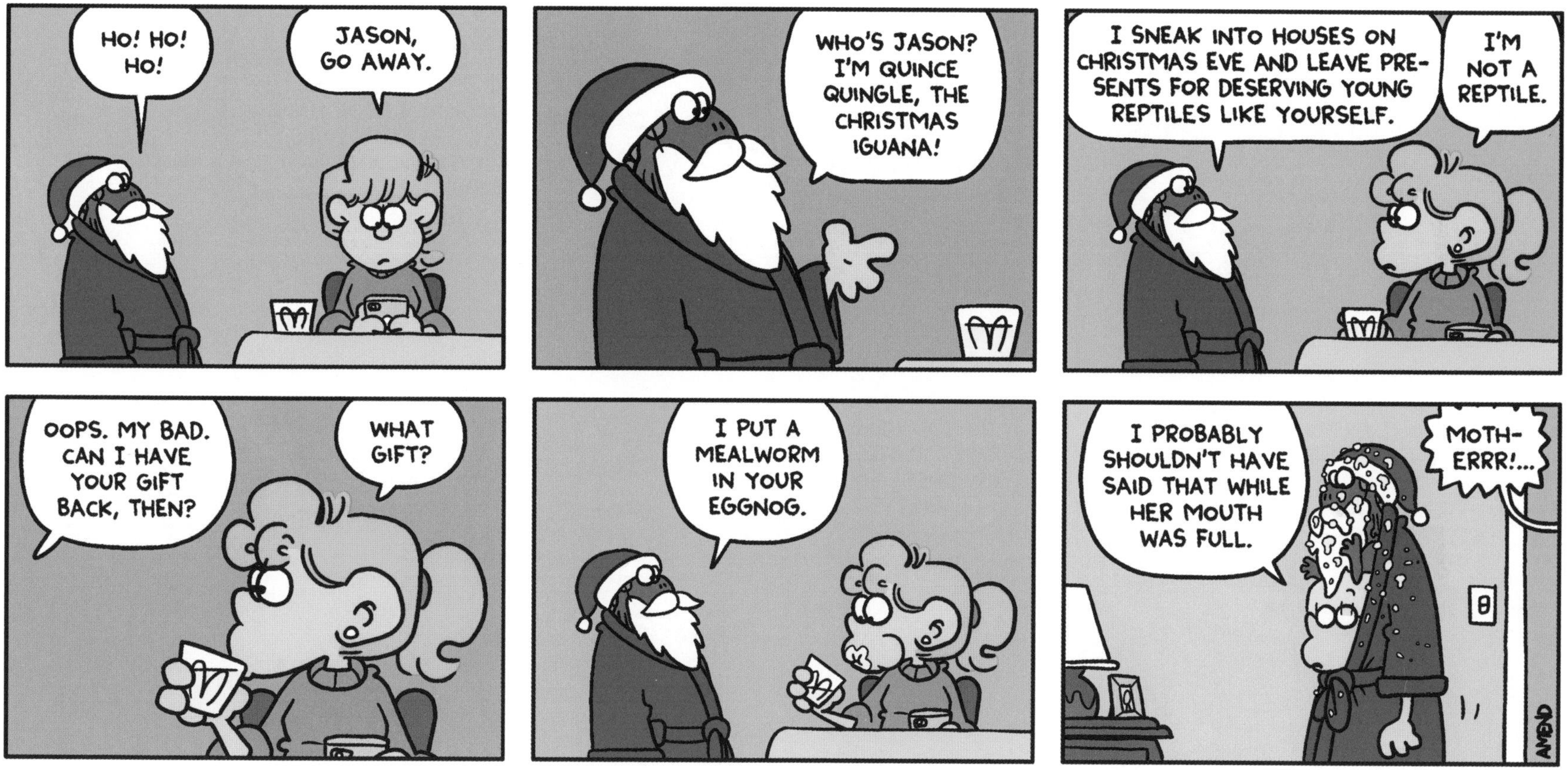
HO! HO! HO!
JASON, GO AWAY.
WHO'S JASON? I'M QUINCE QUINGLE, THE CHRISTMAS IGUANA!
I SNEAK INTO HOUSES ON CHRISTMAS EVE AND LEAVE PRESENTS FOR DESERVING YOUNG REPTILES LIKE YOURSELF.
I'M NOT A REPTILE.
OOPS. MY BAD. CAN I HAVE YOUR GIFT BACK, THEN?
WHAT GIFT?
I PUT A MEALWORM IN YOUR EGGNOG.
I PROBABLY SHOULDN'T HAVE SAID THAT WHILE HER MOUTH WAS FULL.
MOTH-ERRR!...
AMEND

Party of One

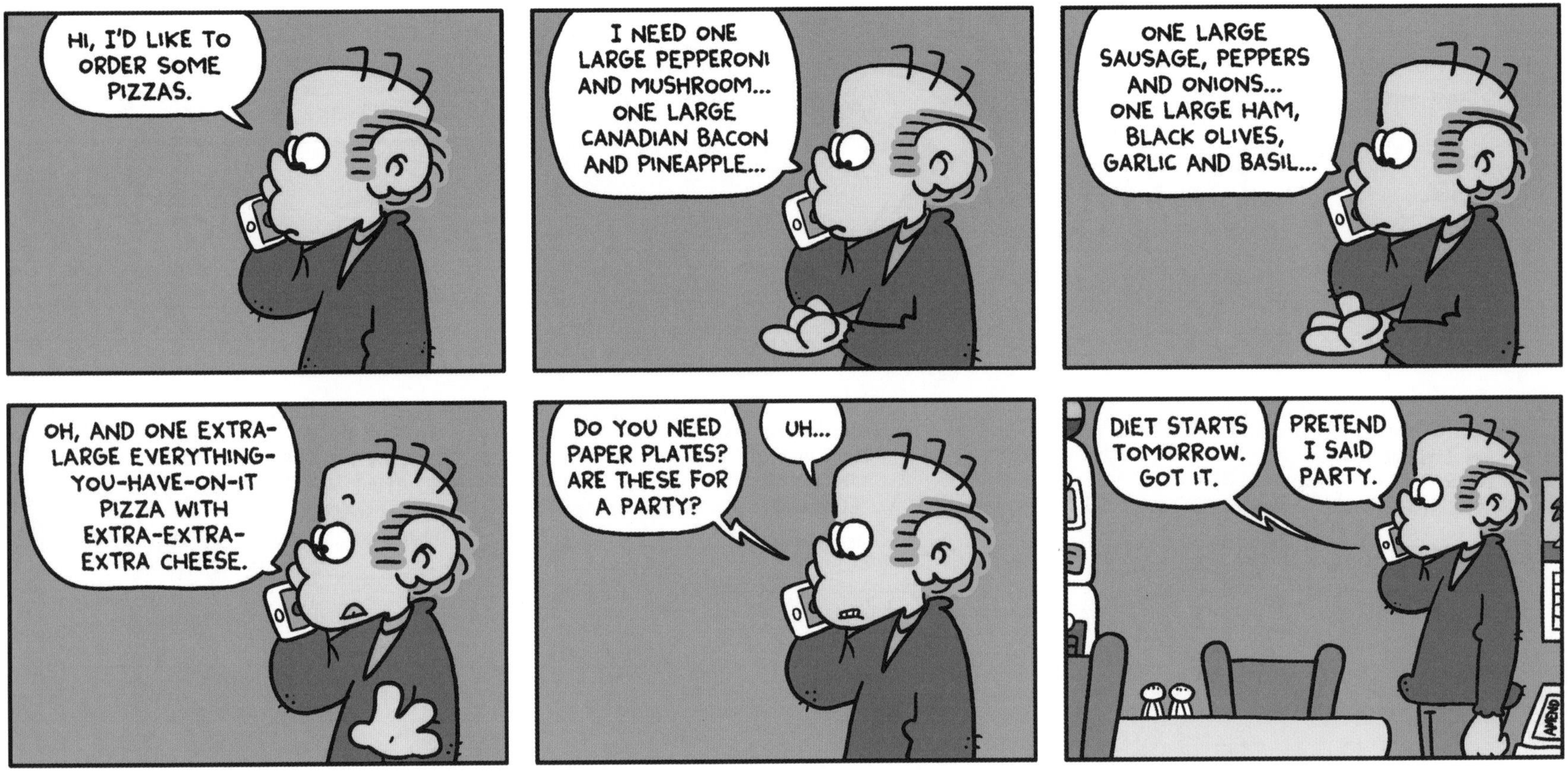
HI, I'D LIKE TO ORDER SOME PIZZAS.
I NEED ONE LARGE PEPPERONI AND MUSHROOM... ONE LARGE CANADIAN BACON AND PINEAPPLE...
ONE LARGE SAUSAGE, PEPPERS AND ONIONS... ONE LARGE HAM, BLACK OLIVES, GARLIC AND BASIL...
OH, AND ONE EXTRA-LARGE EVERYTHING-YOU-HAVE-ON-IT PIZZA WITH EXTRA-EXTRA-EXTRA CHEESE.
DO YOU NEED PAPER PLATES? ARE THESE FOR A PARTY?
UH...
DIET STARTS TOMORROW. GOT IT.
PRETEND I SAID PARTY.

Snowmin

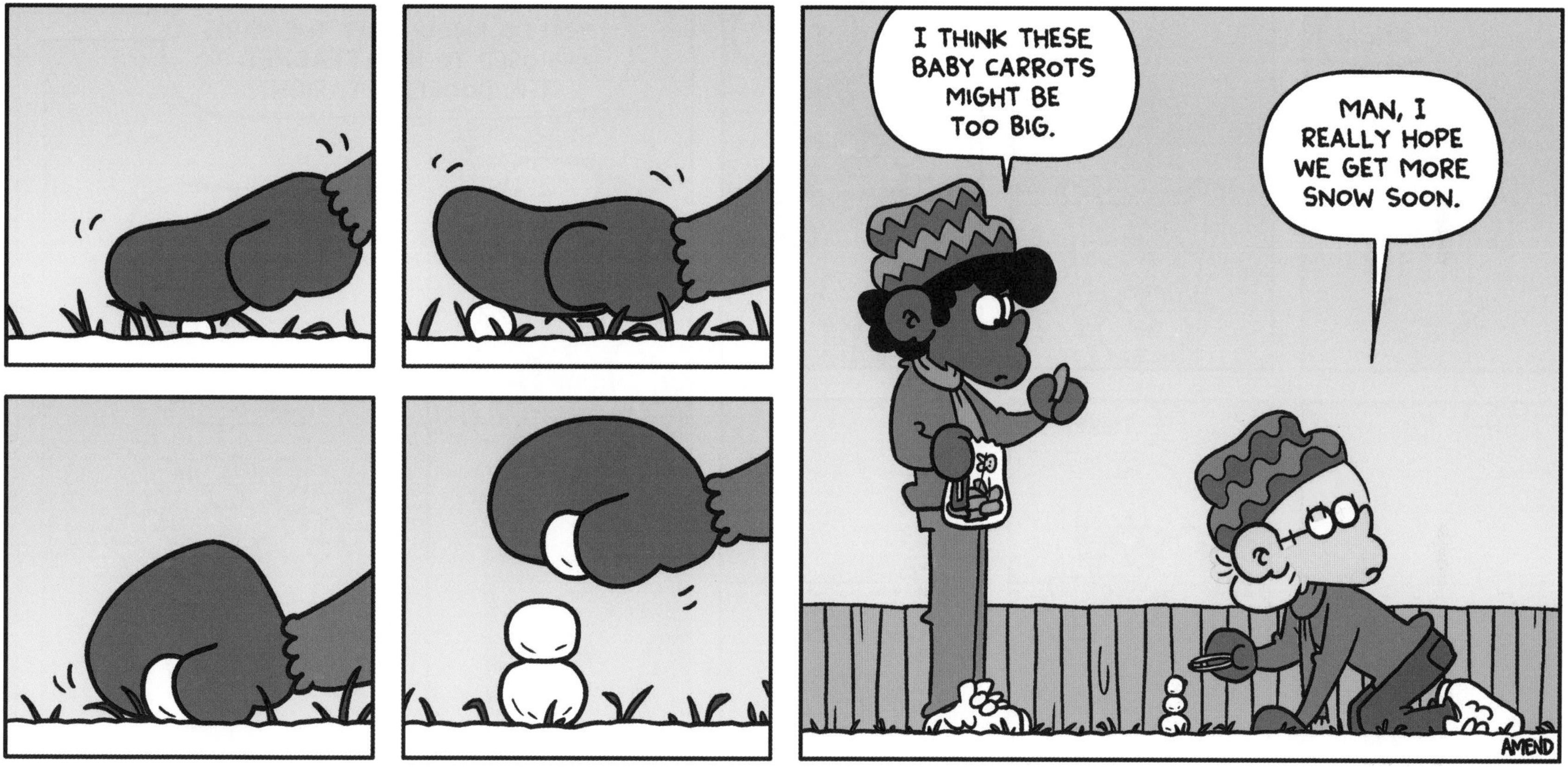

I THINK THESE BABY CARROTS MIGHT BE TOO BIG.
MAN, I REALLY HOPE WE GET MORE SNOW SOON.
AMEND

Bar Easier

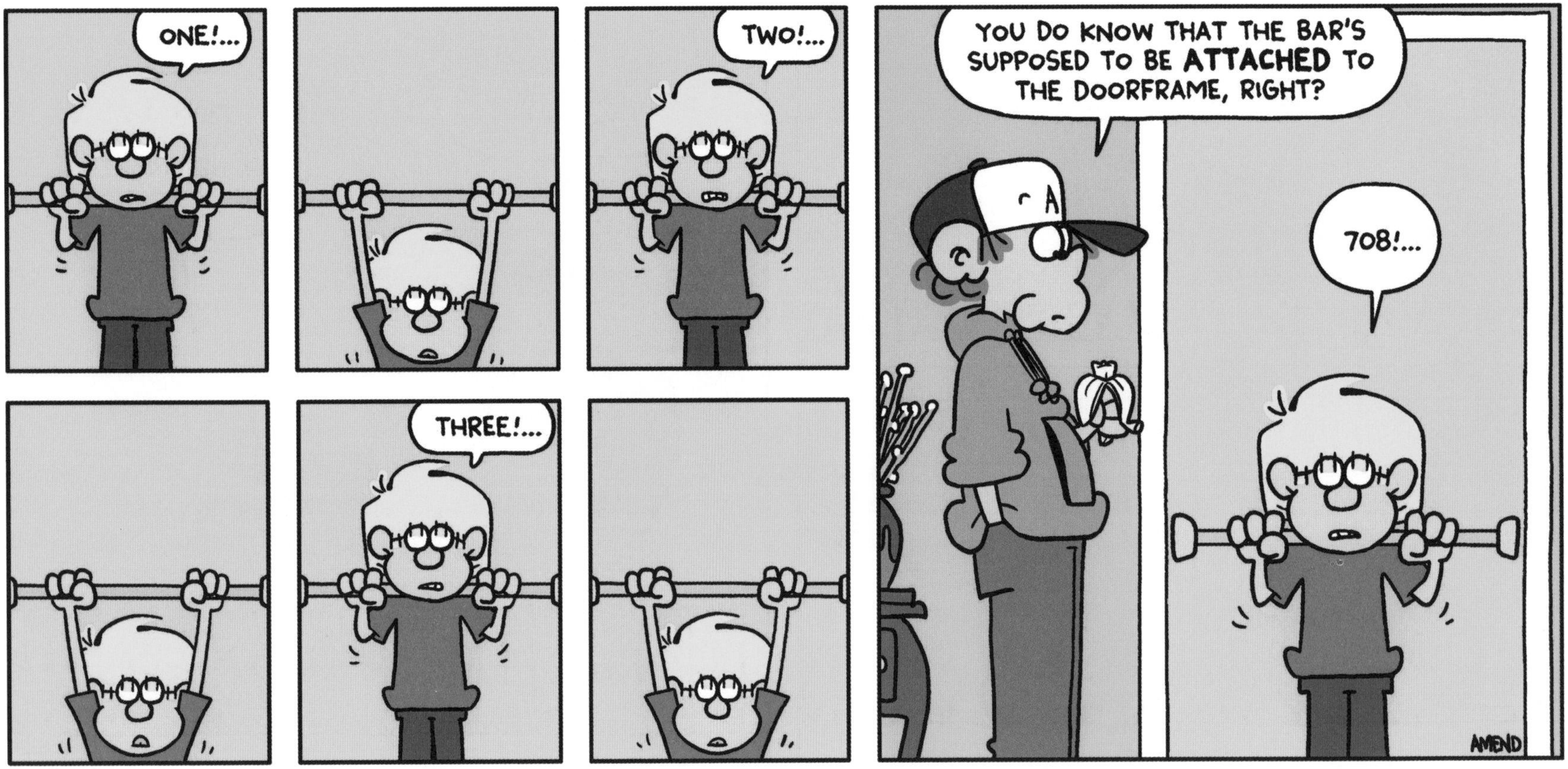

ONE!...
TWO!...
THREE!...
YOU DO KNOW THAT THE BAR'S SUPPOSED TO BE **ATTACHED** TO THE DOORFRAME, RIGHT?
708!...
AMEND

Winter Driving

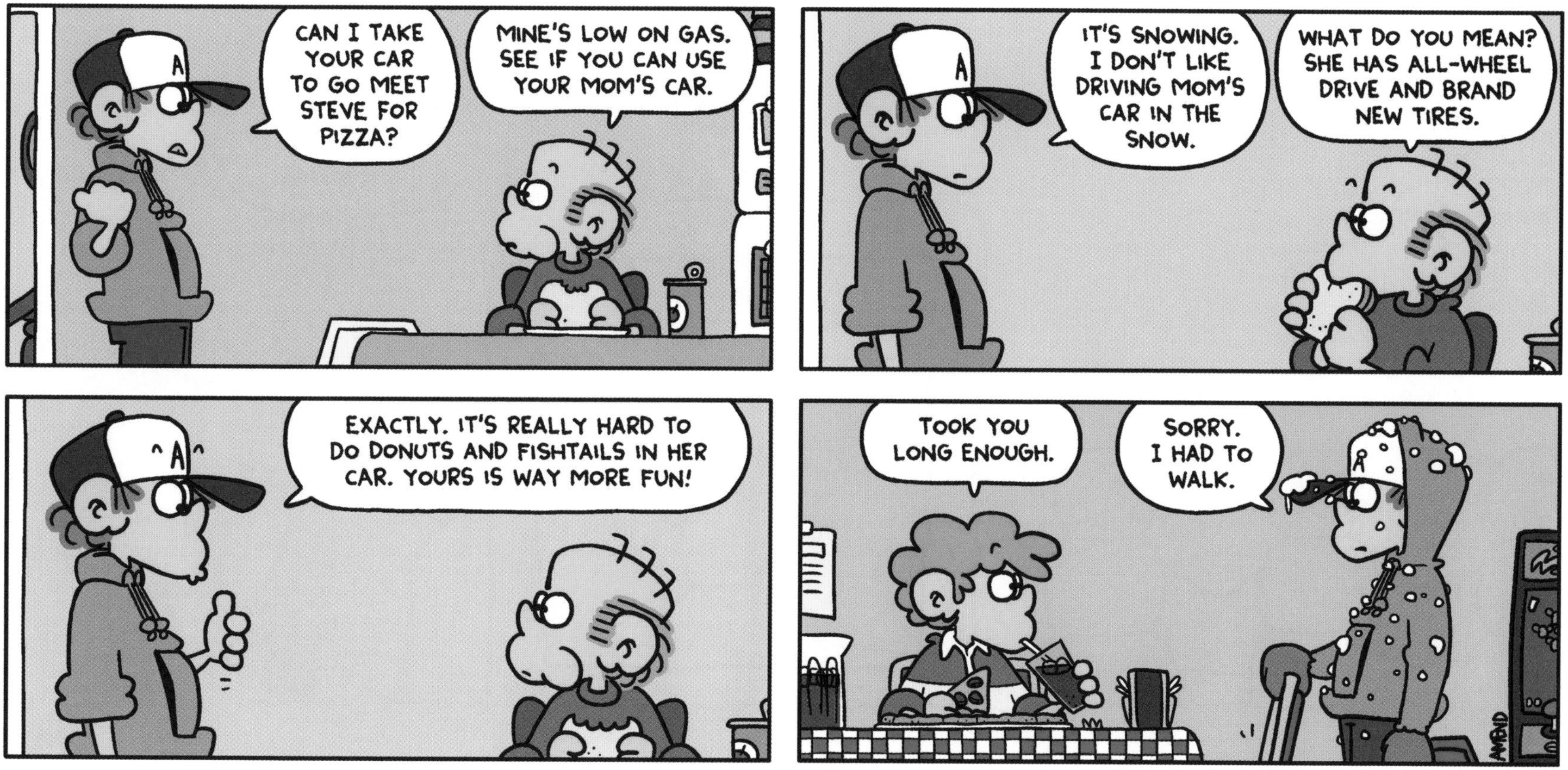
CAN I TAKE YOUR CAR TO GO MEET STEVE FOR PIZZA?
MINE'S LOW ON GAS. SEE IF YOU CAN USE YOUR MOM'S CAR.
IT'S SNOWING. I DON'T LIKE DRIVING MOM'S CAR IN THE SNOW.
WHAT DO YOU MEAN? SHE HAS ALL-WHEEL DRIVE AND BRAND NEW TIRES.
EXACTLY. IT'S REALLY HARD TO DO DONUTS AND FISHTAILS IN HER CAR. YOURS IS WAY MORE FUN!
TOOK YOU LONG ENOUGH.
SORRY. I HAD TO WALK.

Printer Wonderland

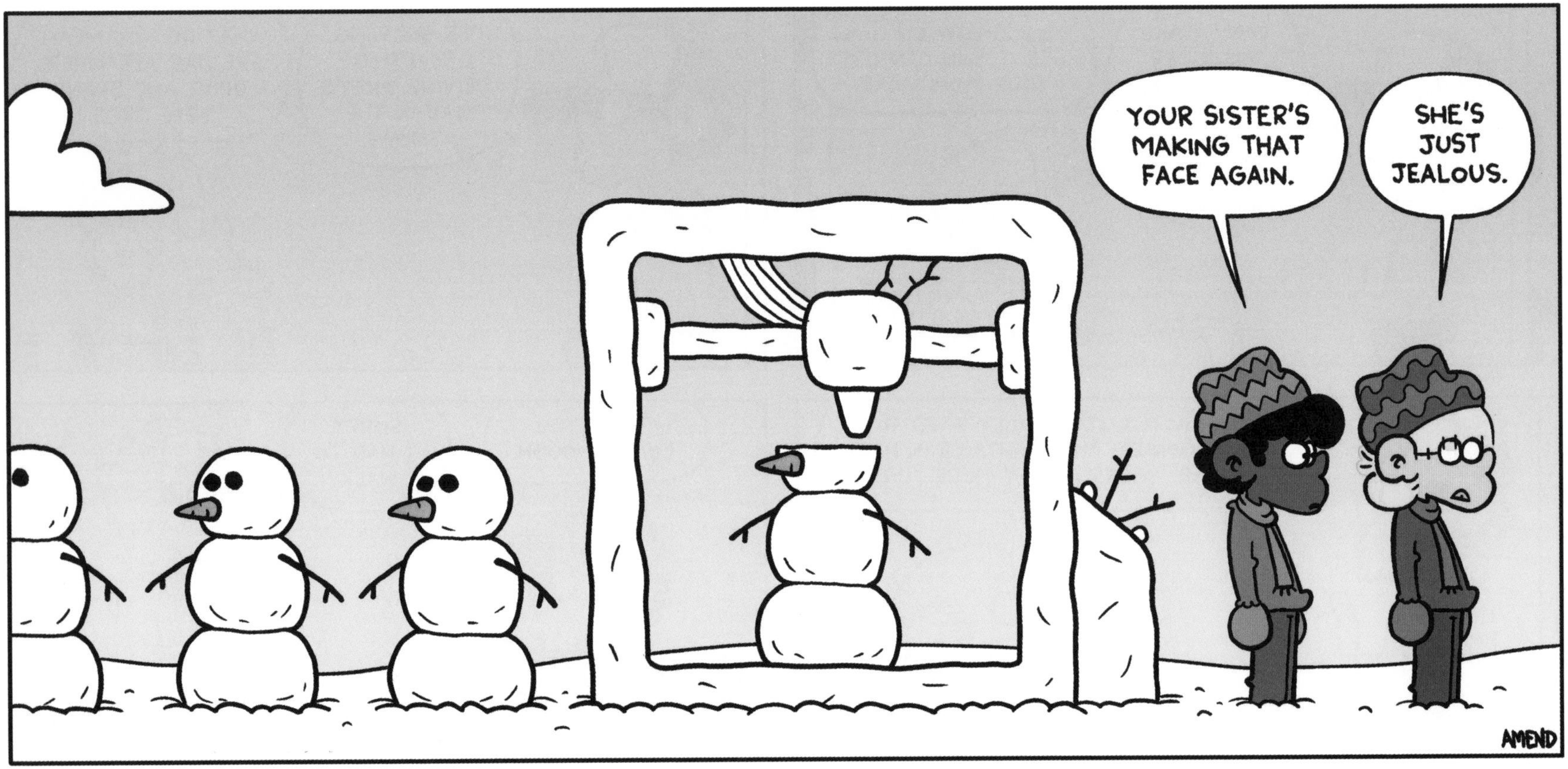
YOUR SISTER'S MAKING THAT FACE AGAIN.
SHE'S JUST JEALOUS.
AMEND

Miserable Code

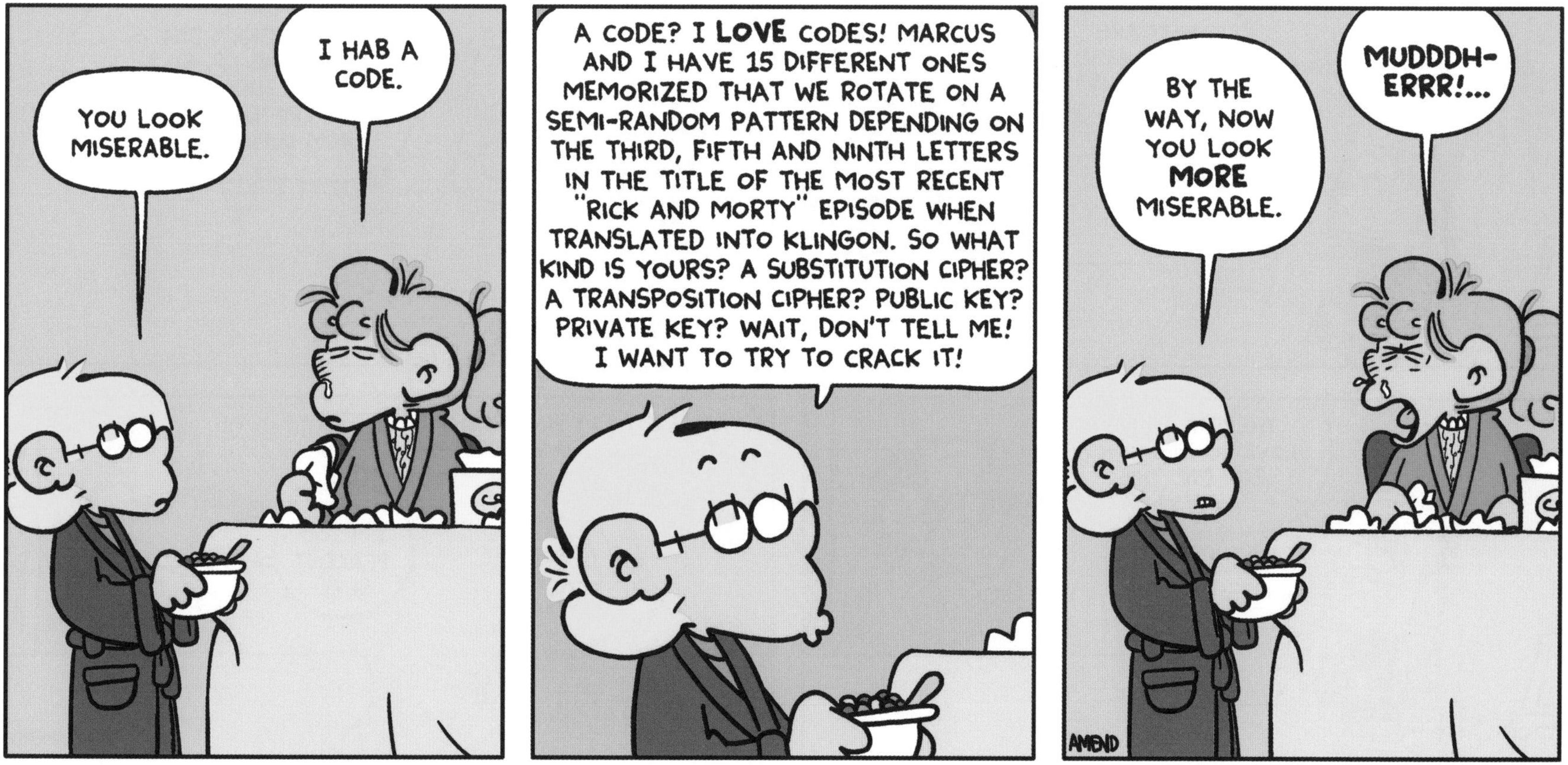
YOU LOOK MISERABLE.
I HAB A CODE.
A CODE? I **LOVE** CODES! MARCUS AND I HAVE 15 DIFFERENT ONES MEMORIZED THAT WE ROTATE ON A SEMI-RANDOM PATTERN DEPENDING ON THE THIRD, FIFTH AND NINTH LETTERS IN THE TITLE OF THE MOST RECENT "RICK AND MORTY" EPISODE WHEN TRANSLATED INTO KLINGON. SO WHAT KIND IS YOURS? A SUBSTITUTION CIPHER? A TRANSPOSITION CIPHER? PUBLIC KEY? PRIVATE KEY? WAIT, DON'T TELL ME! I WANT TO TRY TO CRACK IT!
BY THE WAY, NOW YOU LOOK **MORE** MISERABLE.
MUDDDH-ERRR!...
AMEND

Cupidproof

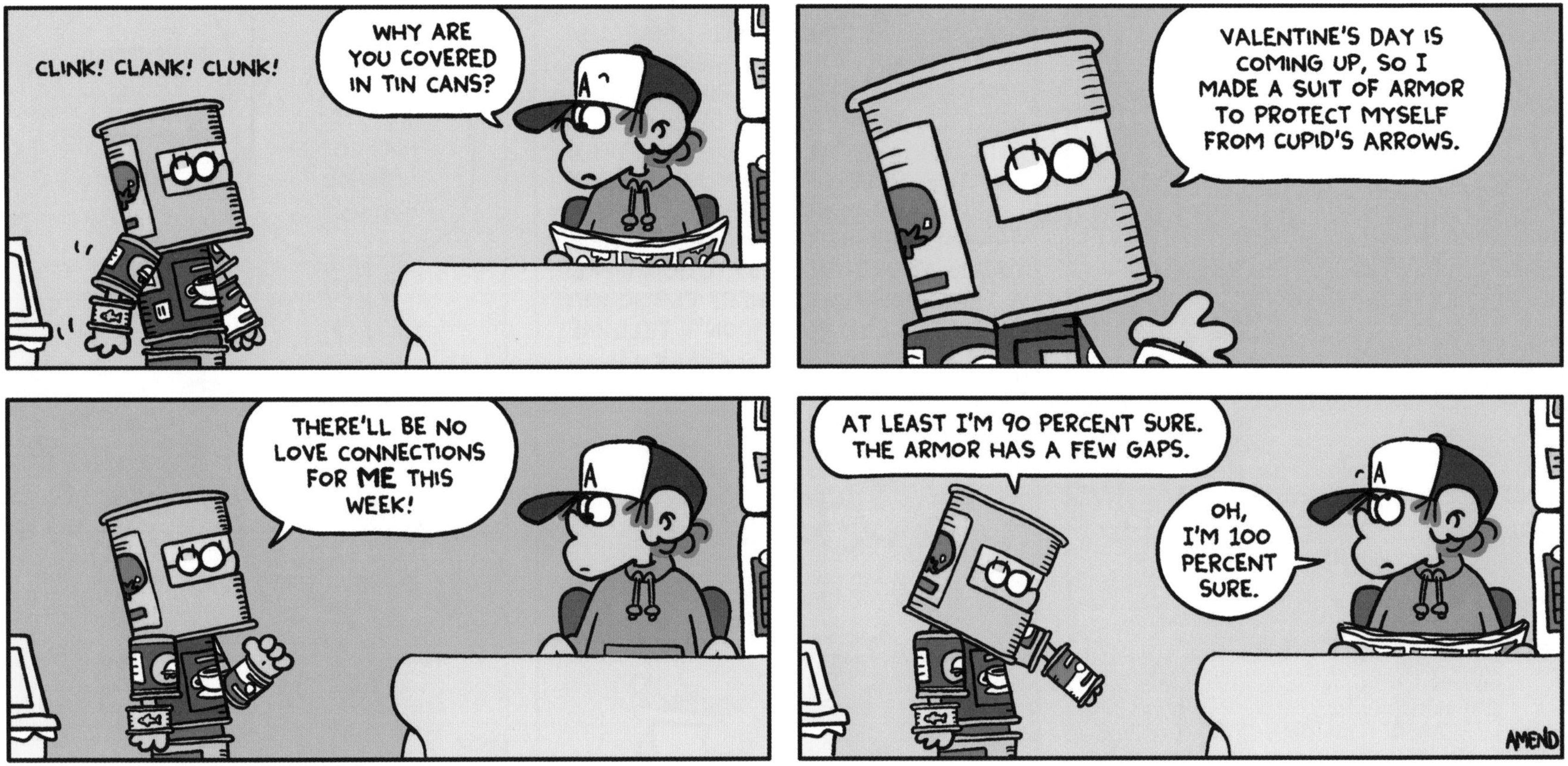

CLINK! CLANK! CLUNK!
WHY ARE YOU COVERED IN TIN CANS?
VALENTINE'S DAY IS COMING UP, SO I MADE A SUIT OF ARMOR TO PROTECT MYSELF FROM CUPID'S ARROWS.
THERE'LL BE NO LOVE CONNECTIONS FOR ME THIS WEEK!
AT LEAST I'M 90 PERCENT SURE. THE ARMOR HAS A FEW GAPS.
OH, I'M 100 PERCENT SURE.
AMEND

Jane Need Help?

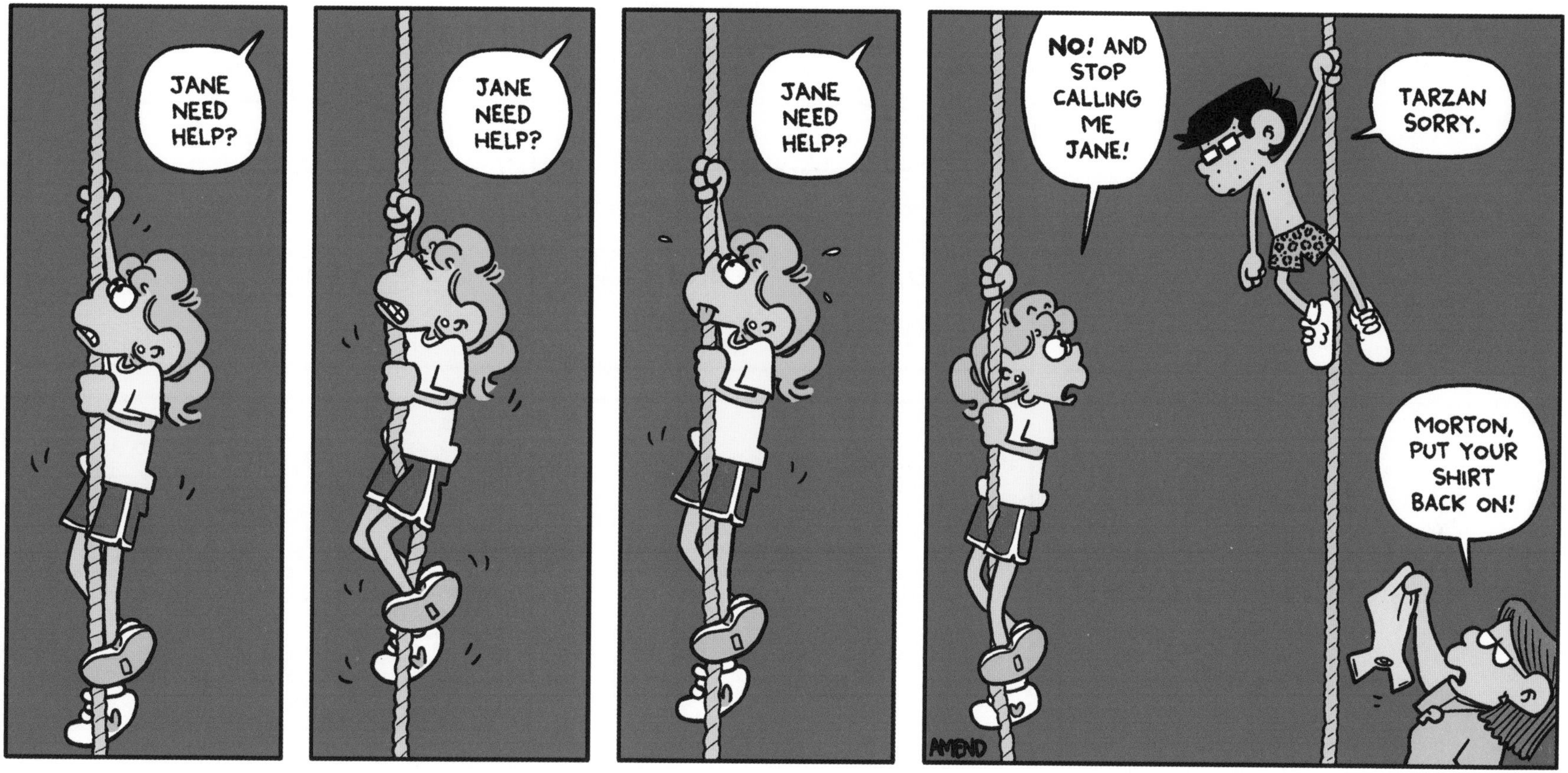
JANE NEED HELP?
JANE NEED HELP?
JANE NEED HELP?
NO! AND STOP CALLING ME JANE!
TARZAN SORRY.
MORTON, PUT YOUR SHIRT BACK ON!
AMEND

UFO Math

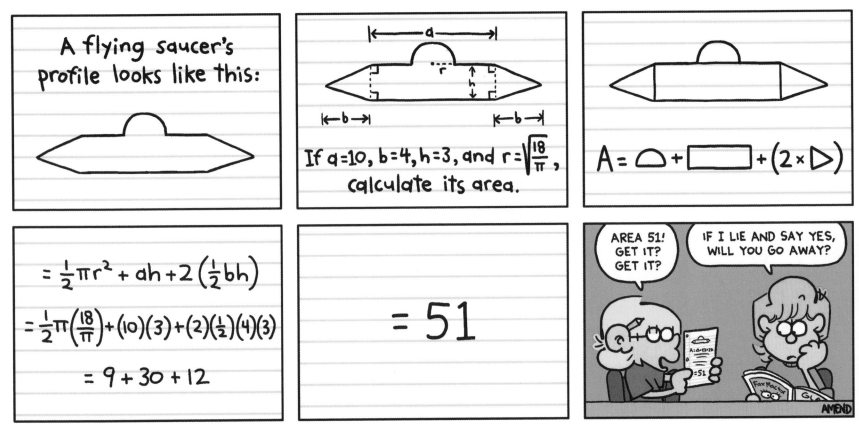

A flying saucer's profile looks like this:

If $a=10$, $b=4$, $h=3$, and $r=\sqrt{\frac{18}{\pi}}$, calculate its area.

$$A = \bigcirc + \rule{1.5cm}{0.4cm} + (2 \times \triangleright)$$

$$= \frac{1}{2}\pi r^2 + ah + 2\left(\frac{1}{2}bh\right)$$

$$= \frac{1}{2}\pi\left(\frac{18}{\pi}\right) + (10)(3) + (2)\left(\frac{1}{2}\right)(4)(3)$$

$$= 9 + 30 + 12$$

$$= 51$$

AREA 51! GET IT? GET IT?

IF I LIE AND SAY YES, WILL YOU GO AWAY?

Loot Boxing

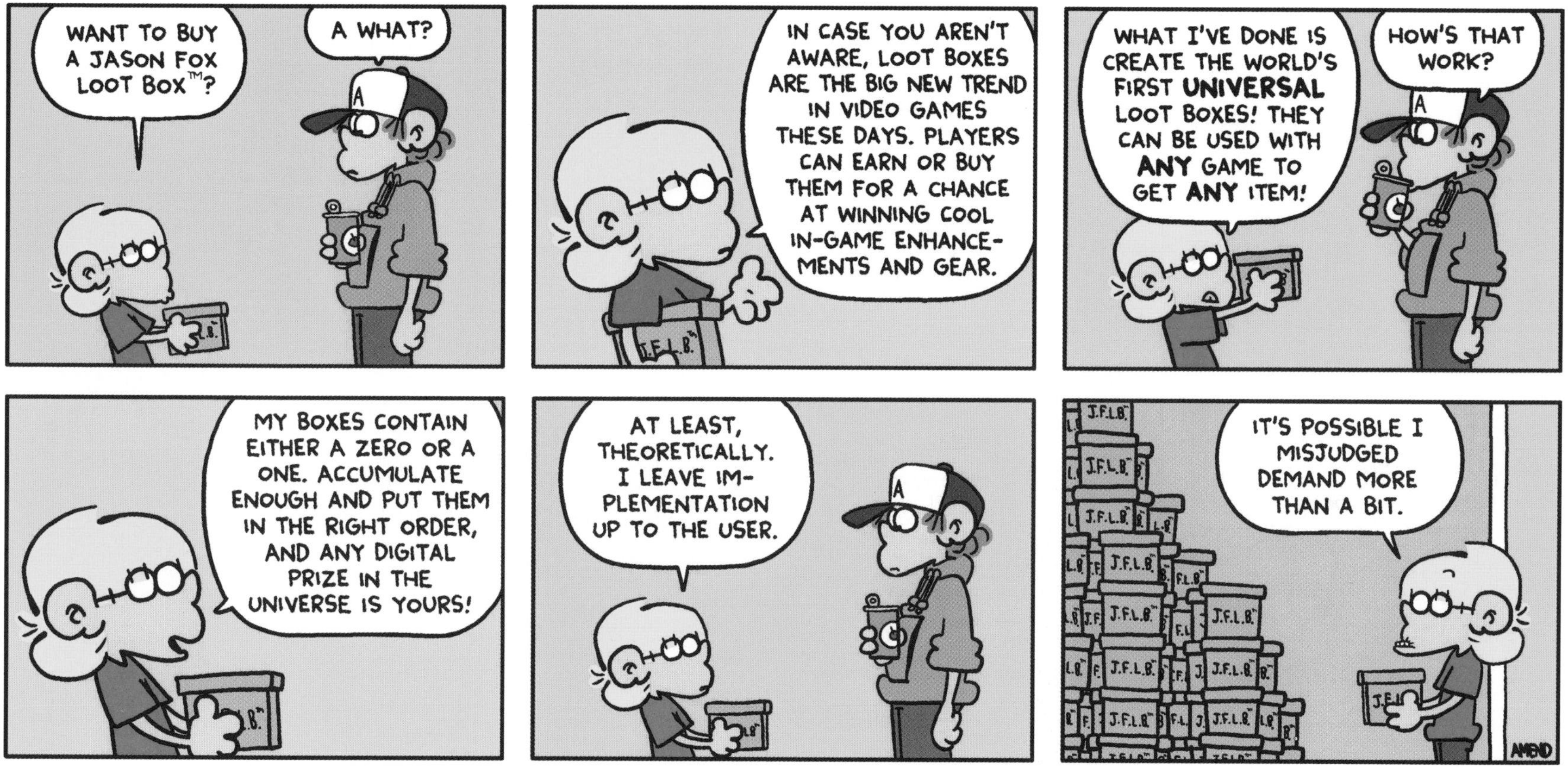
WANT TO BUY A JASON FOX LOOT BOX™?
A WHAT?
IN CASE YOU AREN'T AWARE, LOOT BOXES ARE THE BIG NEW TREND IN VIDEO GAMES THESE DAYS. PLAYERS CAN EARN OR BUY THEM FOR A CHANCE AT WINNING COOL IN-GAME ENHANCEMENTS AND GEAR.
WHAT I'VE DONE IS CREATE THE WORLD'S FIRST **UNIVERSAL** LOOT BOXES! THEY CAN BE USED WITH **ANY** GAME TO GET **ANY** ITEM!
HOW'S THAT WORK?
MY BOXES CONTAIN EITHER A ZERO OR A ONE. ACCUMULATE ENOUGH AND PUT THEM IN THE RIGHT ORDER, AND ANY DIGITAL PRIZE IN THE UNIVERSE IS YOURS!
AT LEAST, THEORETICALLY. I LEAVE IMPLEMENTATION UP TO THE USER.
IT'S POSSIBLE I MISJUDGED DEMAND MORE THAN A BIT.
AMEND

Beeps and Bleeps

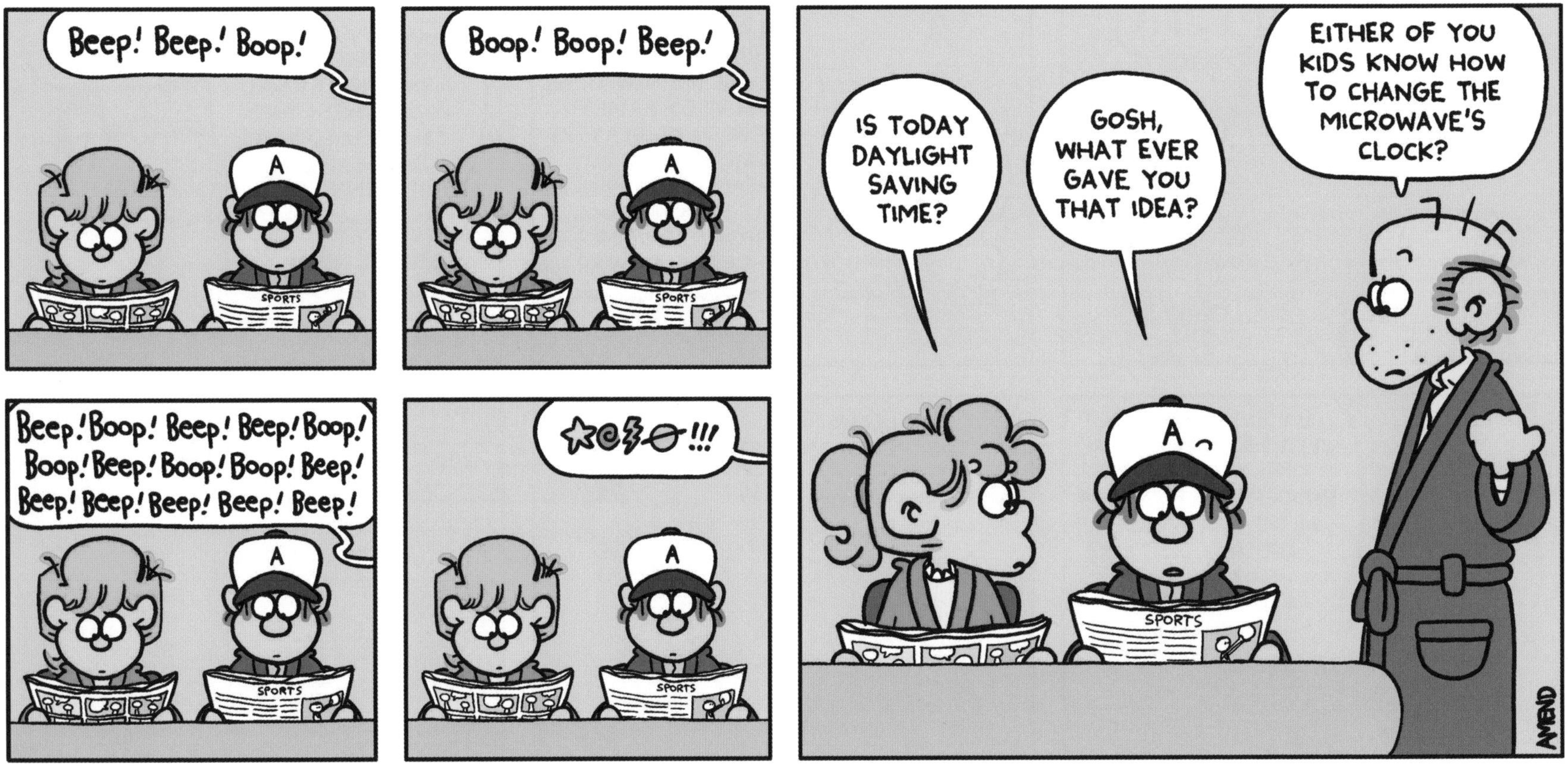

Beep! Beep! Boop!
Boop! Boop! Beep!
Beep! Boop! Beep! Beep! Boop! Boop! Beep! Boop! Boop! Beep! Beep! Beep! Beep! Beep! Beep!
!!!
IS TODAY DAYLIGHT SAVING TIME?
GOSH, WHAT EVER GAVE YOU THAT IDEA?
EITHER OF YOU KIDS KNOW HOW TO CHANGE THE MICROWAVE'S CLOCK?
SPORTS
AMEND

Like a Dream

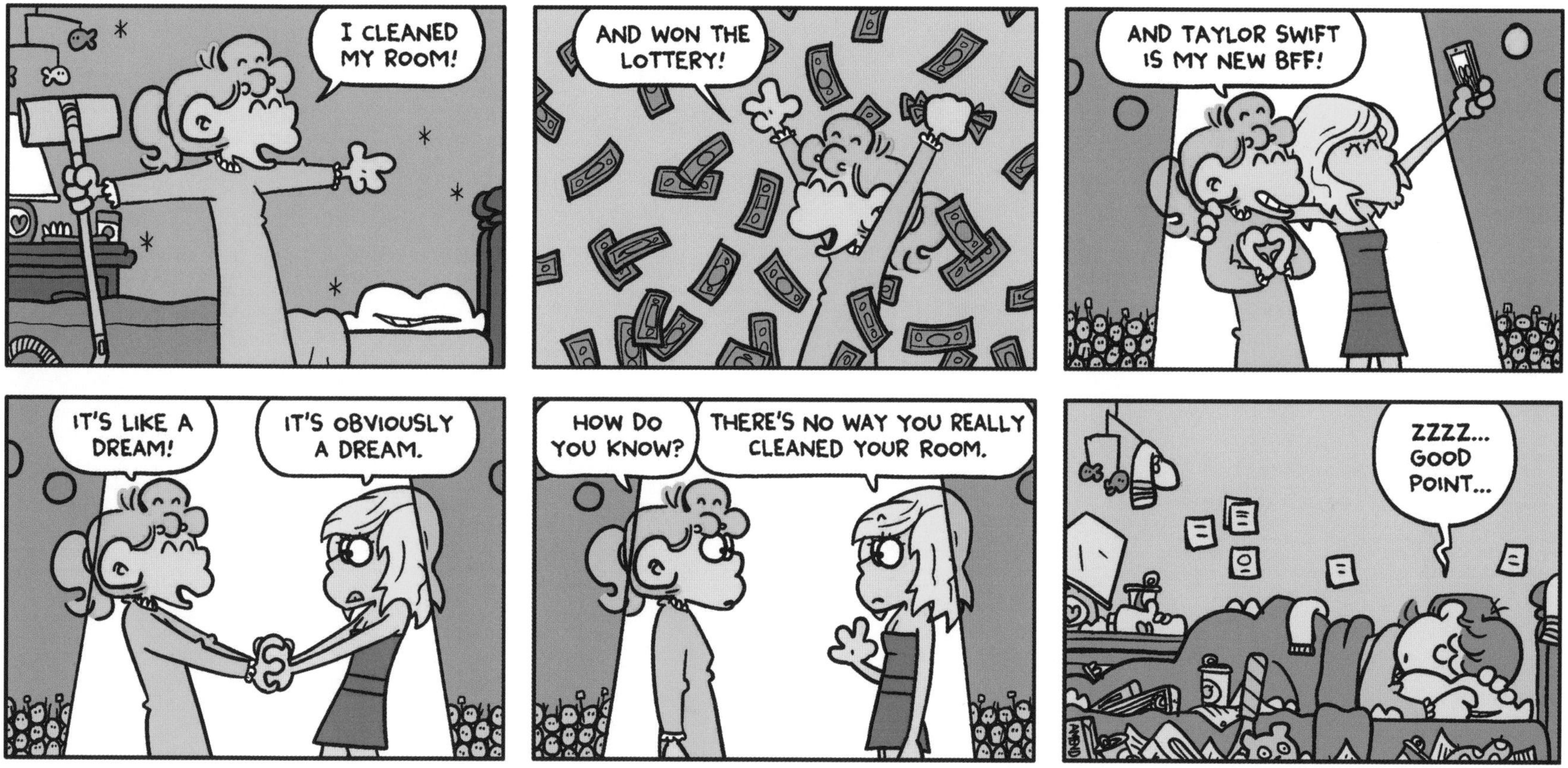
I CLEANED MY ROOM!
AND WON THE LOTTERY!
AND TAYLOR SWIFT IS MY NEW BFF!
IT'S LIKE A DREAM!
IT'S OBVIOUSLY A DREAM.
HOW DO YOU KNOW?
THERE'S NO WAY YOU REALLY CLEANED YOUR ROOM.
ZZZZ... GOOD POINT...

Spring Sports

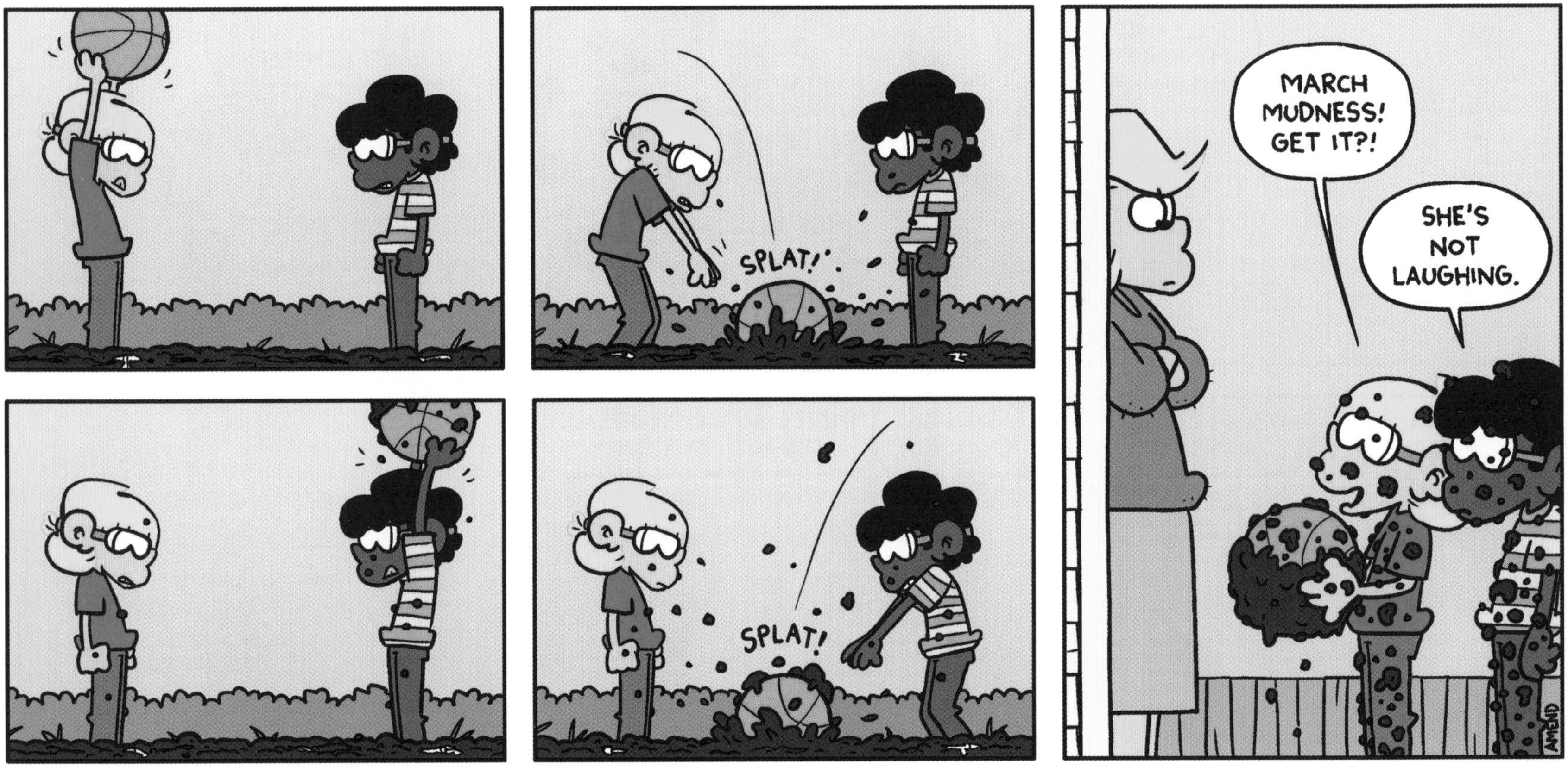
SPLAT!
SPLAT!
MARCH MUDNESS! GET IT?!
SHE'S NOT LAUGHING.
AMEND

Easter Omelettes

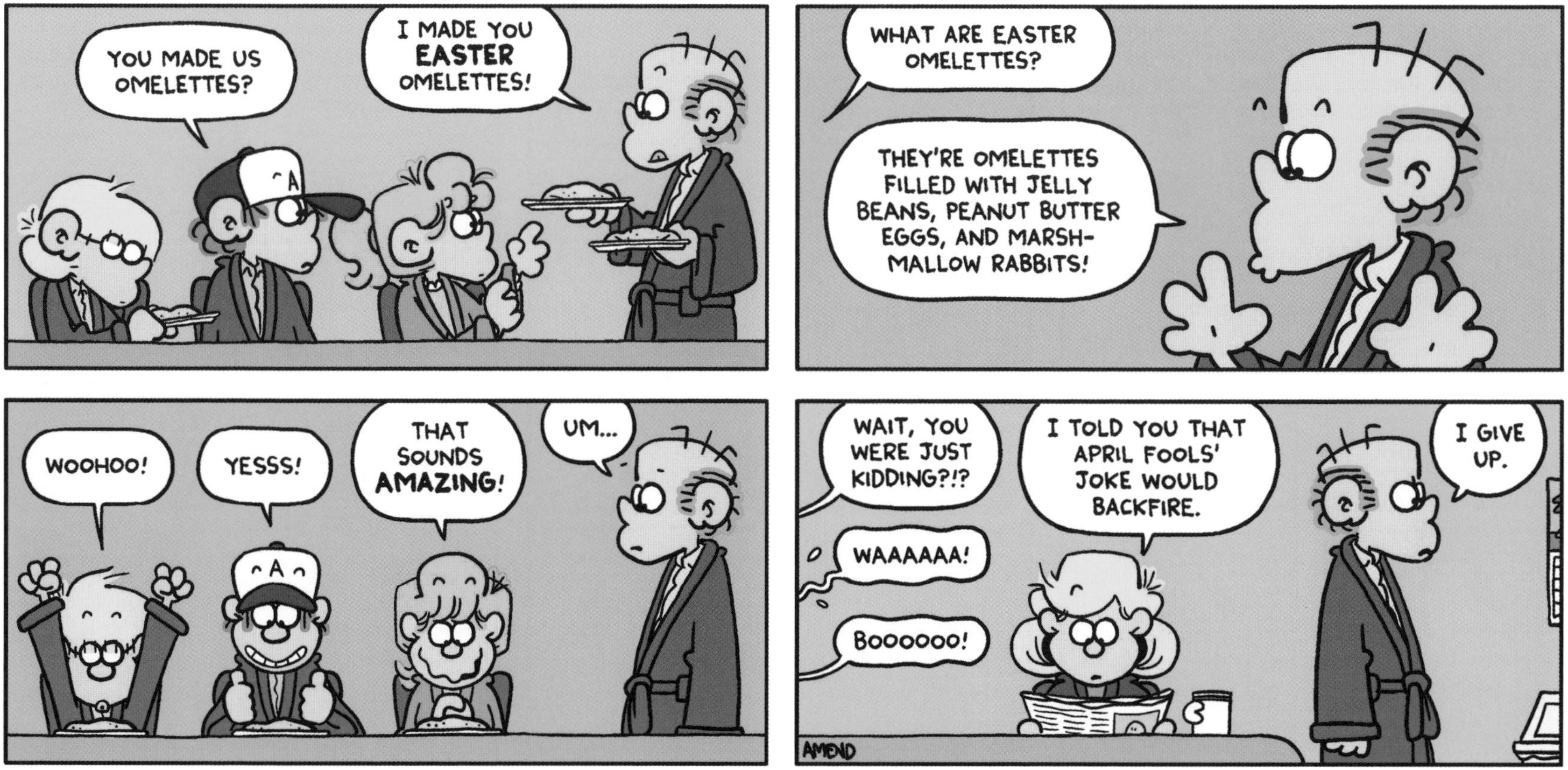
YOU MADE US OMELETTES?
I MADE YOU **EASTER** OMELETTES!
WHAT ARE EASTER OMELETTES?
THEY'RE OMELETTES FILLED WITH JELLY BEANS, PEANUT BUTTER EGGS, AND MARSH-MALLOW RABBITS!
WOOHOO!
YESSS!
THAT SOUNDS **AMAZING**!
UM...
WAIT, YOU WERE JUST KIDDING?!?
WAAAAAA!
BOOOOOO!
I TOLD YOU THAT APRIL FOOLS' JOKE WOULD BACKFIRE.
I GIVE UP.
AMEND

Questioned to Death

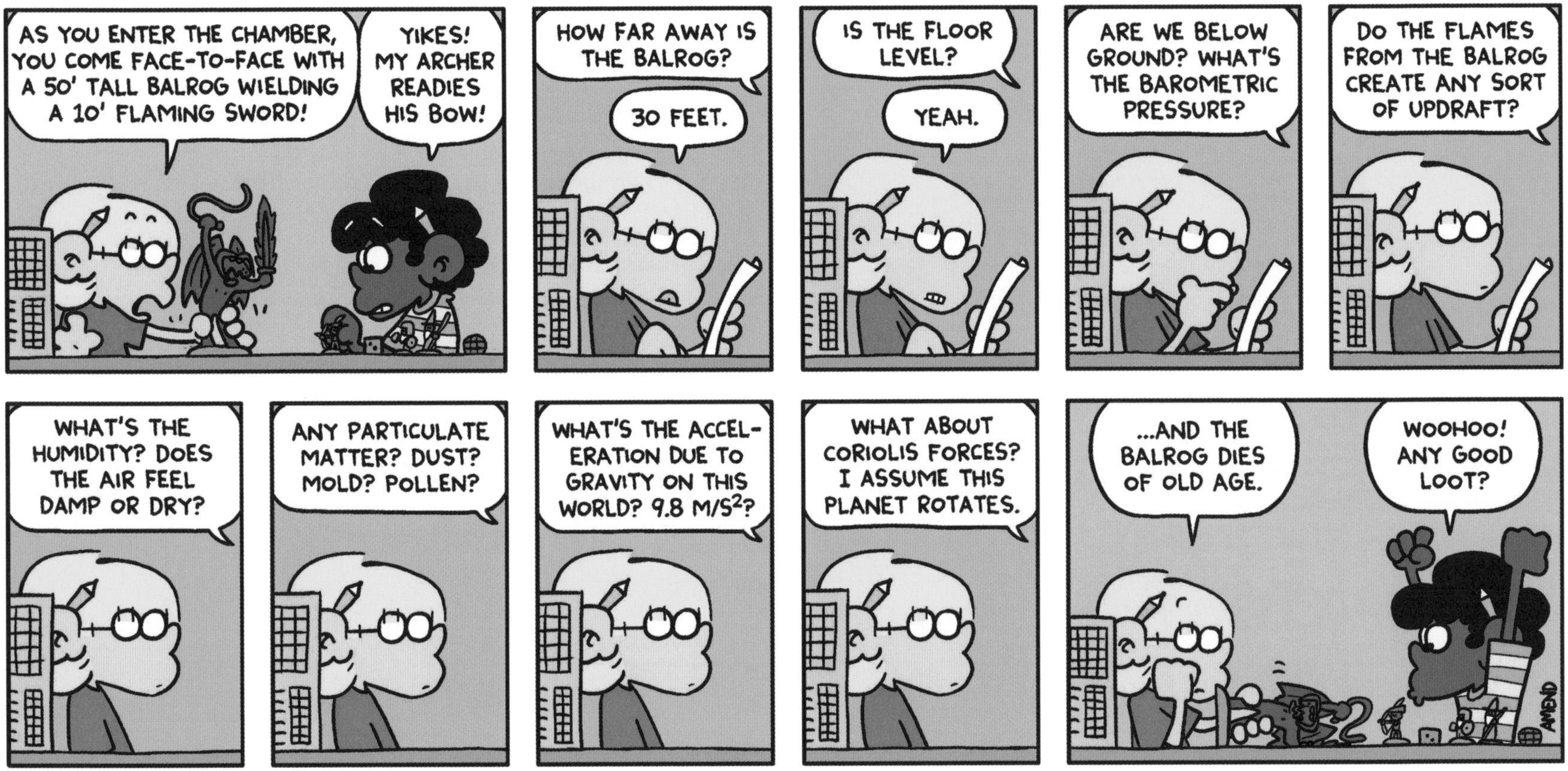

AS YOU ENTER THE CHAMBER, YOU COME FACE-TO-FACE WITH A 50' TALL BALROG WIELDING A 10' FLAMING SWORD!
YIKES! MY ARCHER READIES HIS BOW!
HOW FAR AWAY IS THE BALROG?
30 FEET.
IS THE FLOOR LEVEL?
YEAH.
ARE WE BELOW GROUND? WHAT'S THE BAROMETRIC PRESSURE?
DO THE FLAMES FROM THE BALROG CREATE ANY SORT OF UPDRAFT?
WHAT'S THE HUMIDITY? DOES THE AIR FEEL DAMP OR DRY?
ANY PARTICULATE MATTER? DUST? MOLD? POLLEN?
WHAT'S THE ACCEL-ERATION DUE TO GRAVITY ON THIS WORLD? 9.8 M/S^2?
WHAT ABOUT CORIOLIS FORCES? I ASSUME THIS PLANET ROTATES.
...AND THE BALROG DIES OF OLD AGE.
WOOHOO! ANY GOOD LOOT?
AMEND

Cloudy Vision

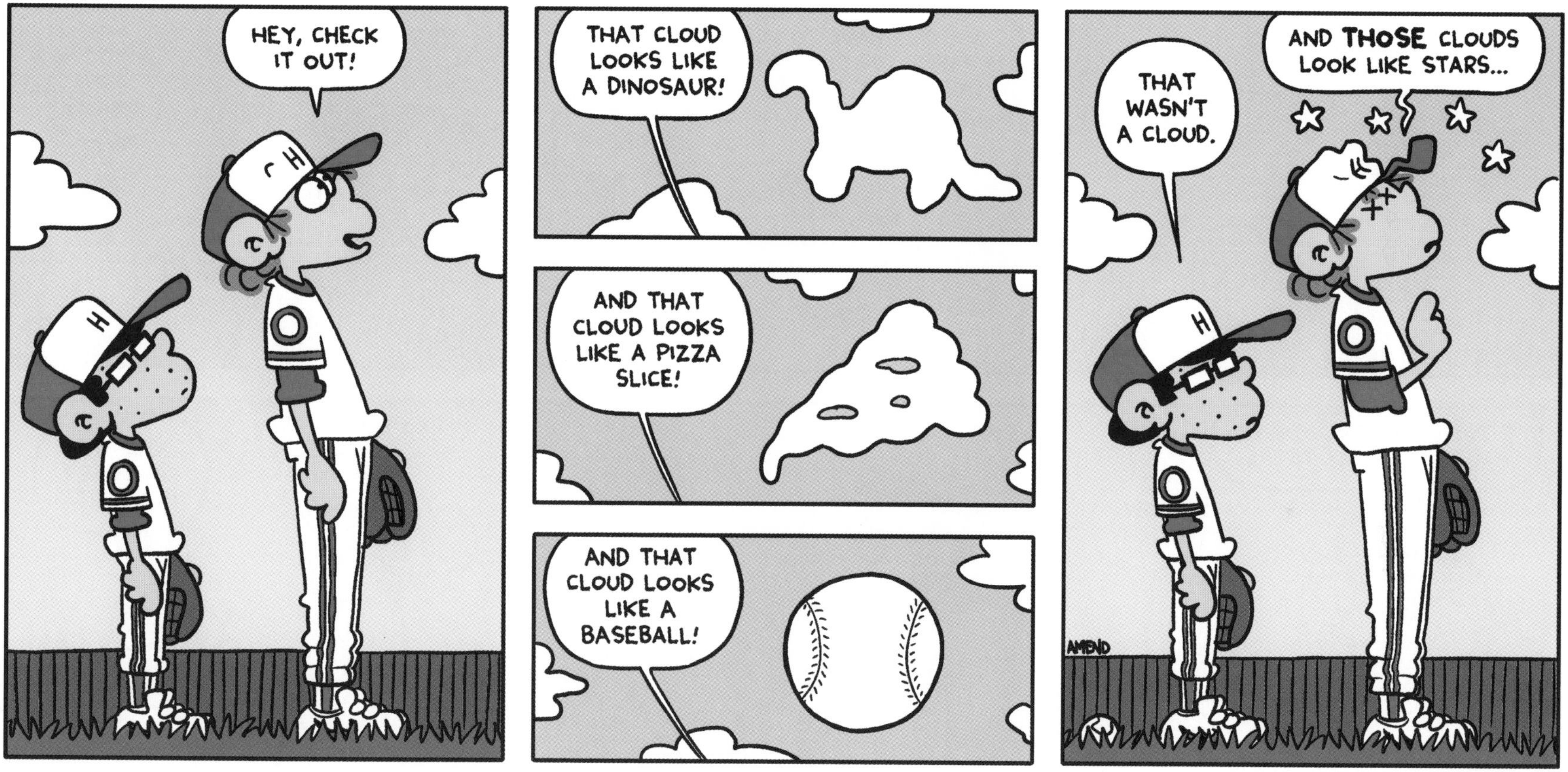
HEY, CHECK IT OUT!
THAT CLOUD LOOKS LIKE A DINOSAUR!
AND THAT CLOUD LOOKS LIKE A PIZZA SLICE!
AND THAT CLOUD LOOKS LIKE A BASEBALL!
THAT WASN'T A CLOUD.
AND THOSE CLOUDS LOOK LIKE STARS...
AMEND

How Much?

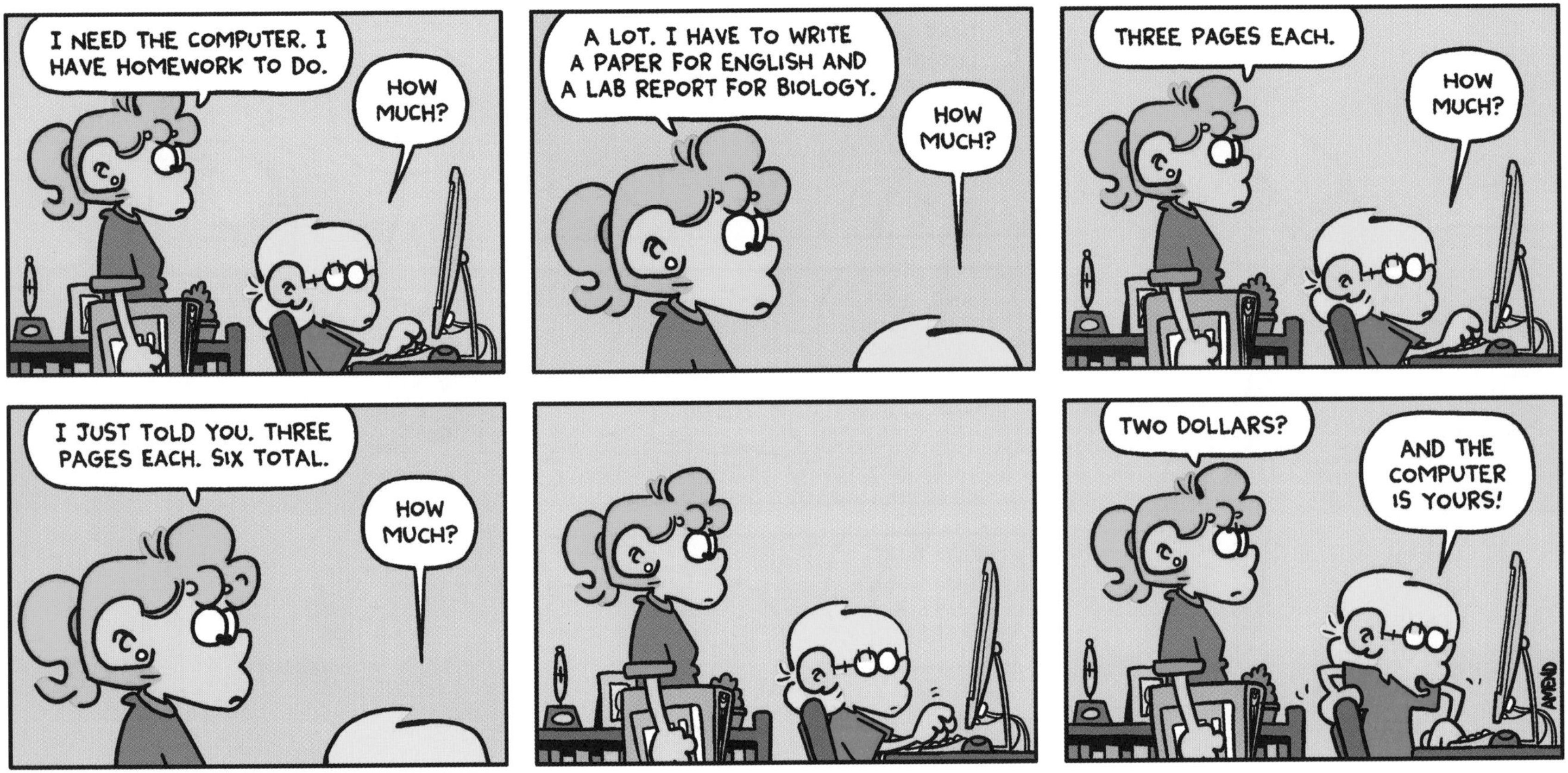
I NEED THE COMPUTER. I HAVE HOMEWORK TO DO.
HOW MUCH?
A LOT. I HAVE TO WRITE A PAPER FOR ENGLISH AND A LAB REPORT FOR BIOLOGY.
HOW MUCH?
THREE PAGES EACH.
HOW MUCH?
I JUST TOLD YOU. THREE PAGES EACH. SIX TOTAL.
HOW MUCH?
TWO DOLLARS?
AND THE COMPUTER IS YOURS!

Aerodumbnamics

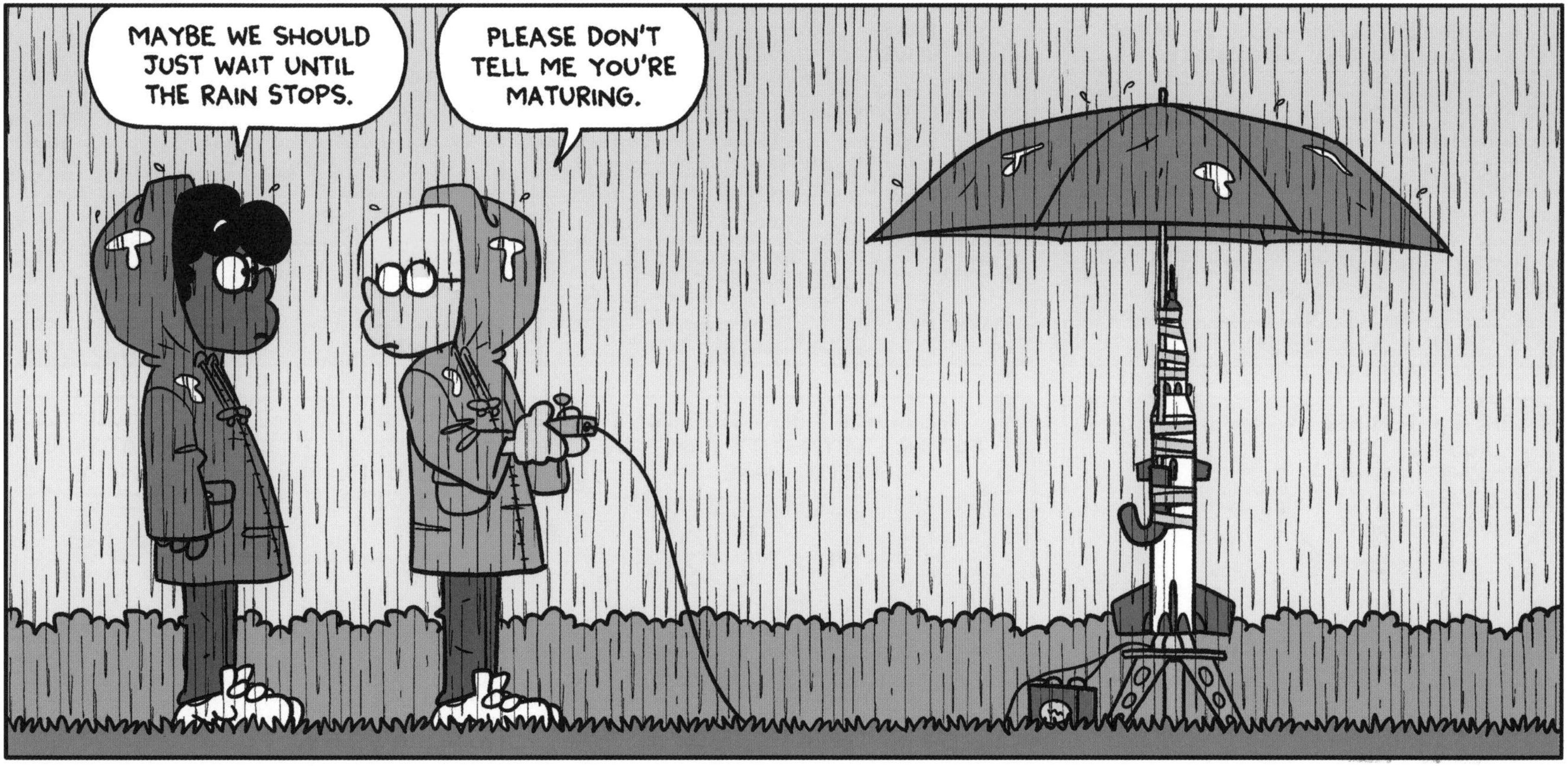
MAYBE WE SHOULD JUST WAIT UNTIL THE RAIN STOPS.
PLEASE DON'T TELL ME YOU'RE MATURING.

Fake News

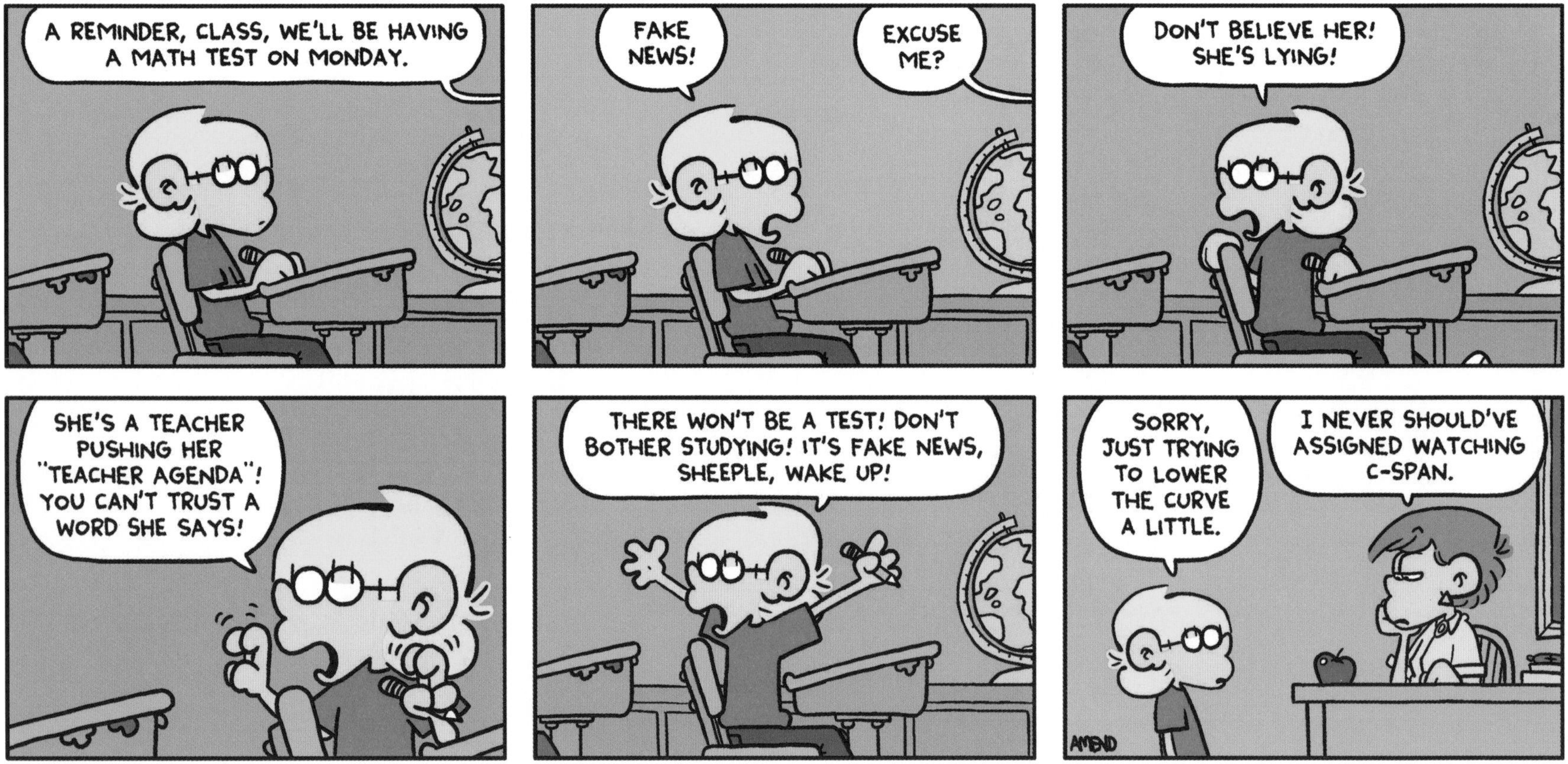
A REMINDER, CLASS, WE'LL BE HAVING A MATH TEST ON MONDAY.
FAKE NEWS!
EXCUSE ME?
DON'T BELIEVE HER! SHE'S LYING!
SHE'S A TEACHER PUSHING HER "TEACHER AGENDA"! YOU CAN'T TRUST A WORD SHE SAYS!
THERE WON'T BE A TEST! DON'T BOTHER STUDYING! IT'S FAKE NEWS, SHEEPLE, WAKE UP!
SORRY, JUST TRYING TO LOWER THE CURVE A LITTLE.
I NEVER SHOULD'VE ASSIGNED WATCHING C-SPAN.
AMEND

Flight Delay

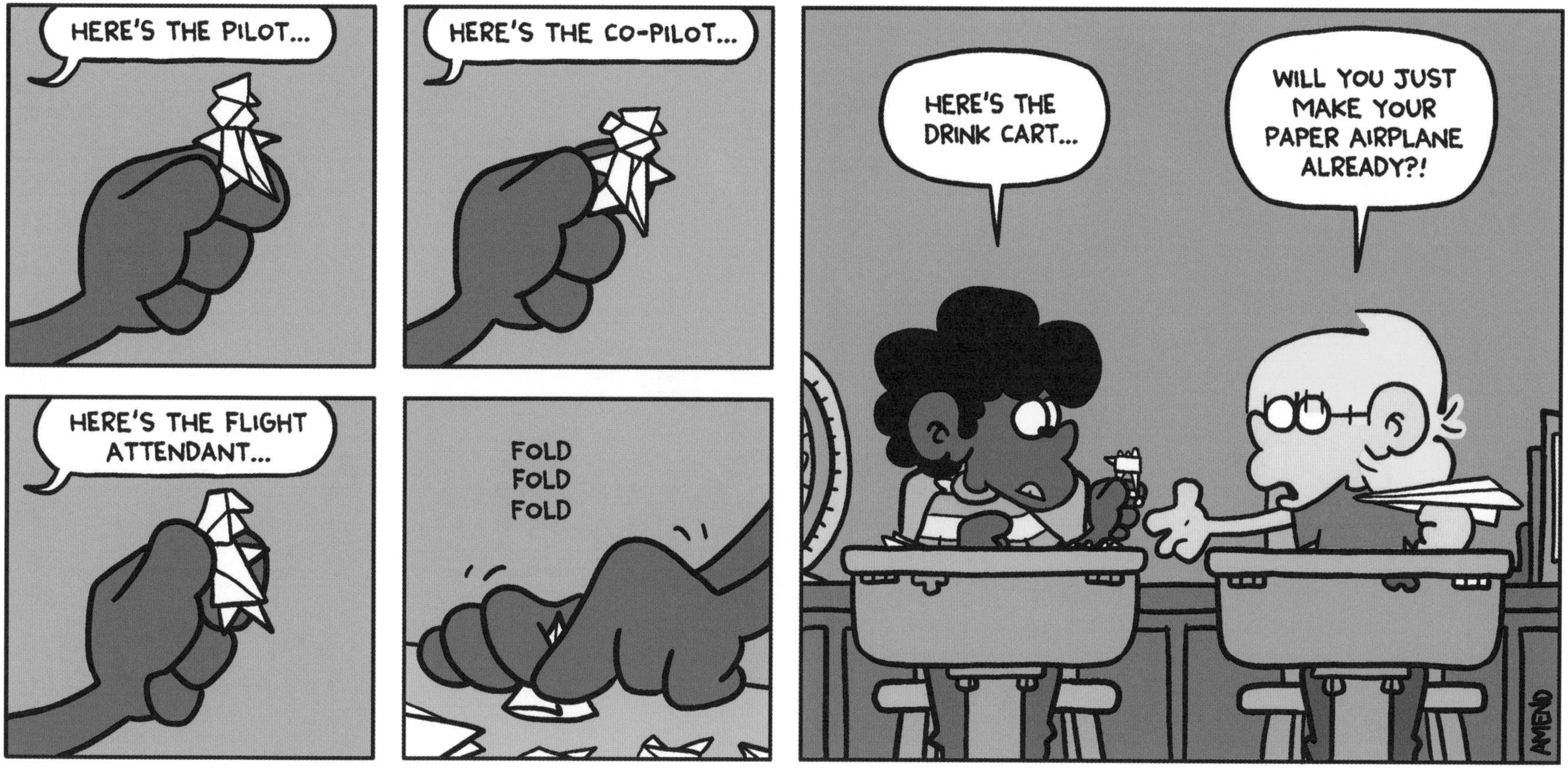
HERE'S THE PILOT...
HERE'S THE CO-PILOT...
HERE'S THE FLIGHT ATTENDANT...
FOLD
FOLD
FOLD
HERE'S THE DRINK CART...
WILL YOU JUST MAKE YOUR PAPER AIRPLANE ALREADY?!
AMEND

Cramming

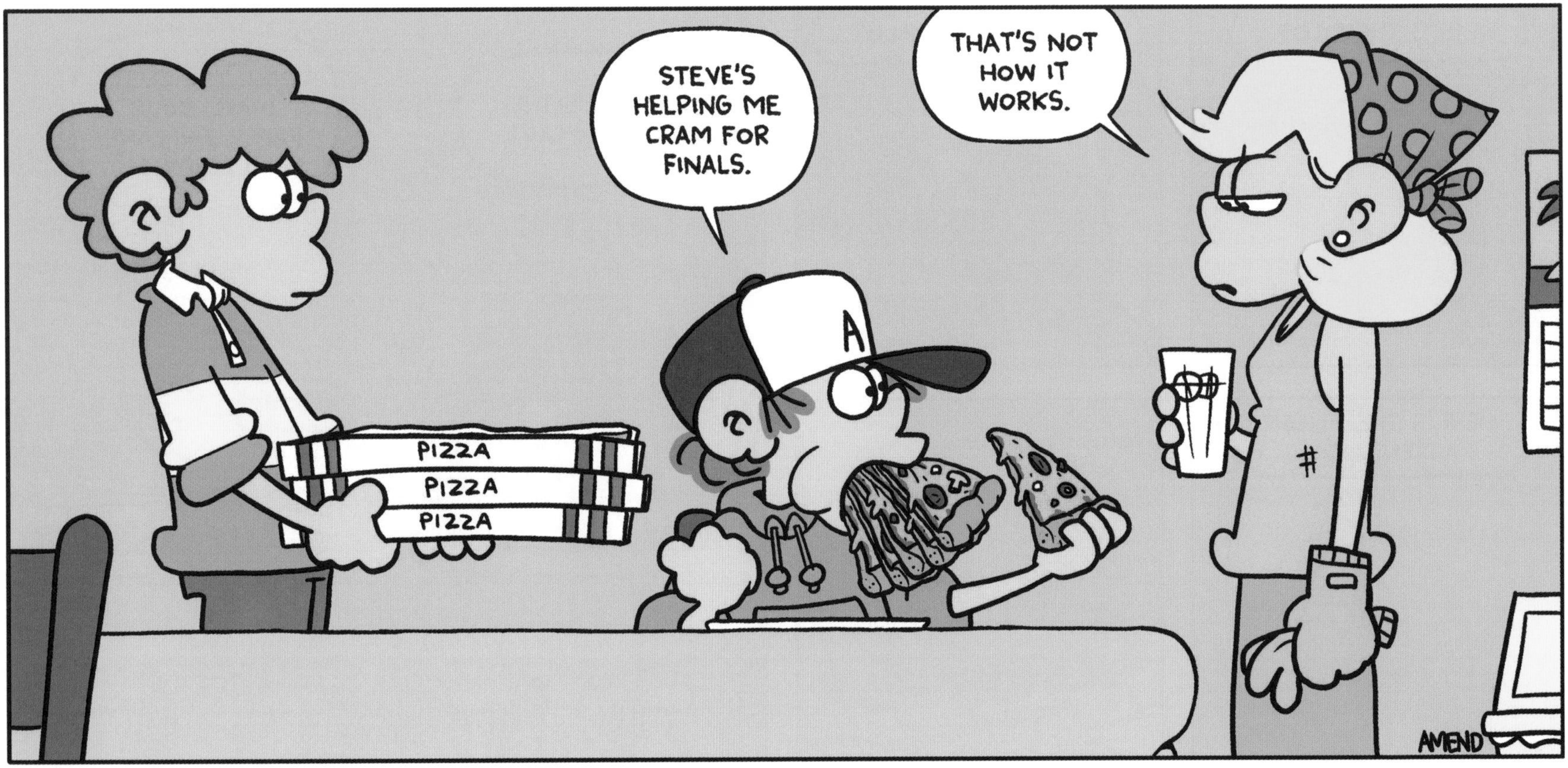
STEVE'S HELPING ME CRAM FOR FINALS.
THAT'S NOT HOW IT WORKS.
PIZZA
PIZZA
PIZZA
A
AMEND

What's Done Is Done

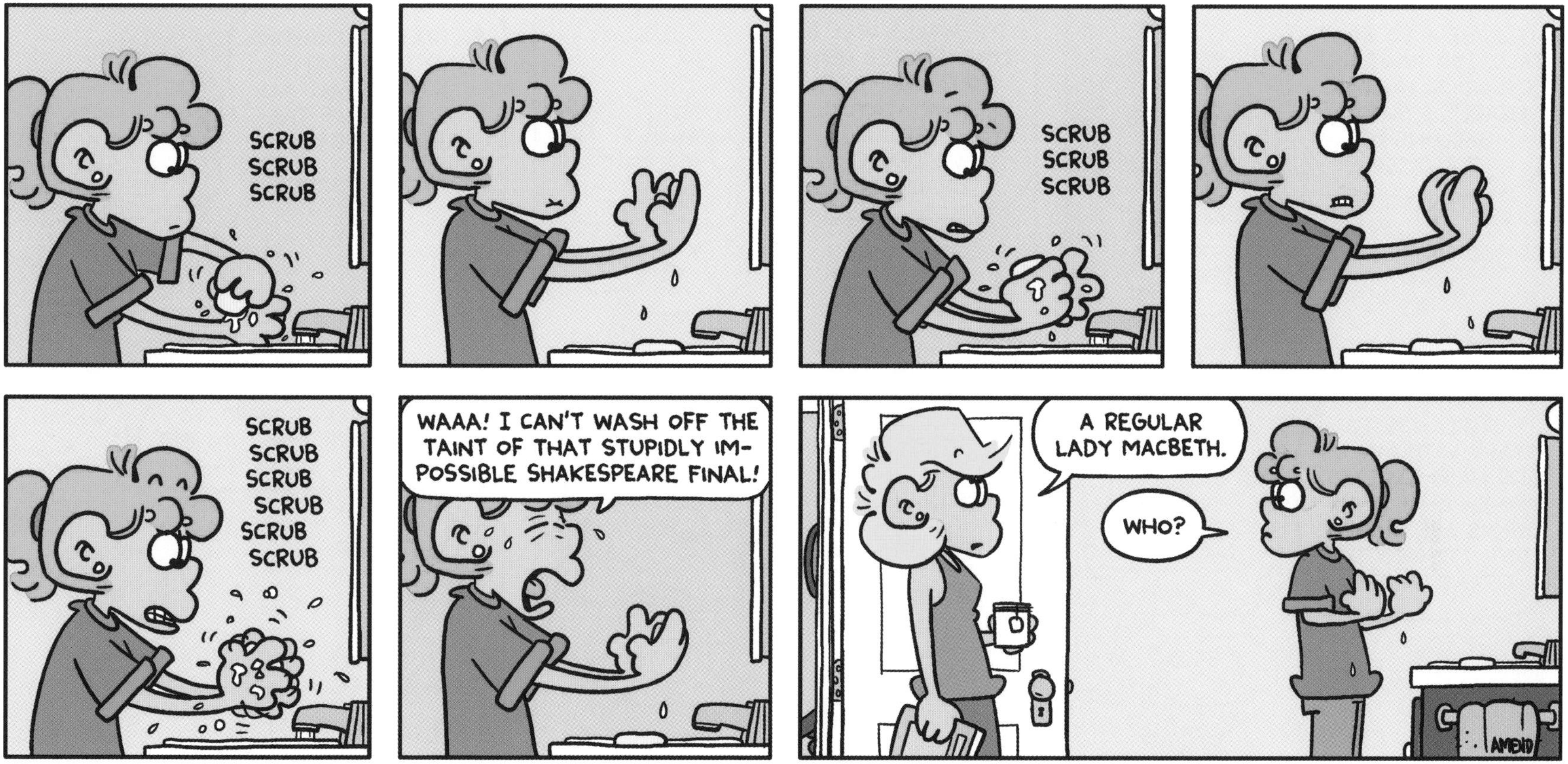
SCRUB
SCRUB
SCRUB
SCRUB
SCRUB
SCRUB
SCRUB
SCRUB
SCRUB
SCRUB
SCRUB
SCRUB
WAAA! I CAN'T WASH OFF THE TAINT OF THAT STUPIDLY IM-POSSIBLE SHAKESPEARE FINAL!
A REGULAR LADY MACBETH.
WHO?

Tank You Very Much

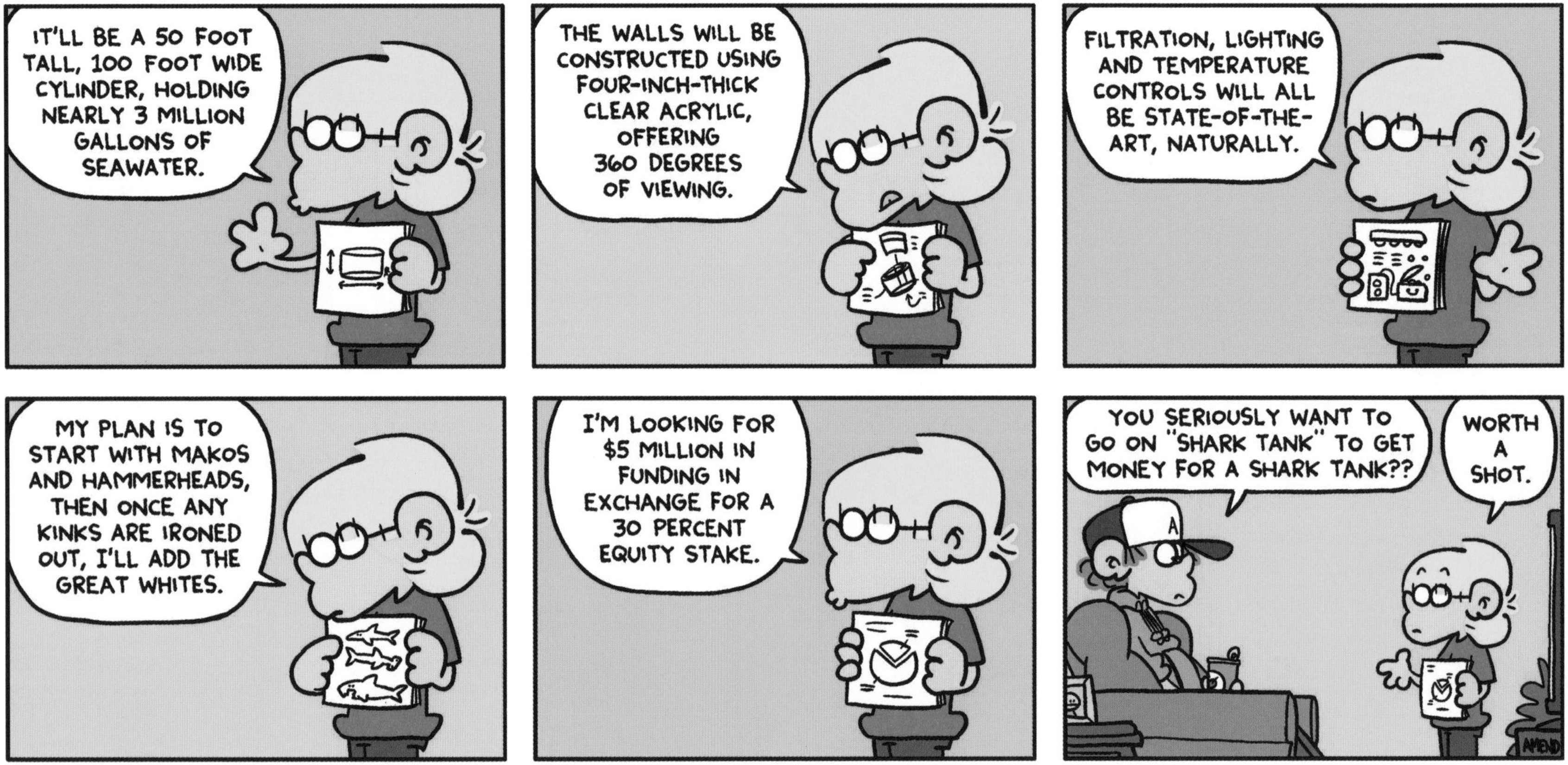
IT'LL BE A 50 FOOT TALL, 100 FOOT WIDE CYLINDER, HOLDING NEARLY 3 MILLION GALLONS OF SEAWATER.
THE WALLS WILL BE CONSTRUCTED USING FOUR-INCH-THICK CLEAR ACRYLIC, OFFERING 360 DEGREES OF VIEWING.
FILTRATION, LIGHTING AND TEMPERATURE CONTROLS WILL ALL BE STATE-OF-THE-ART, NATURALLY.
MY PLAN IS TO START WITH MAKOS AND HAMMERHEADS, THEN ONCE ANY KINKS ARE IRONED OUT, I'LL ADD THE GREAT WHITES.
I'M LOOKING FOR $5 MILLION IN FUNDING IN EXCHANGE FOR A 30 PERCENT EQUITY STAKE.
YOU SERIOUSLY WANT TO GO ON "SHARK TANK" TO GET MONEY FOR A SHARK TANK??
WORTH A SHOT.
AMEND

The Right Medium

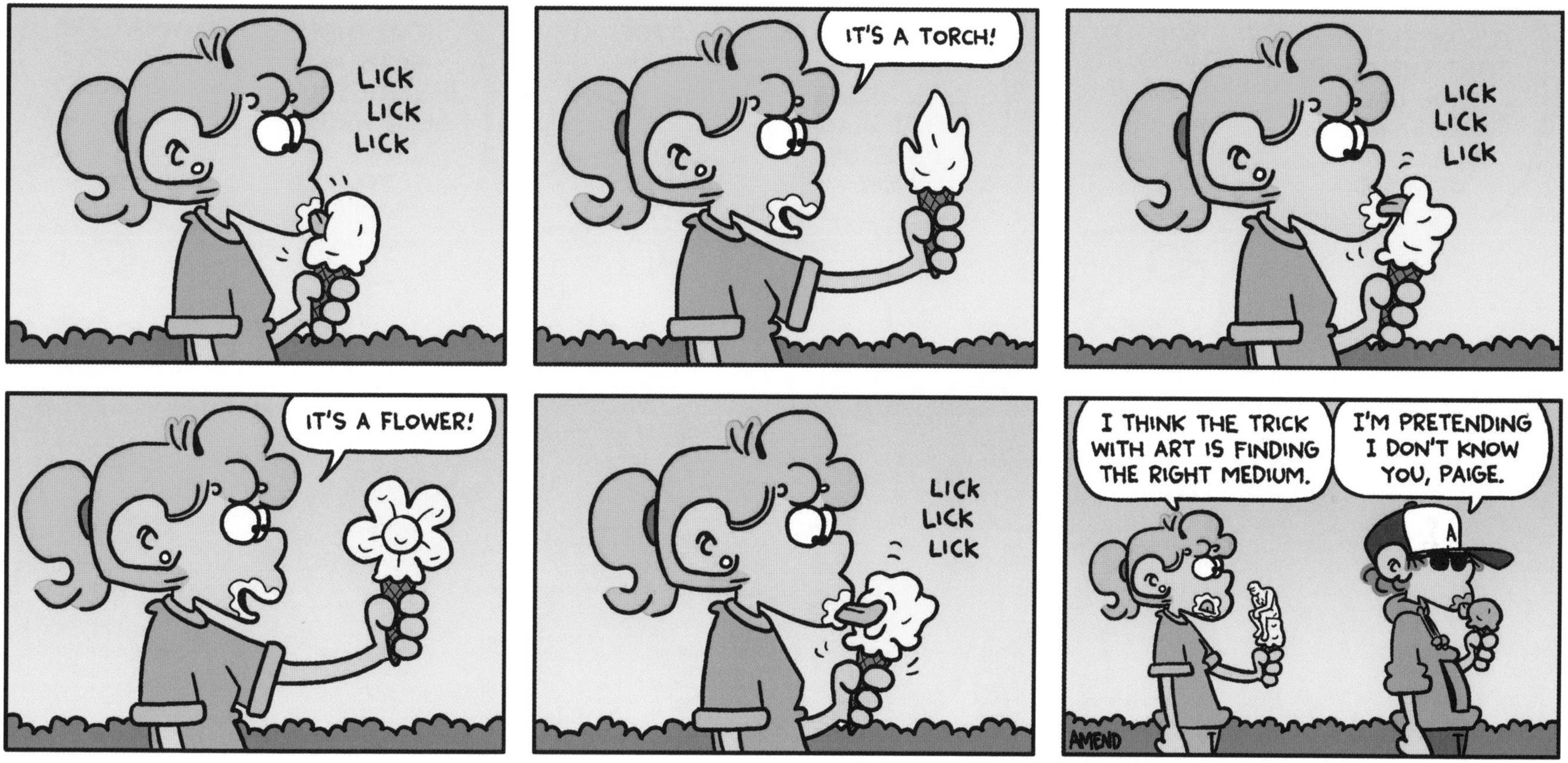
LICK LICK LICK
IT'S A TORCH!
LICK LICK LICK
IT'S A FLOWER!
LICK LICK LICK
I THINK THE TRICK WITH ART IS FINDING THE RIGHT MEDIUM.
I'M PRETENDING I DON'T KNOW YOU, PAIGE.
AMEND

Golfspeak

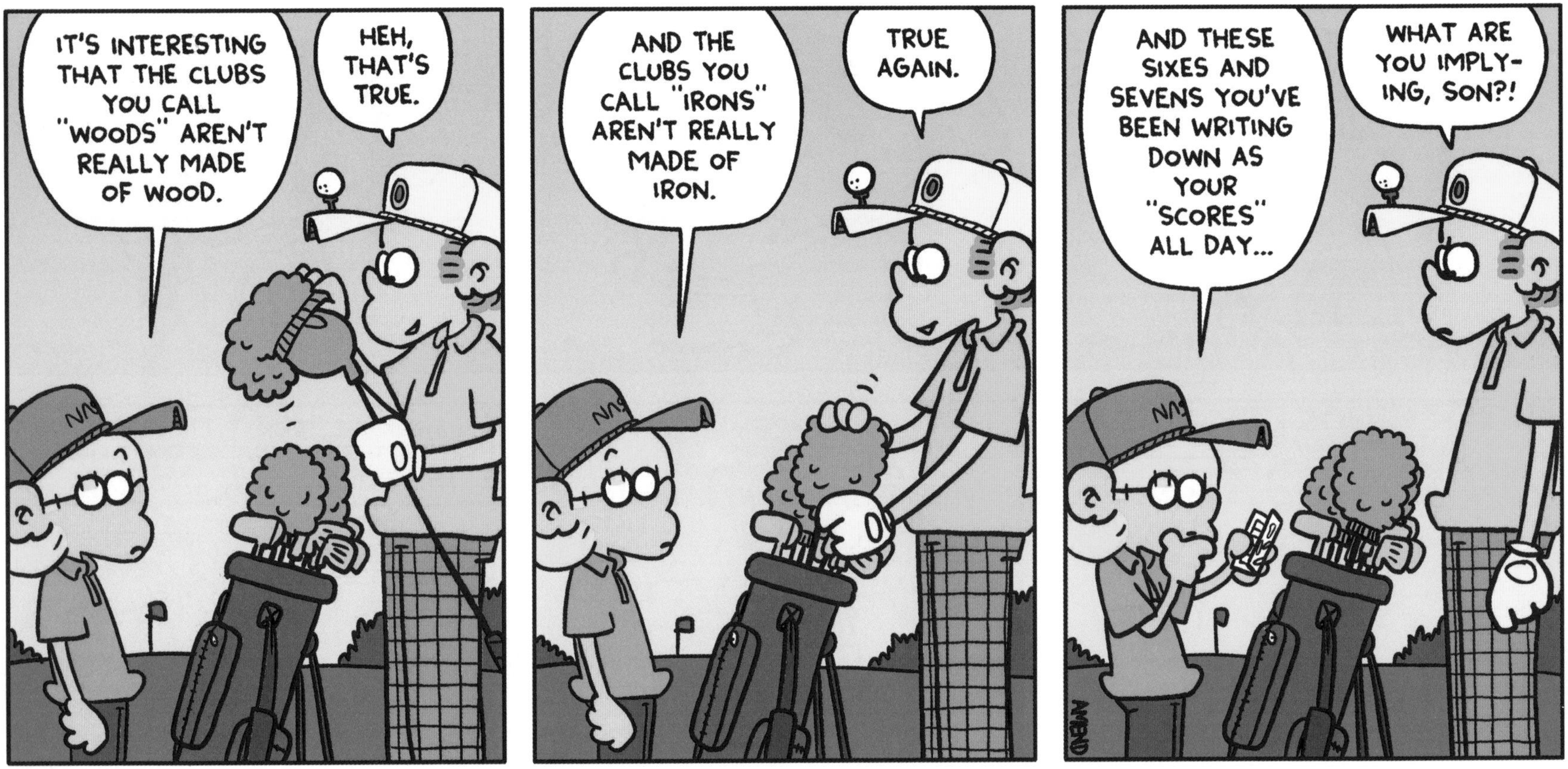
IT'S INTERESTING THAT THE CLUBS YOU CALL "WOODS" AREN'T REALLY MADE OF WOOD.
HEH, THAT'S TRUE.
AND THE CLUBS YOU CALL "IRONS" AREN'T REALLY MADE OF IRON.
TRUE AGAIN.
AND THESE SIXES AND SEVENS YOU'VE BEEN WRITING DOWN AS YOUR "SCORES" ALL DAY...
WHAT ARE YOU IMPLYING, SON?!
AMEND

Balloon Science

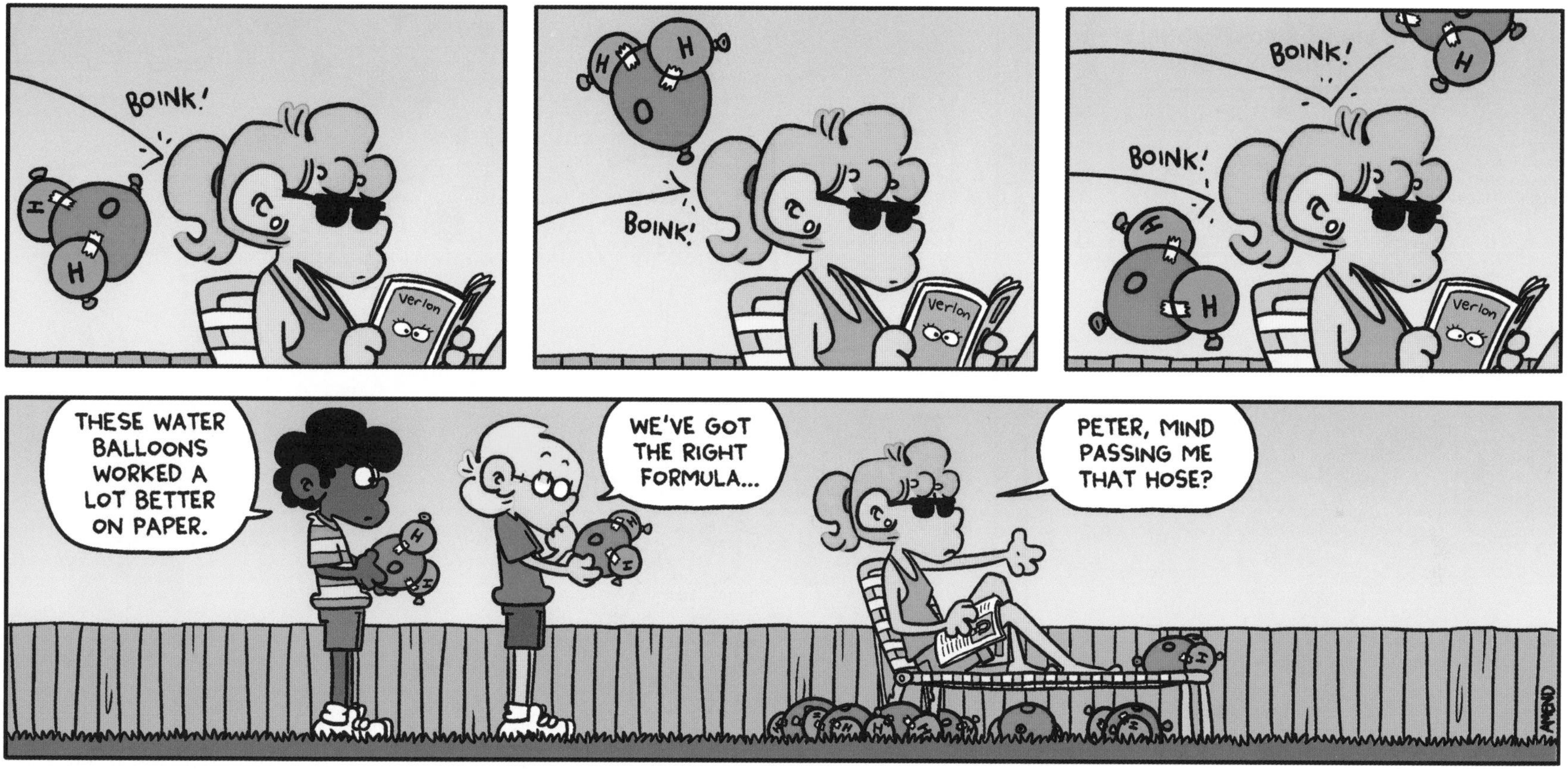
BOINK!
BOINK!
BOINK!
BOINK!
BOINK!
THESE WATER BALLOONS WORKED A LOT BETTER ON PAPER.
WE'VE GOT THE RIGHT FORMULA...
PETER, MIND PASSING ME THAT HOSE?

Smoke Signals

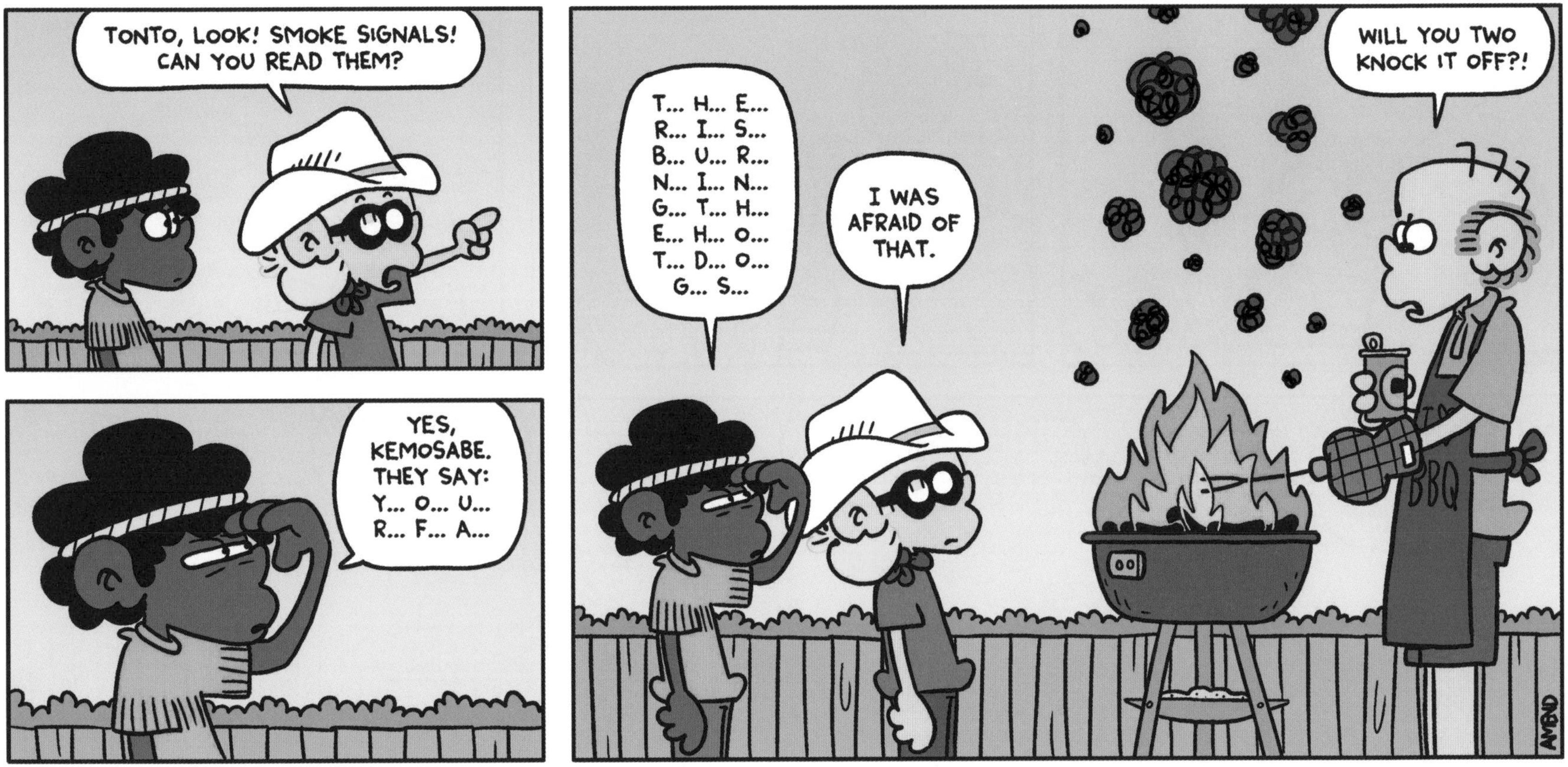

TONTO, LOOK! SMOKE SIGNALS! CAN YOU READ THEM?
YES, KEMOSABE. THEY SAY: Y... O... U... R... F... A...
T... H... E... R... I... S... B... U... R... N... I... N... G... T... H... E... H... O... T... D... O... G... S...
I WAS AFRAID OF THAT.
WILL YOU TWO KNOCK IT OFF?!
BBQ
AMEND

Make It Quick

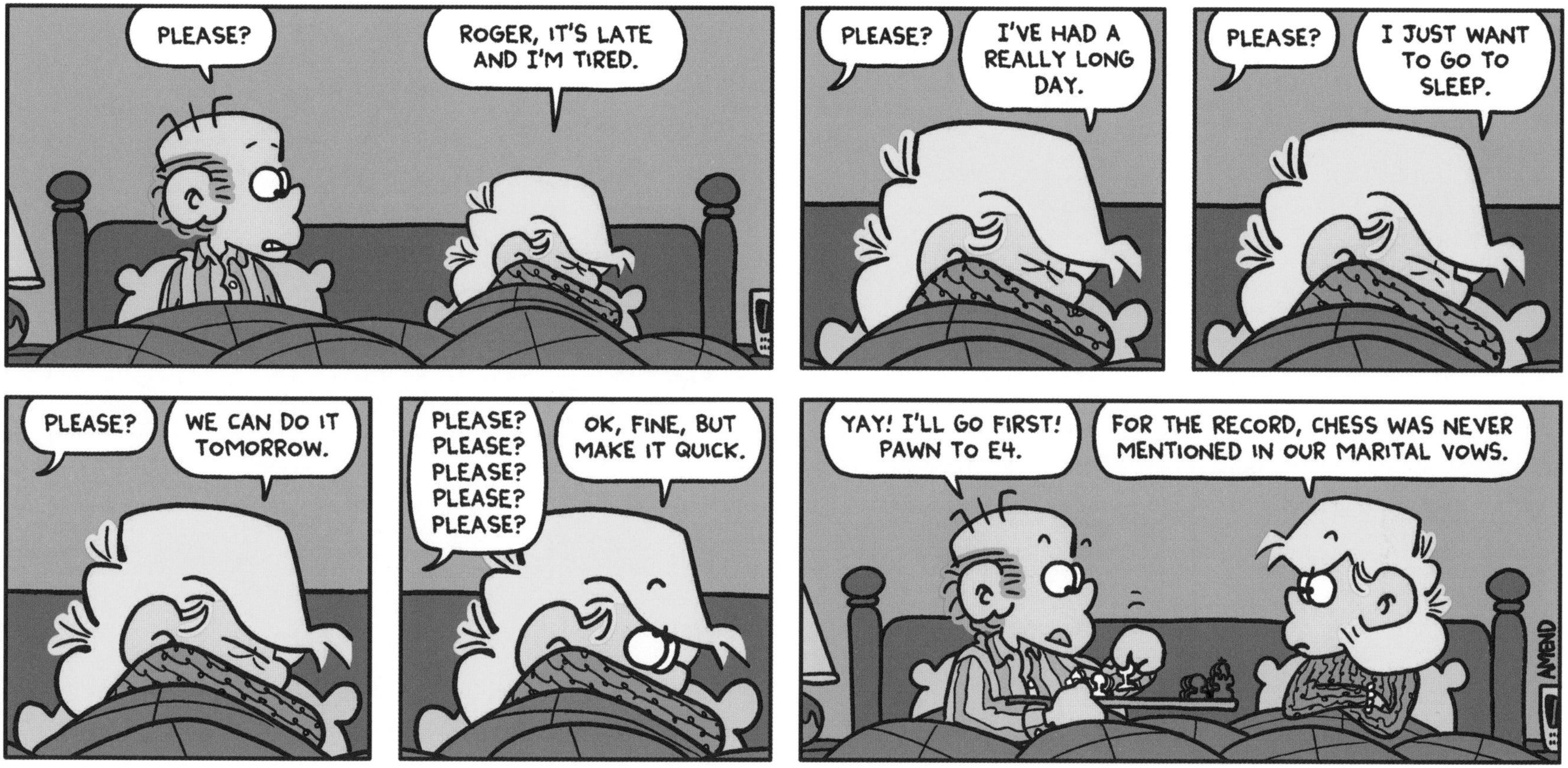
PLEASE?
ROGER, IT'S LATE AND I'M TIRED.
PLEASE?
I'VE HAD A REALLY LONG DAY.
PLEASE?
I JUST WANT TO GO TO SLEEP.
PLEASE?
WE CAN DO IT TOMORROW.
PLEASE? PLEASE? PLEASE? PLEASE? PLEASE?
OK, FINE, BUT MAKE IT QUICK.
YAY! I'LL GO FIRST! PAWN TO E4.
FOR THE RECORD, CHESS WAS NEVER MENTIONED IN OUR MARITAL VOWS.
AMEND

Shoe, Bee!

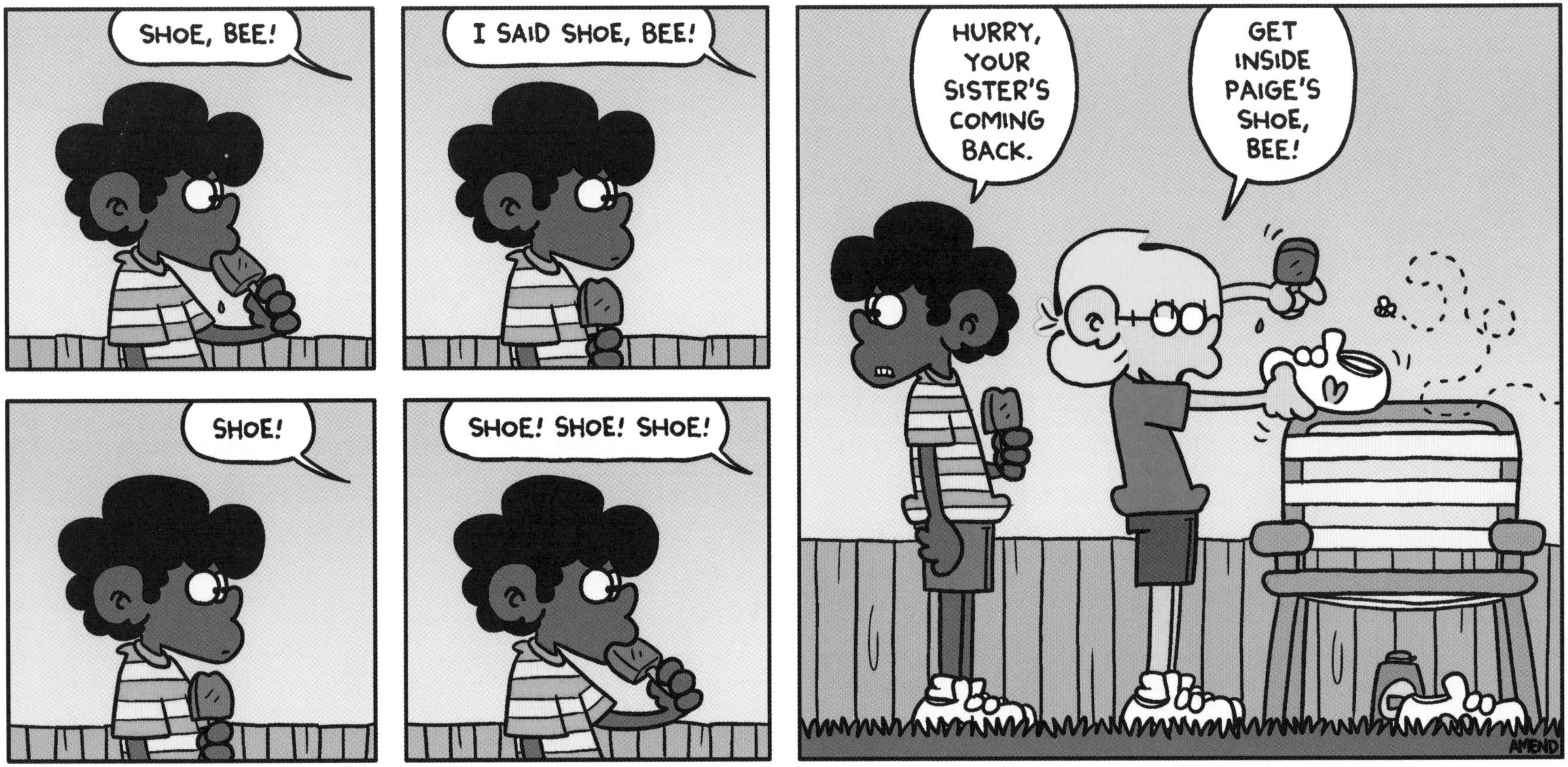
SHOE, BEE!
I SAID SHOE, BEE!
SHOE!
SHOE! SHOE! SHOE!
HURRY, YOUR SISTER'S COMING BACK.
GET INSIDE PAIGE'S SHOE, BEE!
AMEND

Dim City

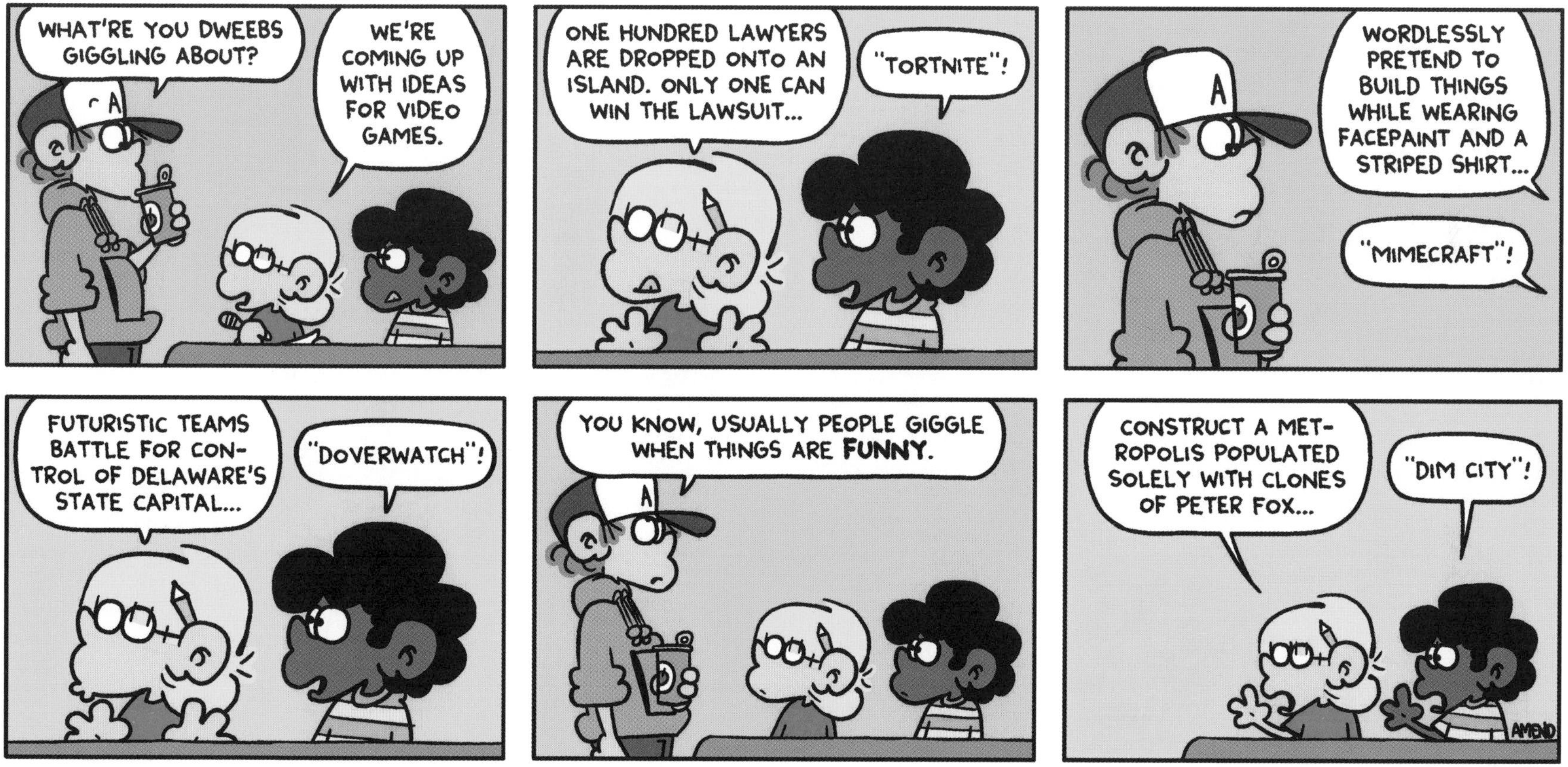
WHAT'RE YOU DWEEBS GIGGLING ABOUT?
WE'RE COMING UP WITH IDEAS FOR VIDEO GAMES.
ONE HUNDRED LAWYERS ARE DROPPED ONTO AN ISLAND. ONLY ONE CAN WIN THE LAWSUIT...
"TORTNITE"!
WORDLESSLY PRETEND TO BUILD THINGS WHILE WEARING FACEPAINT AND A STRIPED SHIRT...
"MIMECRAFT"!
FUTURISTIC TEAMS BATTLE FOR CONTROL OF DELAWARE'S STATE CAPITAL...
"DOVERWATCH"!
YOU KNOW, USUALLY PEOPLE GIGGLE WHEN THINGS ARE FUNNY.
CONSTRUCT A METROPOLIS POPULATED SOLELY WITH CLONES OF PETER FOX...
"DIM CITY"!
AMEND

Playerlist

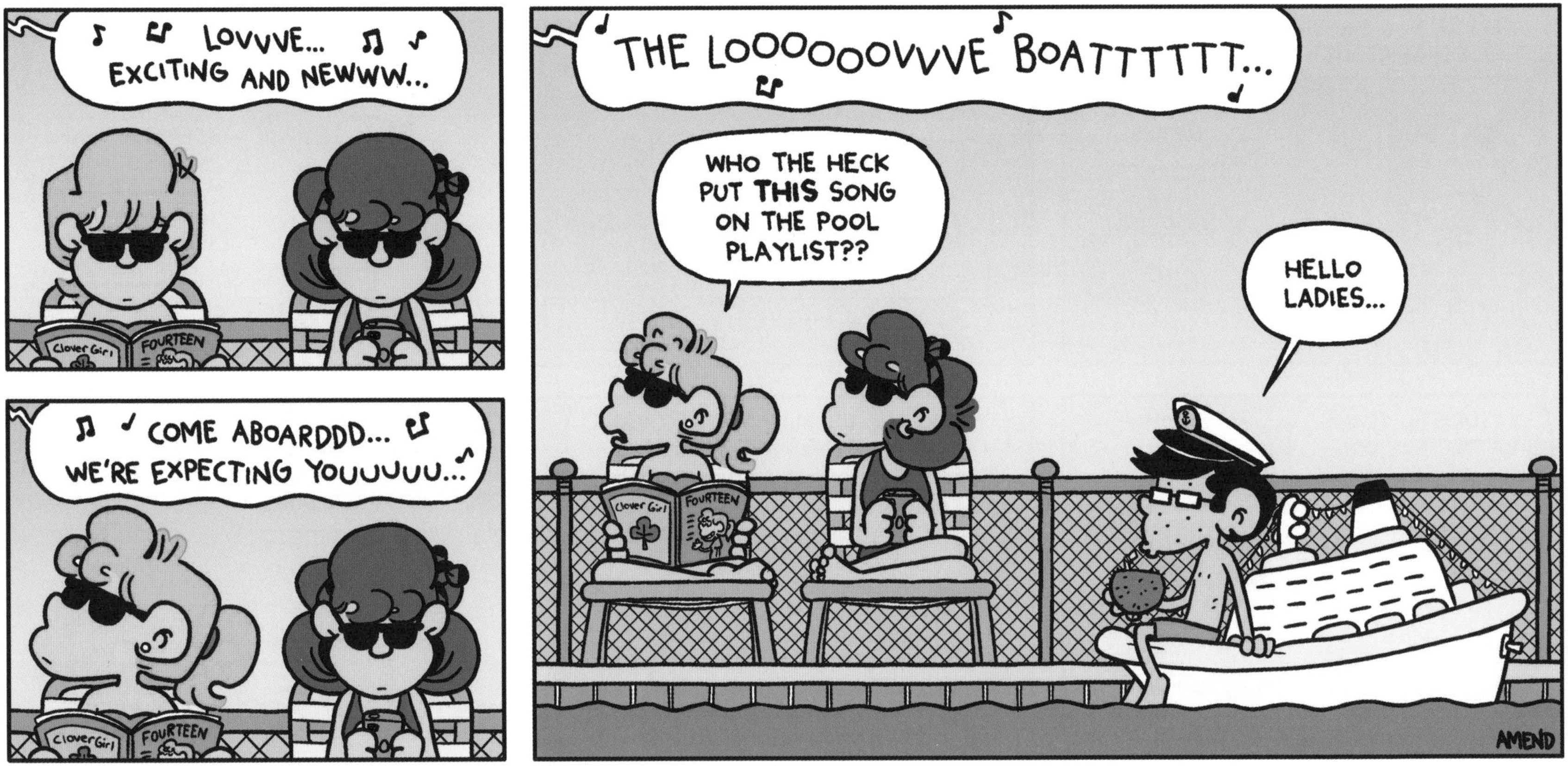

LOVVVE... EXCITING AND NEWWW...
COME ABOARDDD... WE'RE EXPECTING YOUUUUU...
THE LOOOOOOVVVE BOATTTTTT...
WHO THE HECK PUT **THIS** SONG ON THE POOL PLAYLIST??
HELLO LADIES...
Clover Girl
FOURTEEN
AMEND

Corn Dog Amusement

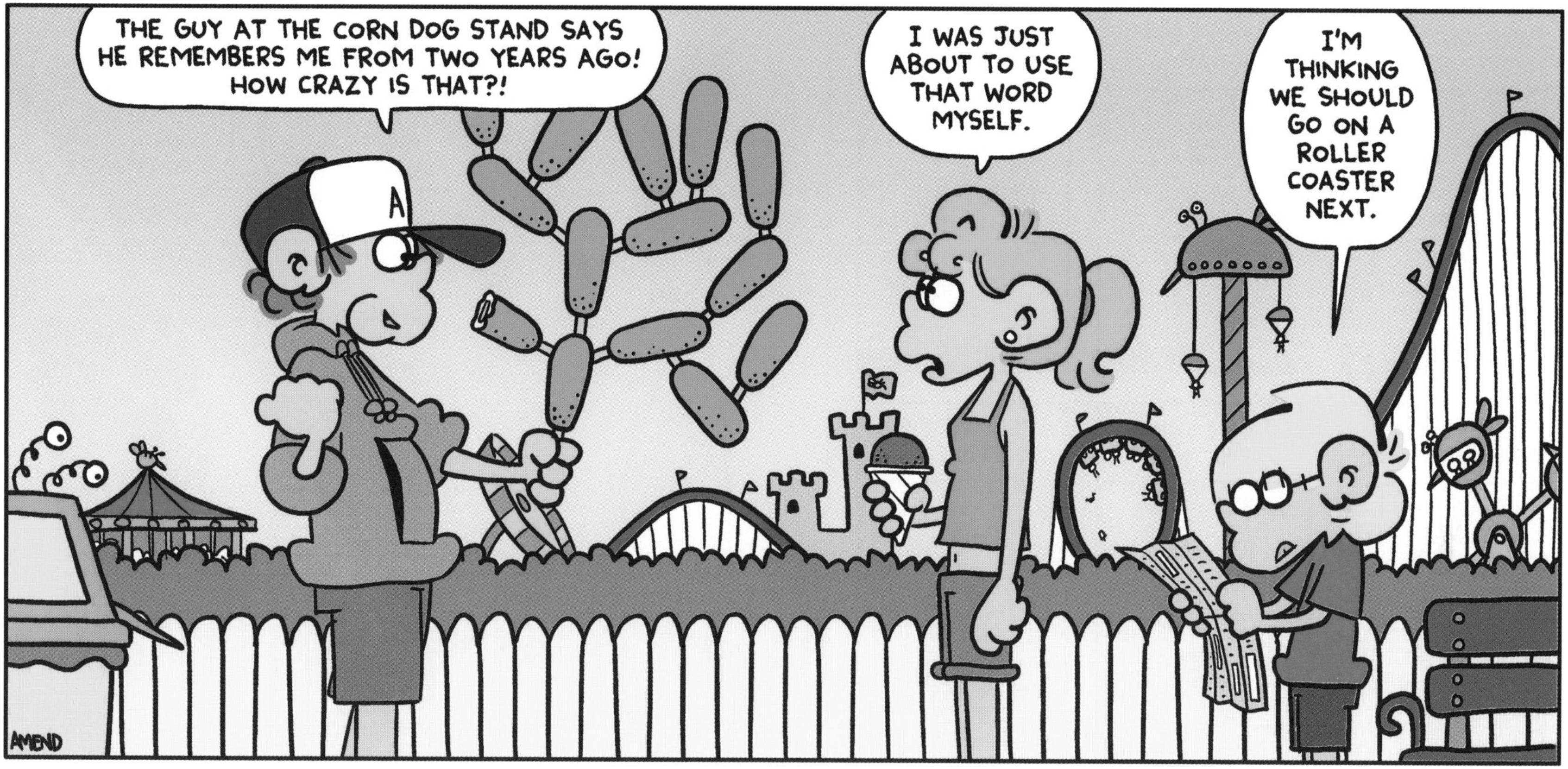
THE GUY AT THE CORN DOG STAND SAYS HE REMEMBERS ME FROM TWO YEARS AGO! HOW CRAZY IS THAT?!
I WAS JUST ABOUT TO USE THAT WORD MYSELF.
I'M THINKING WE SHOULD GO ON A ROLLER COASTER NEXT.
AMEND

Low Pressure

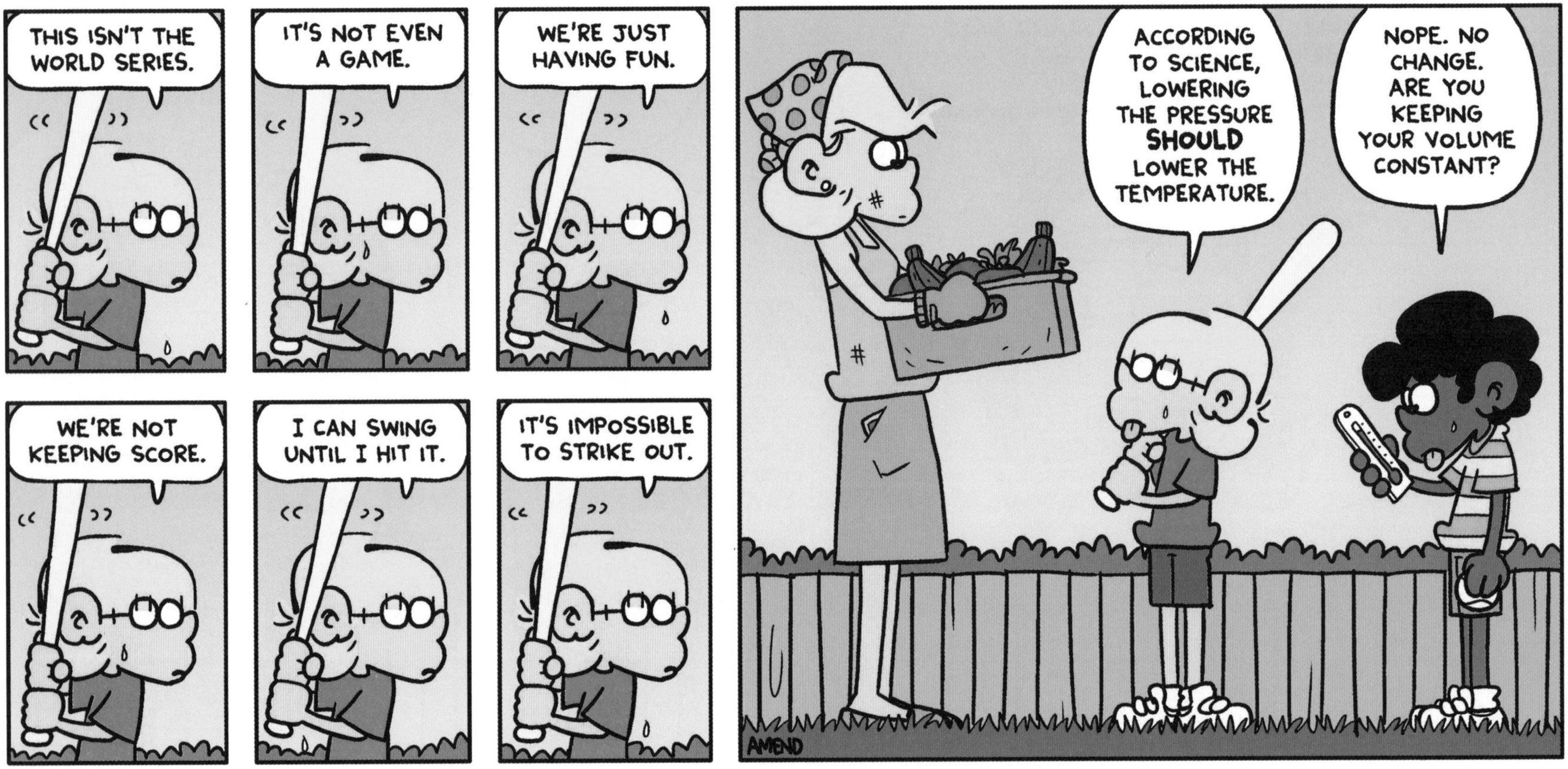
THIS ISN'T THE WORLD SERIES.
IT'S NOT EVEN A GAME.
WE'RE JUST HAVING FUN.
WE'RE NOT KEEPING SCORE.
I CAN SWING UNTIL I HIT IT.
IT'S IMPOSSIBLE TO STRIKE OUT.
ACCORDING TO SCIENCE, LOWERING THE PRESSURE **SHOULD** LOWER THE TEMPERATURE.
NOPE. NO CHANGE. ARE YOU KEEPING YOUR VOLUME CONSTANT?
AMEND

Rub It In

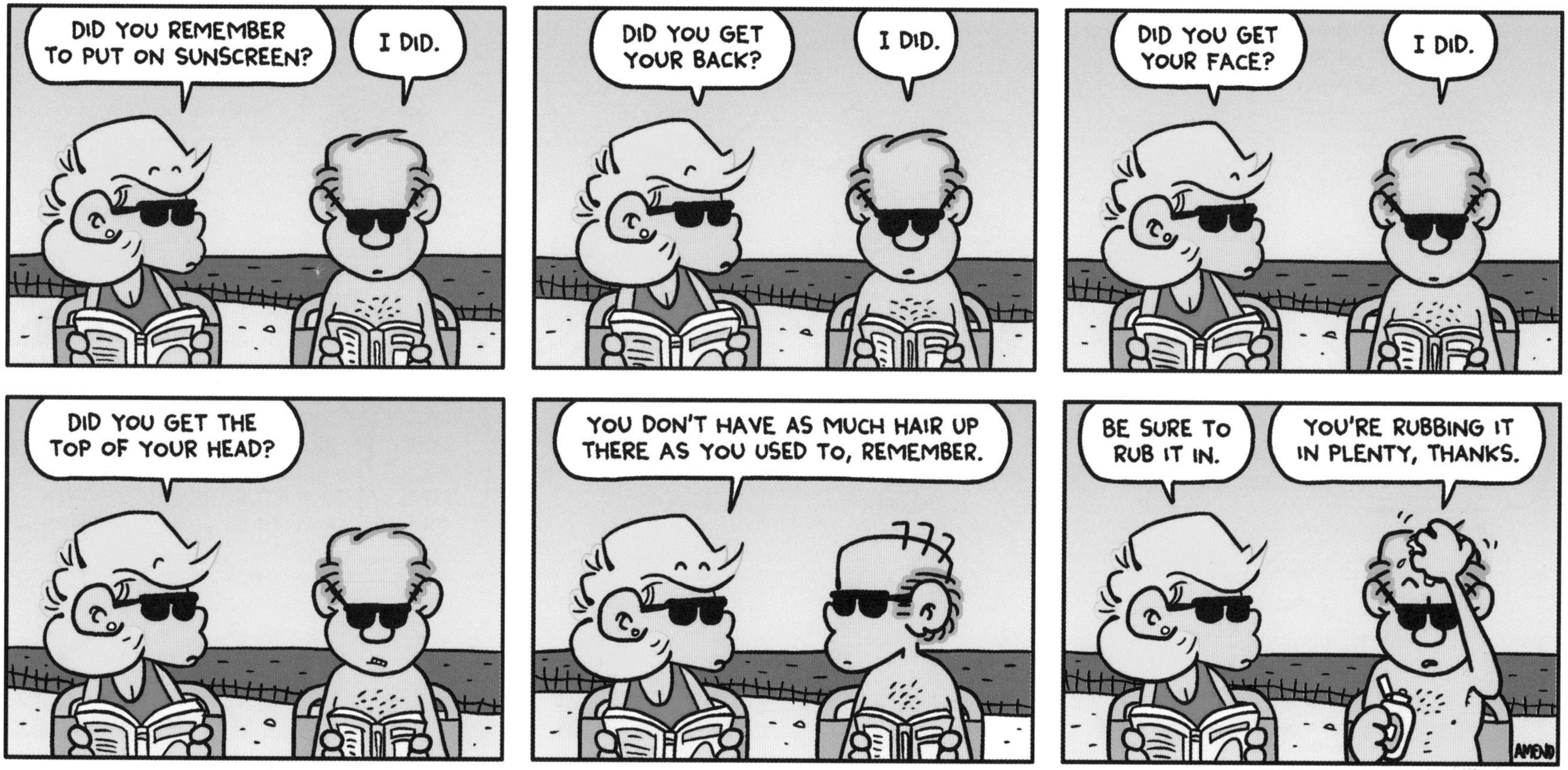
DID YOU REMEMBER TO PUT ON SUNSCREEN?
I DID.
DID YOU GET YOUR BACK?
I DID.
DID YOU GET YOUR FACE?
I DID.
DID YOU GET THE TOP OF YOUR HEAD?
YOU DON'T HAVE AS MUCH HAIR UP THERE AS YOU USED TO, REMEMBER.
BE SURE TO RUB IT IN.
YOU'RE RUBBING IT IN PLENTY, THANKS.
AMEND

Stab Me

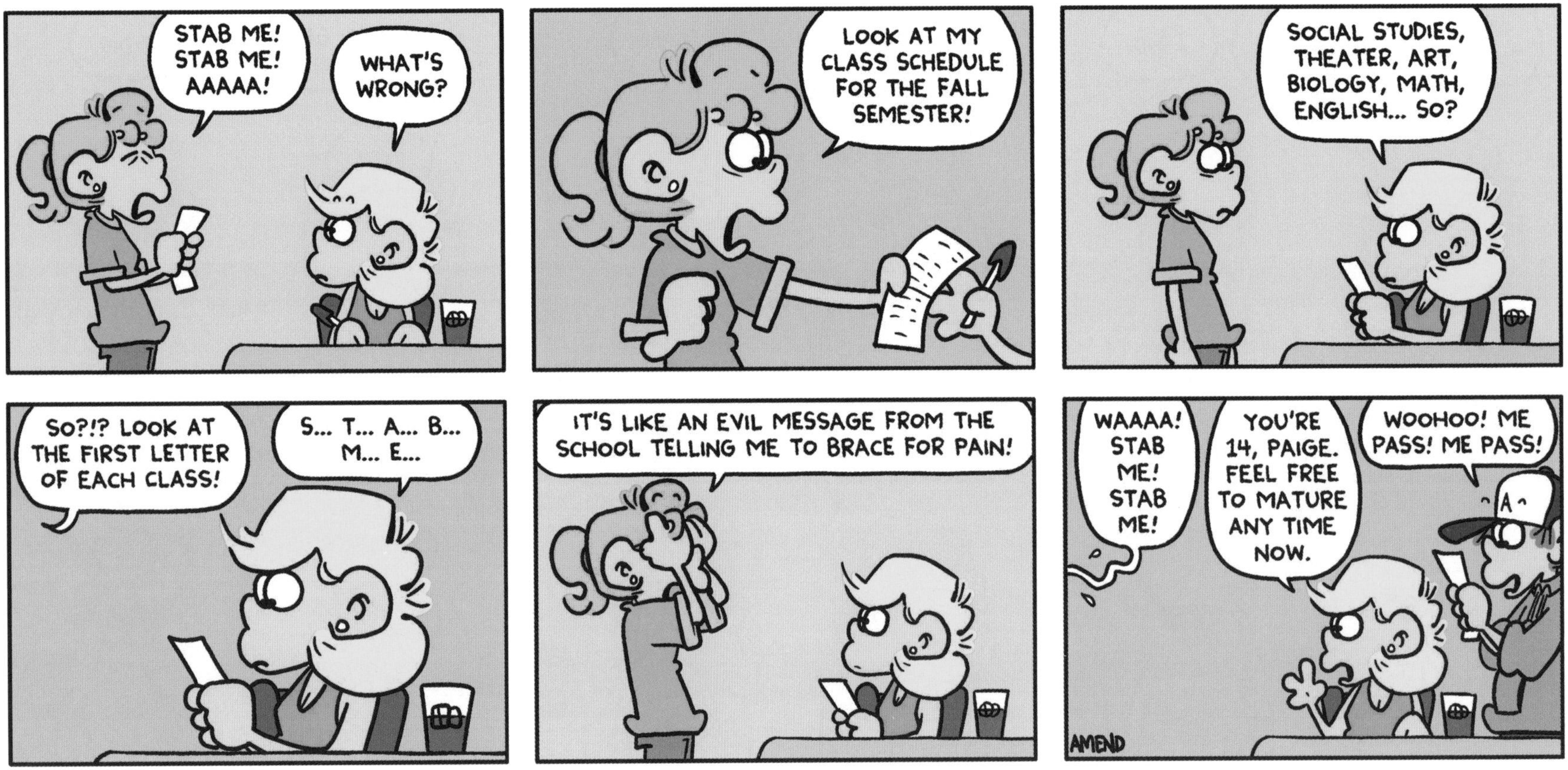
STAB ME! STAB ME! AAAAA!
WHAT'S WRONG?
LOOK AT MY CLASS SCHEDULE FOR THE FALL SEMESTER!
SOCIAL STUDIES, THEATER, ART, BIOLOGY, MATH, ENGLISH... SO?
SO?!? LOOK AT THE FIRST LETTER OF EACH CLASS!
S... T... A... B... M... E...
IT'S LIKE AN EVIL MESSAGE FROM THE SCHOOL TELLING ME TO BRACE FOR PAIN!
WAAAA! STAB ME! STAB ME!
YOU'RE 14, PAIGE. FEEL FREE TO MATURE ANY TIME NOW.
WOOHOO! ME PASS! ME PASS!
AMEND

Shoulda Seen It

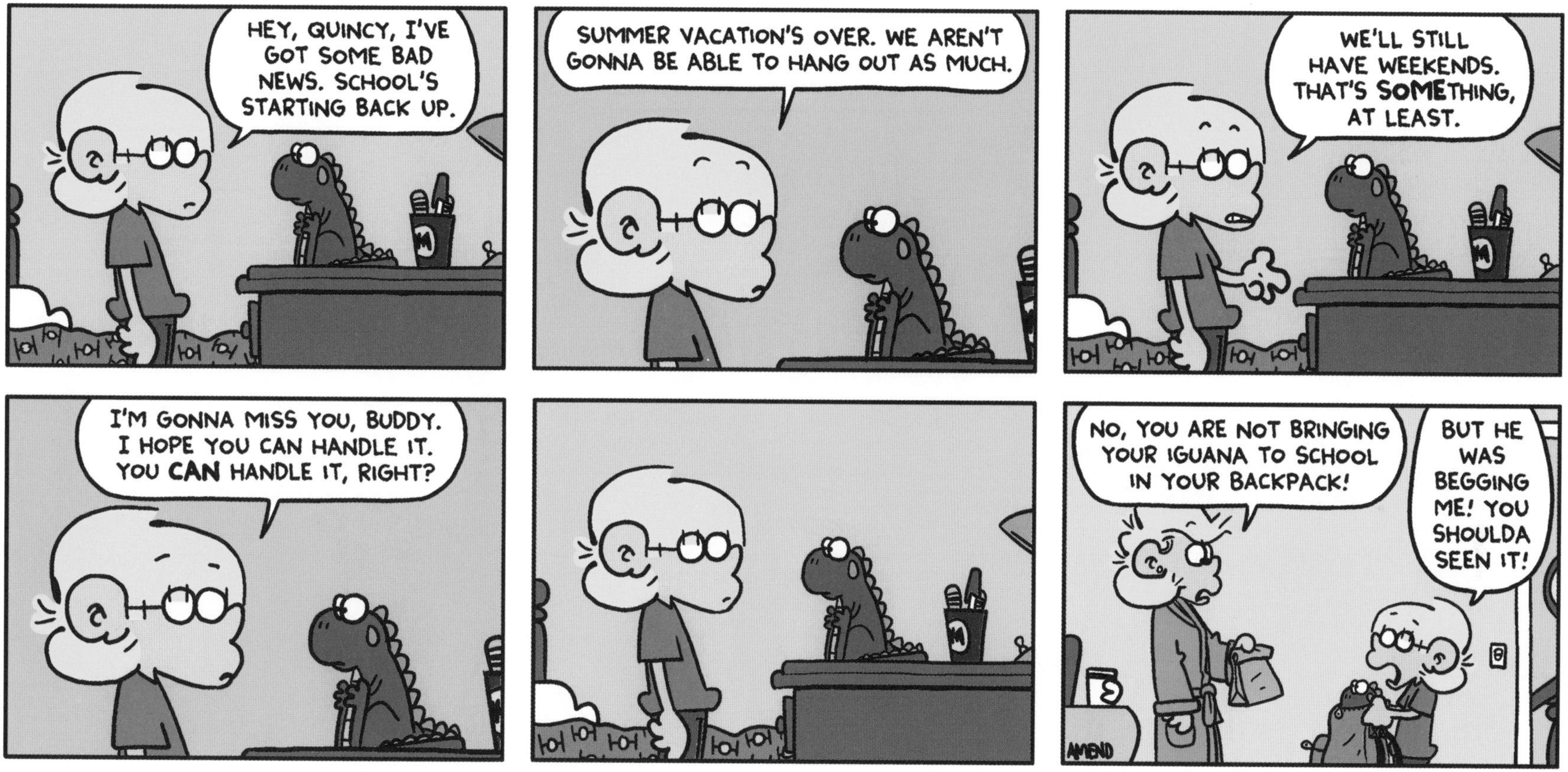

HEY, QUINCY, I'VE GOT SOME BAD NEWS. SCHOOL'S STARTING BACK UP.
SUMMER VACATION'S OVER. WE AREN'T GONNA BE ABLE TO HANG OUT AS MUCH.
WE'LL STILL HAVE WEEKENDS. THAT'S SOMETHING, AT LEAST.
I'M GONNA MISS YOU, BUDDY. I HOPE YOU CAN HANDLE IT. YOU CAN HANDLE IT, RIGHT?
NO, YOU ARE NOT BRINGING YOUR IGUANA TO SCHOOL IN YOUR BACKPACK!
BUT HE WAS BEGGING ME! YOU SHOULDA SEEN IT!
AMEND

He Bobs! He Weaves!

PETER FOX CUTS TO HIS LEFT! HE CUTS TO HIS RIGHT! HE ZIG-ZAGS ACROSS MIDFIELD!

HE BOBS! HE WEAVES! HE JUKES! HE SPINS! NO ONE HAS EVER SEEN MOVES LIKE THESE!

HE CROSSES THE 50! THE 40! THE 30! HE... COULD... GO... ALL... THE... WAY...

...TO WHERE THE TEAM IS WAITING FOR HIM TO DELIVER THEIR WATER!

COACH SAYS I CAN START SUITING UP IN PADS AND A HELMET.

YOU'RE THE TEAM MANAGER. IS THAT NORMAL?

A Mere Quadrillion

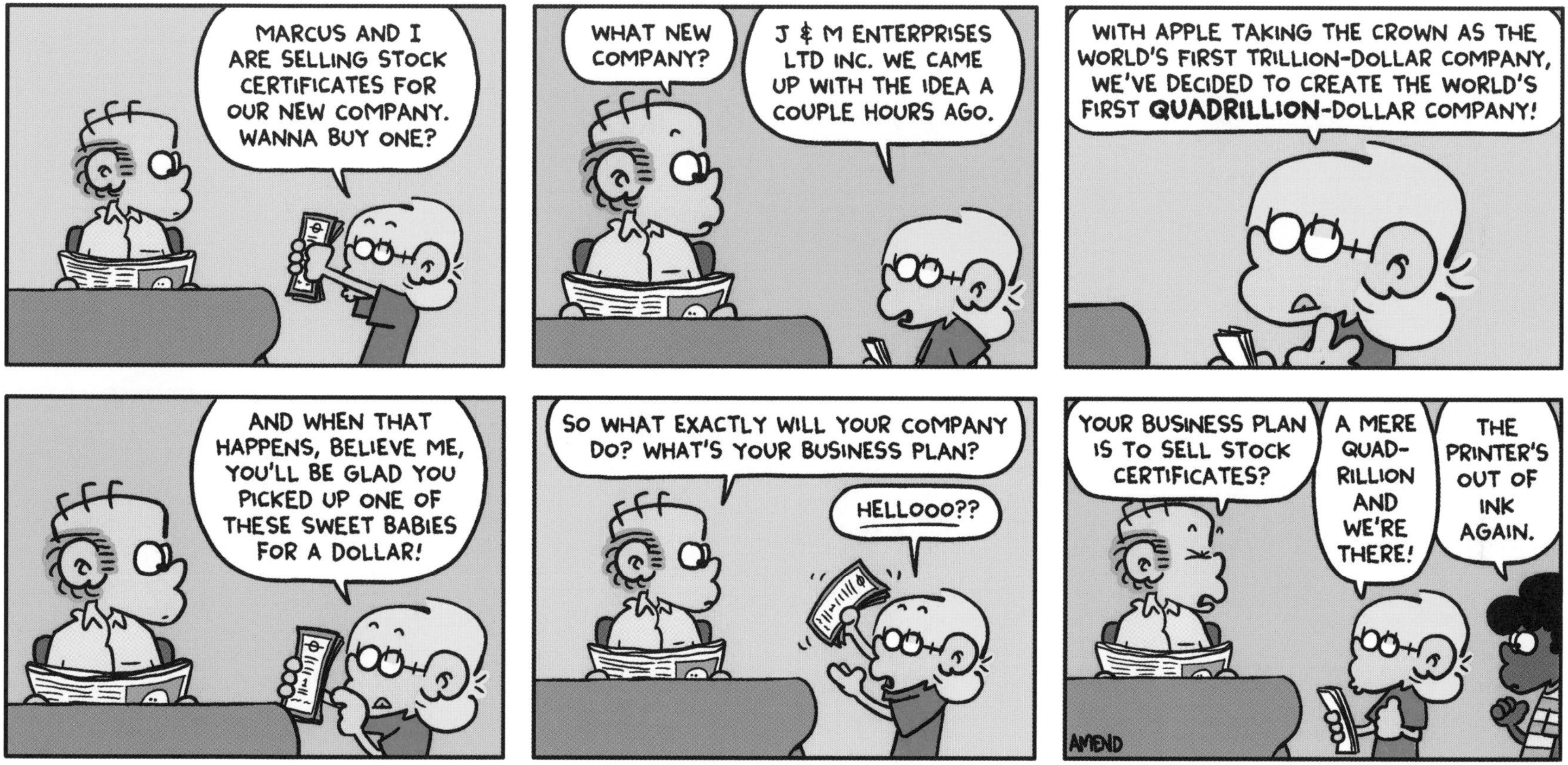
MARCUS AND I ARE SELLING STOCK CERTIFICATES FOR OUR NEW COMPANY. WANNA BUY ONE?
WHAT NEW COMPANY?
J & M ENTERPRISES LTD INC. WE CAME UP WITH THE IDEA A COUPLE HOURS AGO.
WITH APPLE TAKING THE CROWN AS THE WORLD'S FIRST TRILLION-DOLLAR COMPANY, WE'VE DECIDED TO CREATE THE WORLD'S FIRST **QUADRILLION**-DOLLAR COMPANY!
AND WHEN THAT HAPPENS, BELIEVE ME, YOU'LL BE GLAD YOU PICKED UP ONE OF THESE SWEET BABIES FOR A DOLLAR!
SO WHAT EXACTLY WILL YOUR COMPANY DO? WHAT'S YOUR BUSINESS PLAN?
HELLOOO??
YOUR BUSINESS PLAN IS TO SELL STOCK CERTIFICATES?
A MERE QUAD-RILLION AND WE'RE THERE!
THE PRINTER'S OUT OF INK AGAIN.
AMEND

Jacks

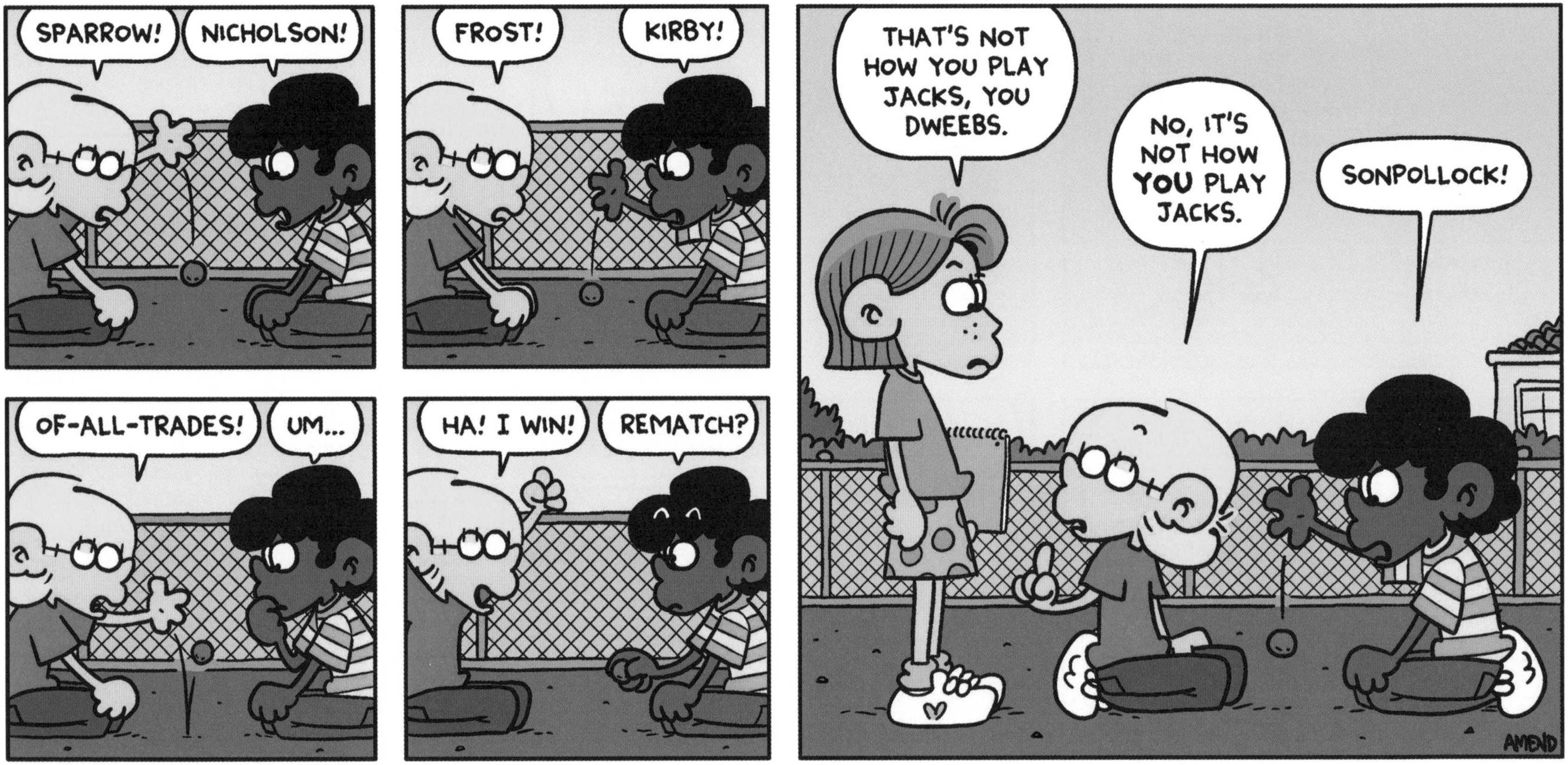
SPARROW!
NICHOLSON!
FROST!
KIRBY!
OF-ALL-TRADES!
UM...
HA! I WIN!
REMATCH?
THAT'S NOT HOW YOU PLAY JACKS, YOU DWEEBS.
NO, IT'S NOT HOW YOU PLAY JACKS.
SONPOLLOCK!
AMEND

Slow Phone

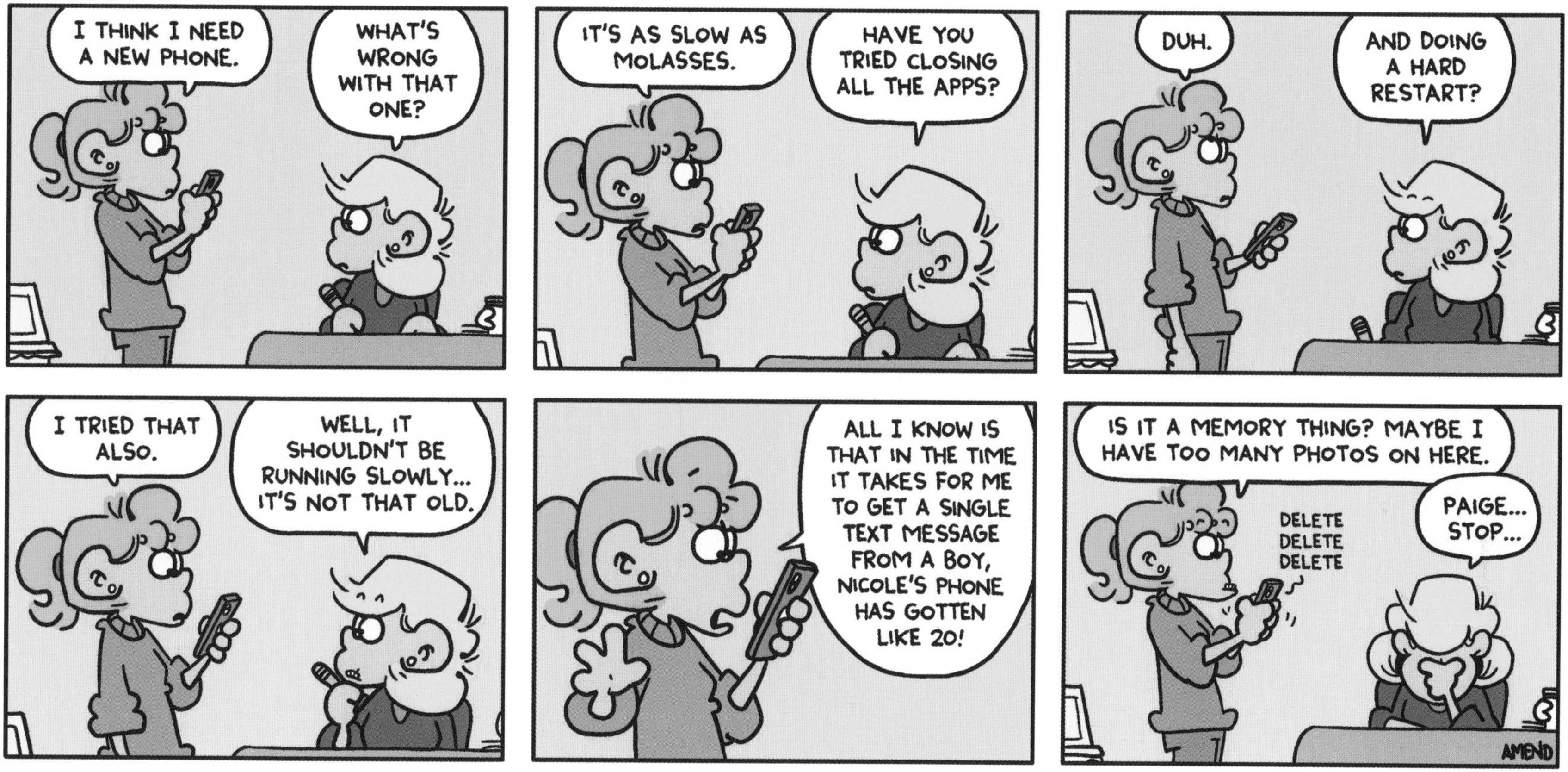
I THINK I NEED A NEW PHONE.
WHAT'S WRONG WITH THAT ONE?
IT'S AS SLOW AS MOLASSES.
HAVE YOU TRIED CLOSING ALL THE APPS?
DUH.
AND DOING A HARD RESTART?
I TRIED THAT ALSO.
WELL, IT SHOULDN'T BE RUNNING SLOWLY... IT'S NOT THAT OLD.
ALL I KNOW IS THAT IN THE TIME IT TAKES FOR ME TO GET A SINGLE TEXT MESSAGE FROM A BOY, NICOLE'S PHONE HAS GOTTEN LIKE 20!
IS IT A MEMORY THING? MAYBE I HAVE TOO MANY PHOTOS ON HERE.
DELETE DELETE DELETE
PAIGE... STOP...
AMEND

Energy Boost

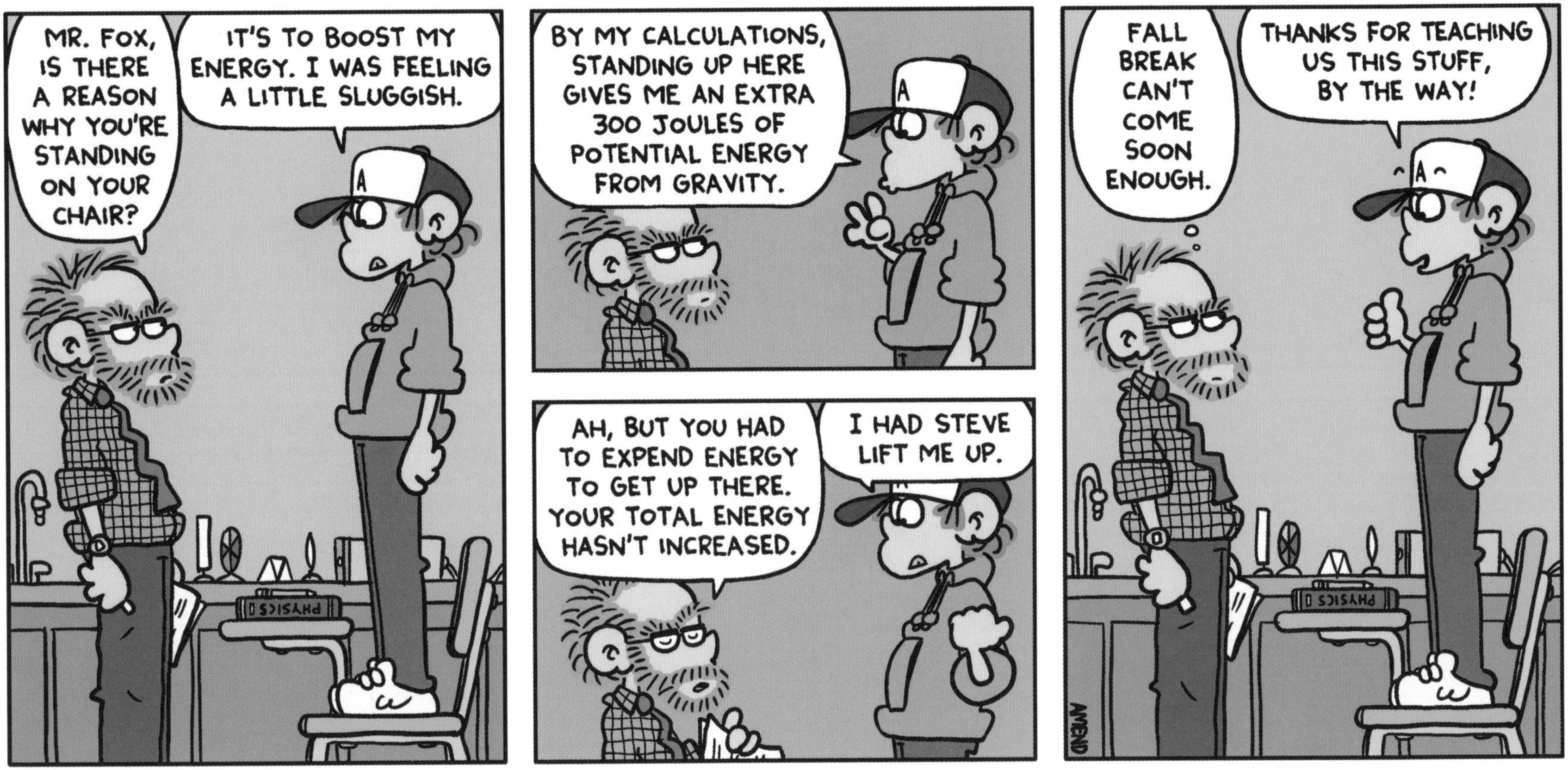
MR. FOX, IS THERE A REASON WHY YOU'RE STANDING ON YOUR CHAIR?
IT'S TO BOOST MY ENERGY. I WAS FEELING A LITTLE SLUGGISH.
PHYSICS
BY MY CALCULATIONS, STANDING UP HERE GIVES ME AN EXTRA 300 JOULES OF POTENTIAL ENERGY FROM GRAVITY.
AH, BUT YOU HAD TO EXPEND ENERGY TO GET UP THERE. YOUR TOTAL ENERGY HASN'T INCREASED.
I HAD STEVE LIFT ME UP.
FALL BREAK CAN'T COME SOON ENOUGH.
THANKS FOR TEACHING US THIS STUFF, BY THE WAY!
PHYSICS
AMEND

TIE Food

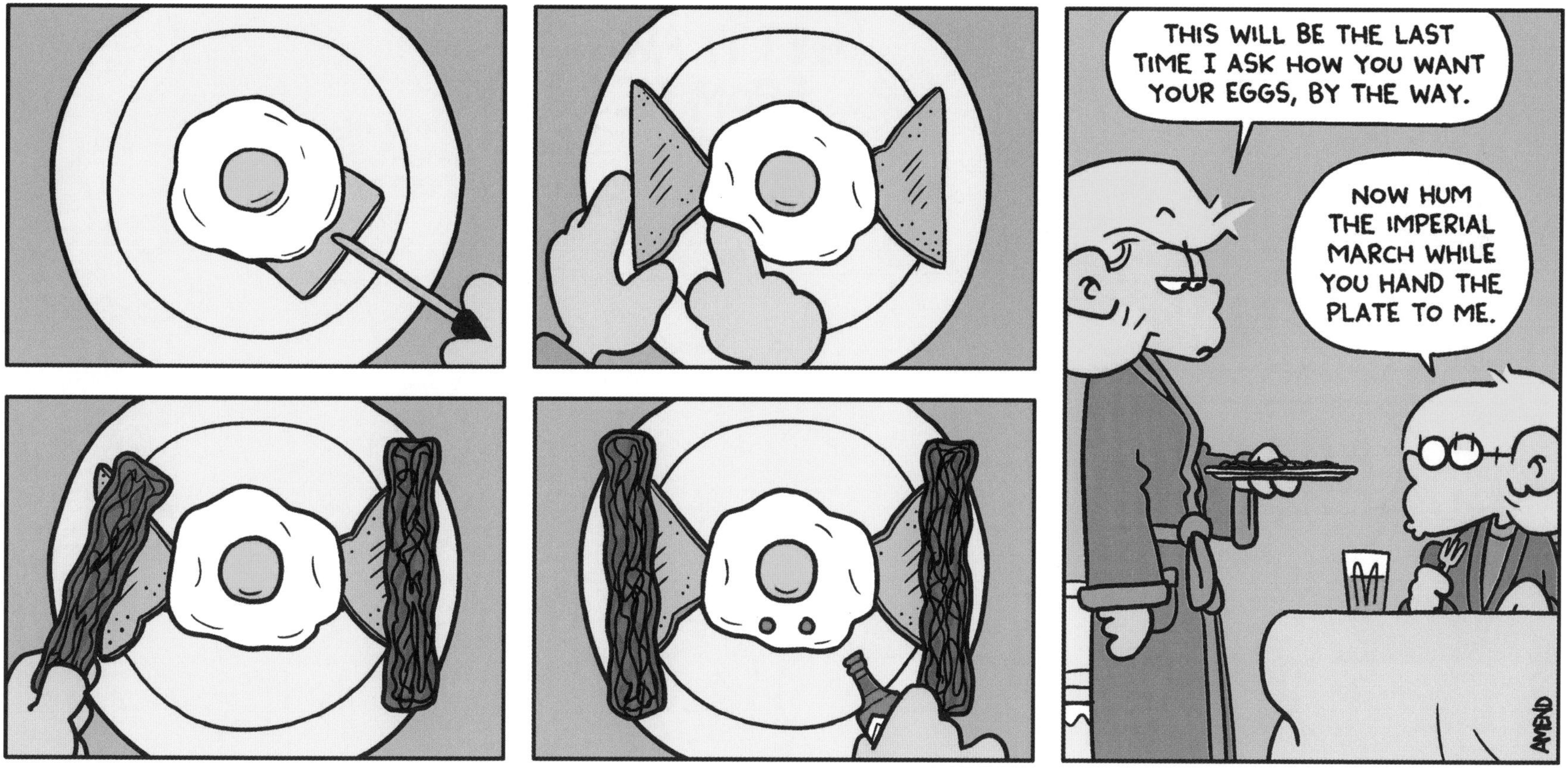
THIS WILL BE THE LAST TIME I ASK HOW YOU WANT YOUR EGGS, BY THE WAY.
NOW HUM THE IMPERIAL MARCH WHILE YOU HAND THE PLATE TO ME.
AMEND

Scary Pumpkin

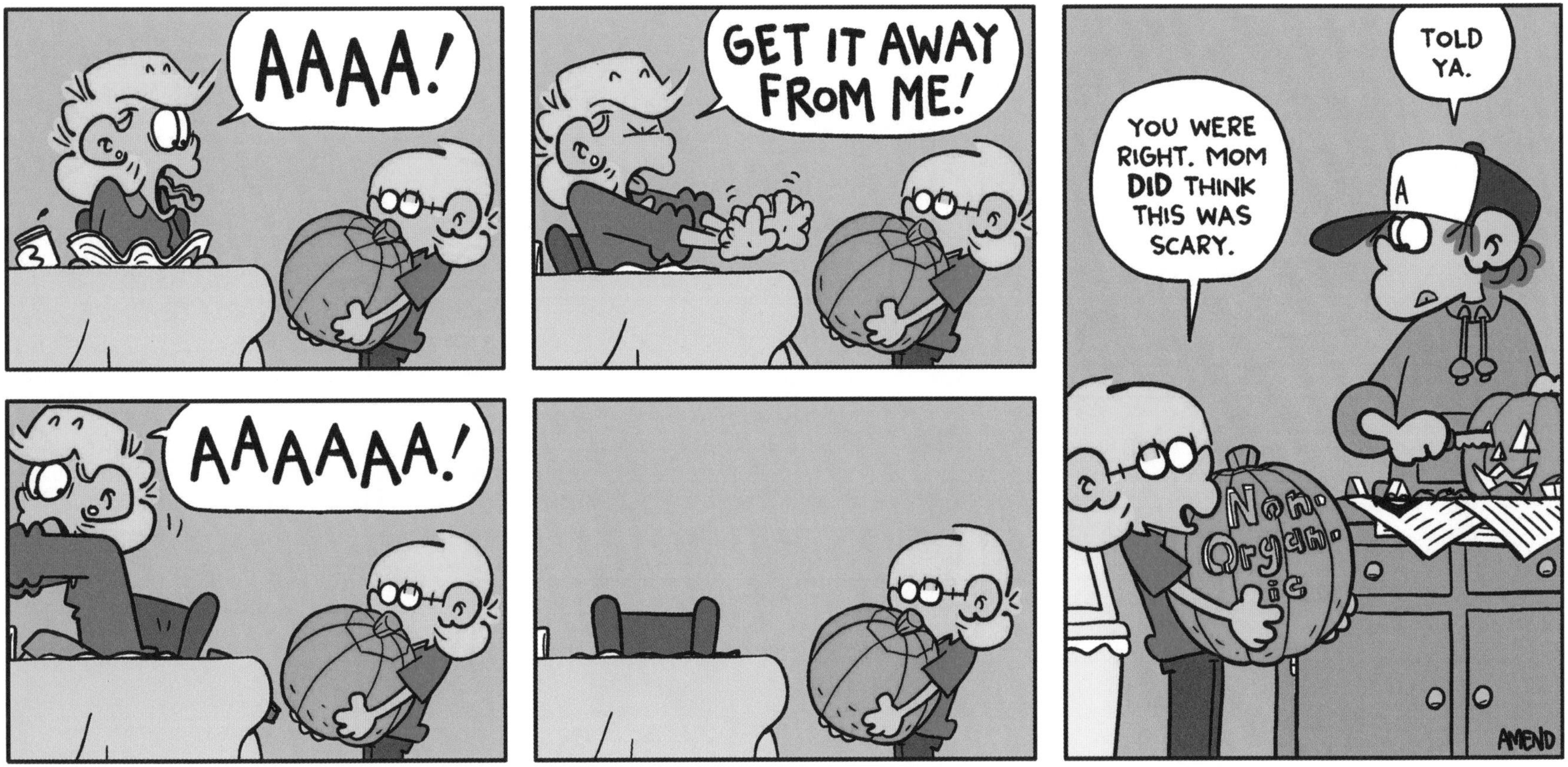
AAAA!
GET IT AWAY FROM ME!
AAAAAA!
YOU WERE RIGHT. MOM DID THINK THIS WAS SCARY.
TOLD YA.
Non-Organic
AMEND

Not Very Imaginative

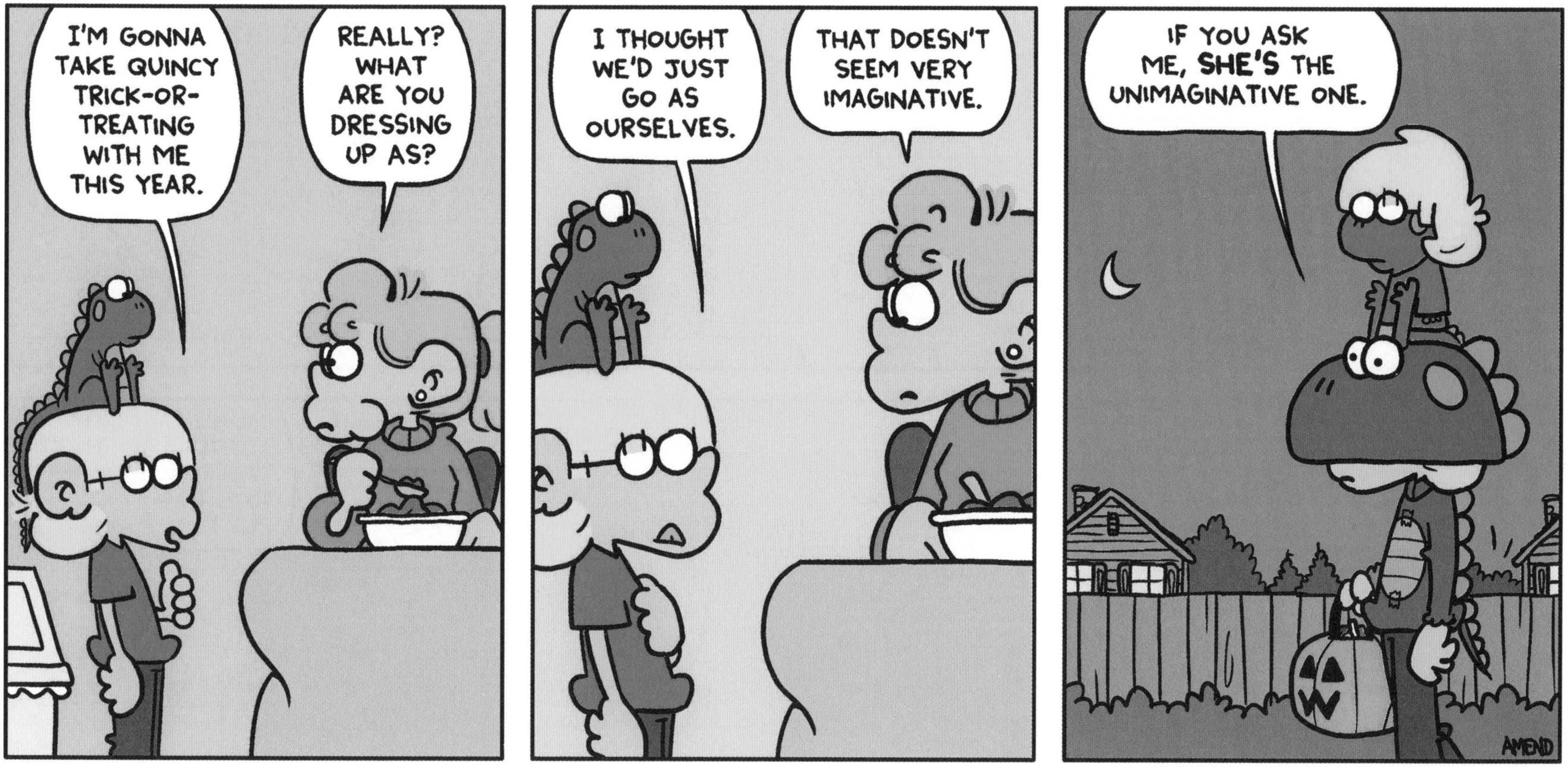
I'M GONNA TAKE QUINCY TRICK-OR-TREATING WITH ME THIS YEAR.
REALLY? WHAT ARE YOU DRESSING UP AS?
I THOUGHT WE'D JUST GO AS OURSELVES.
THAT DOESN'T SEEM VERY IMAGINATIVE.
IF YOU ASK ME, **SHE'S** THE UNIMAGINATIVE ONE.
AMEND

Tuesday

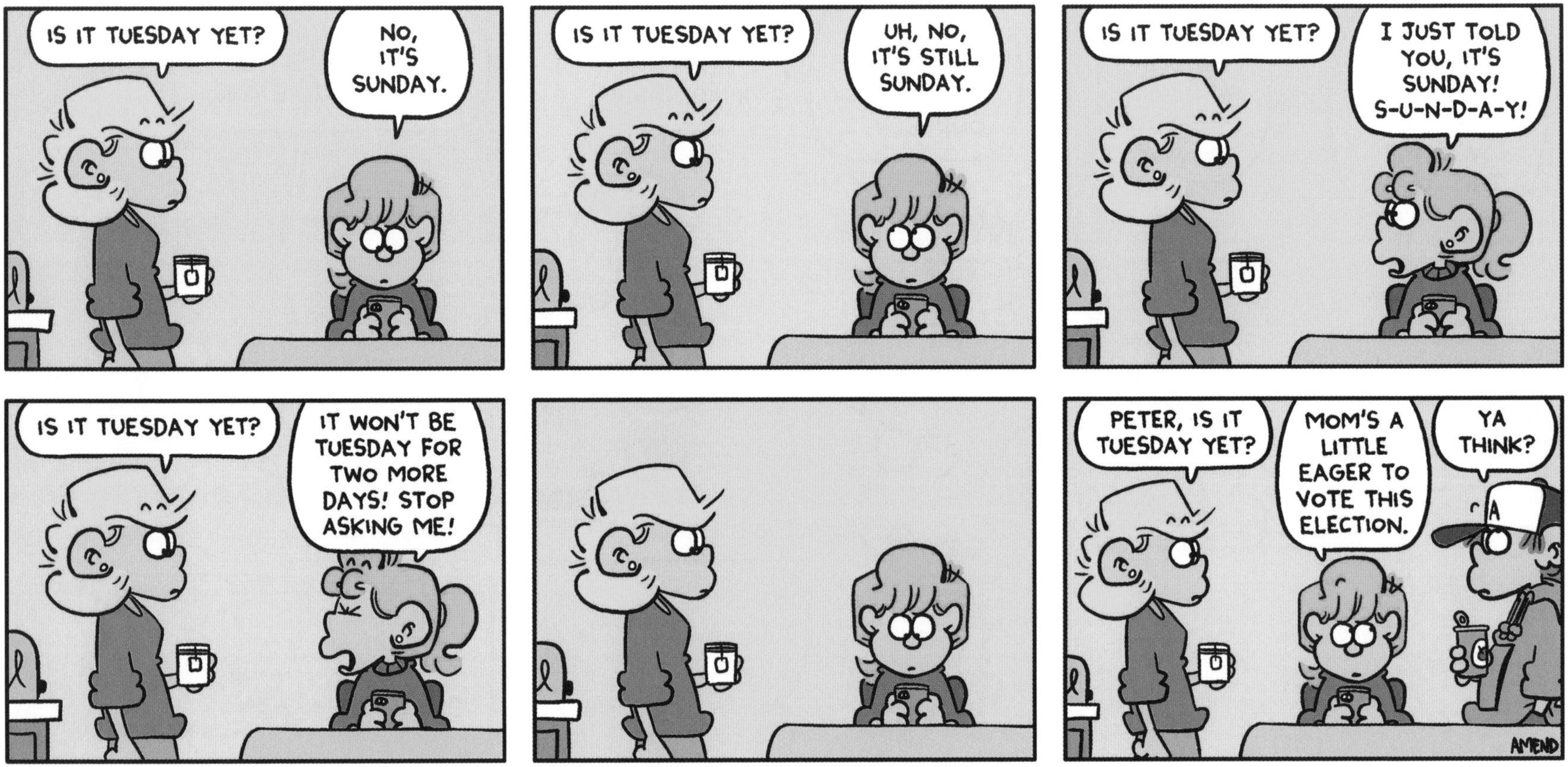
IS IT TUESDAY YET?
NO, IT'S SUNDAY.
IS IT TUESDAY YET?
UH, NO, IT'S STILL SUNDAY.
IS IT TUESDAY YET?
I JUST TOLD YOU, IT'S SUNDAY! S-U-N-D-A-Y!
IS IT TUESDAY YET?
IT WON'T BE TUESDAY FOR TWO MORE DAYS! STOP ASKING ME!
PETER, IS IT TUESDAY YET?
MOM'S A LITTLE EAGER TO VOTE THIS ELECTION.
YA THINK?
AMEND

Dungeon Crawler

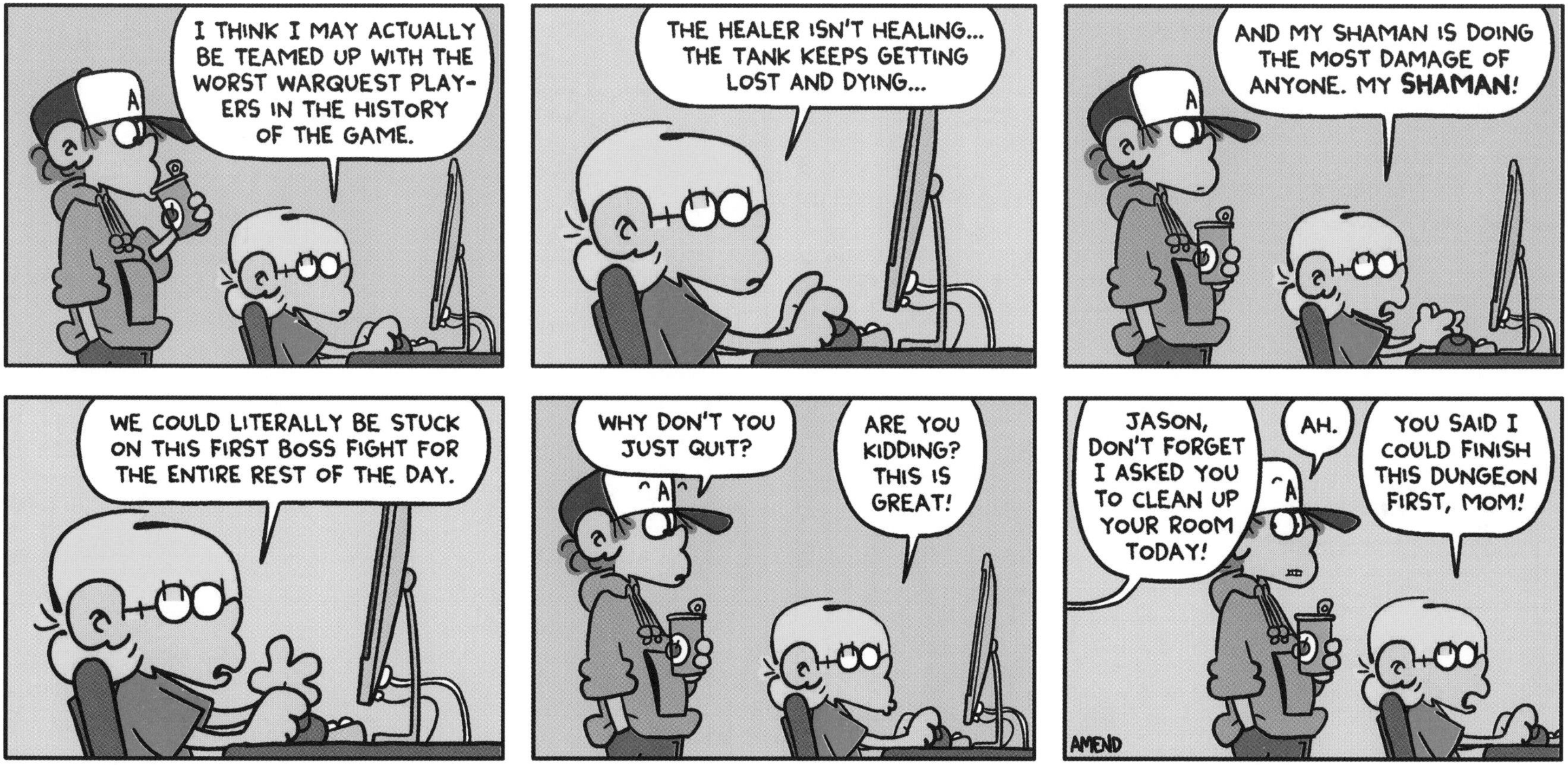
I THINK I MAY ACTUALLY BE TEAMED UP WITH THE WORST WARQUEST PLAYERS IN THE HISTORY OF THE GAME.
THE HEALER ISN'T HEALING... THE TANK KEEPS GETTING LOST AND DYING...
AND MY SHAMAN IS DOING THE MOST DAMAGE OF ANYONE. MY **SHAMAN**!
WE COULD LITERALLY BE STUCK ON THIS FIRST BOSS FIGHT FOR THE ENTIRE REST OF THE DAY.
WHY DON'T YOU JUST QUIT?
ARE YOU KIDDING? THIS IS GREAT!
JASON, DON'T FORGET I ASKED YOU TO CLEAN UP YOUR ROOM TODAY!
AH.
YOU SAID I COULD FINISH THIS DUNGEON FIRST, MOM!
AMEND

Drumstick

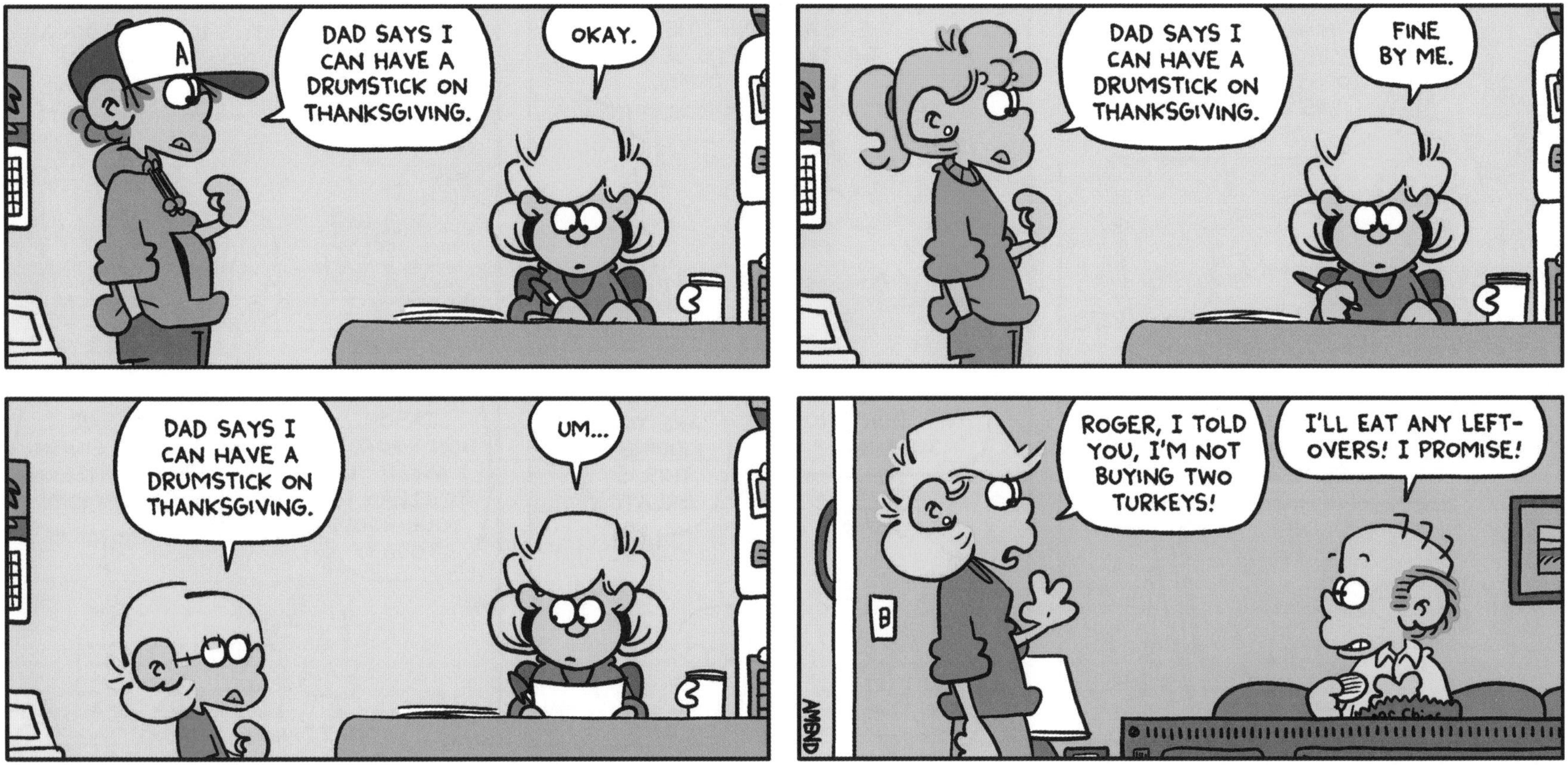
DAD SAYS I CAN HAVE A DRUMSTICK ON THANKSGIVING.
OKAY.
DAD SAYS I CAN HAVE A DRUMSTICK ON THANKSGIVING.
FINE BY ME.
DAD SAYS I CAN HAVE A DRUMSTICK ON THANKSGIVING.
UM...
ROGER, I TOLD YOU, I'M NOT BUYING TWO TURKEYS!
I'LL EAT ANY LEFT-OVERS! I PROMISE!
AMEND

Rakish

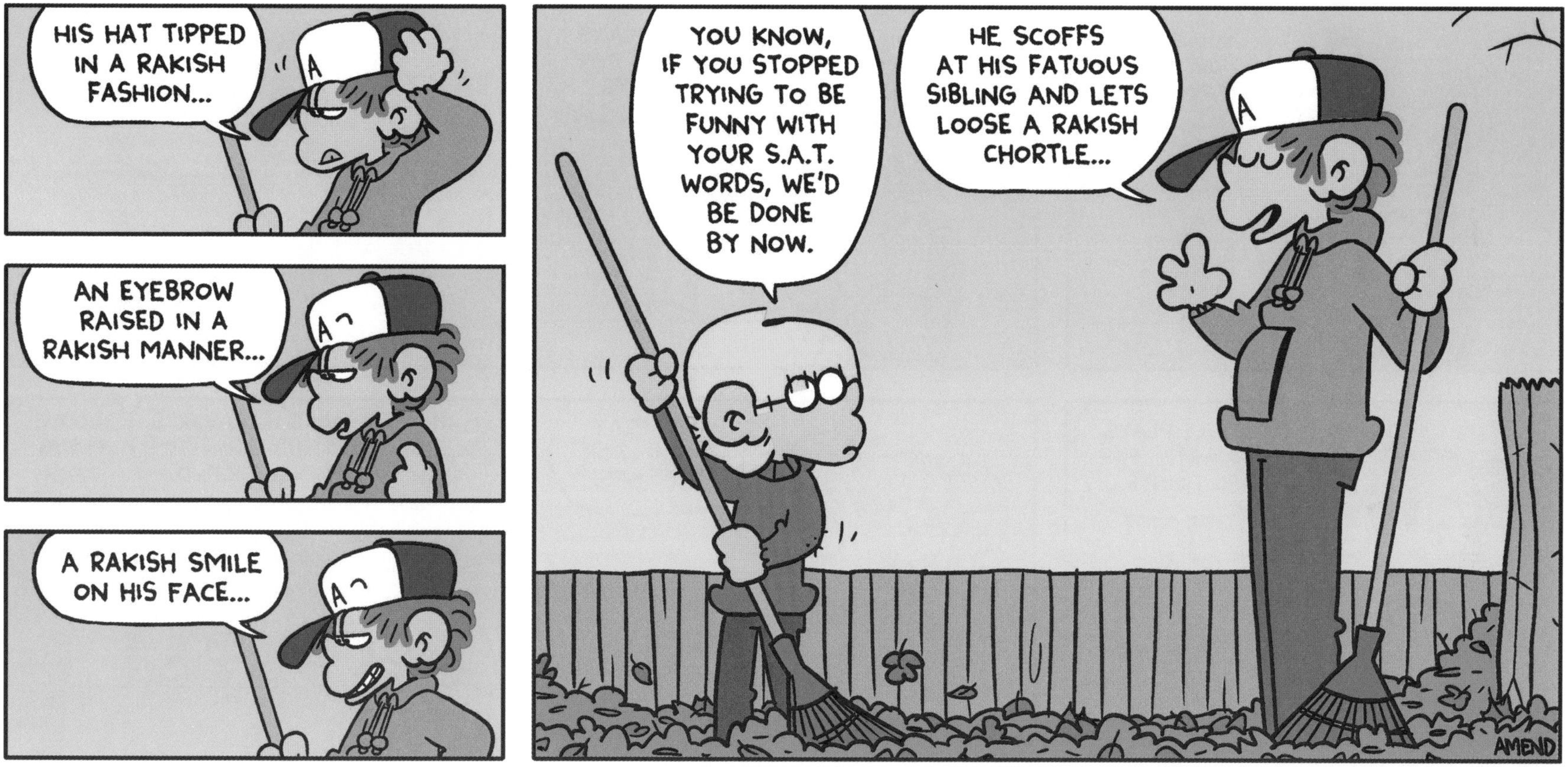

HIS HAT TIPPED IN A RAKISH FASHION...
AN EYEBROW RAISED IN A RAKISH MANNER...
A RAKISH SMILE ON HIS FACE...
HE SCOFFS AT HIS FATUOUS SIBLING AND LETS LOOSE A RAKISH CHORTLE...
YOU KNOW, IF YOU STOPPED TRYING TO BE FUNNY WITH YOUR S.A.T. WORDS, WE'D BE DONE BY NOW.
AMEND

Fightin' Words

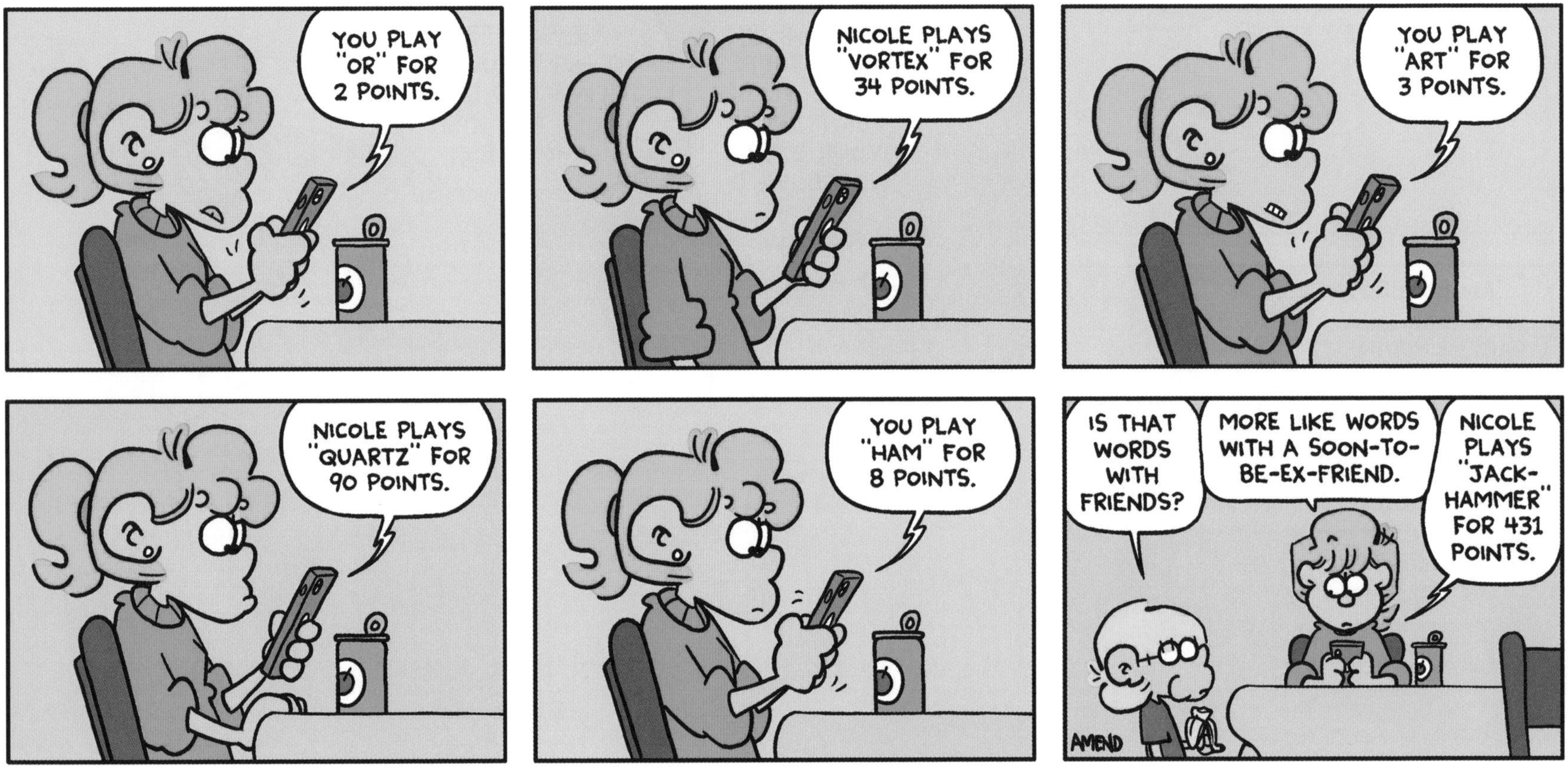
YOU PLAY "OR" FOR 2 POINTS.
NICOLE PLAYS "VORTEX" FOR 34 POINTS.
YOU PLAY "ART" FOR 3 POINTS.
NICOLE PLAYS "QUARTZ" FOR 90 POINTS.
YOU PLAY "HAM" FOR 8 POINTS.
IS THAT WORDS WITH FRIENDS?
MORE LIKE WORDS WITH A SOON-TO-BE-EX-FRIEND.
NICOLE PLAYS "JACK-HAMMER" FOR 431 POINTS.
AMEND

Not So Frosty

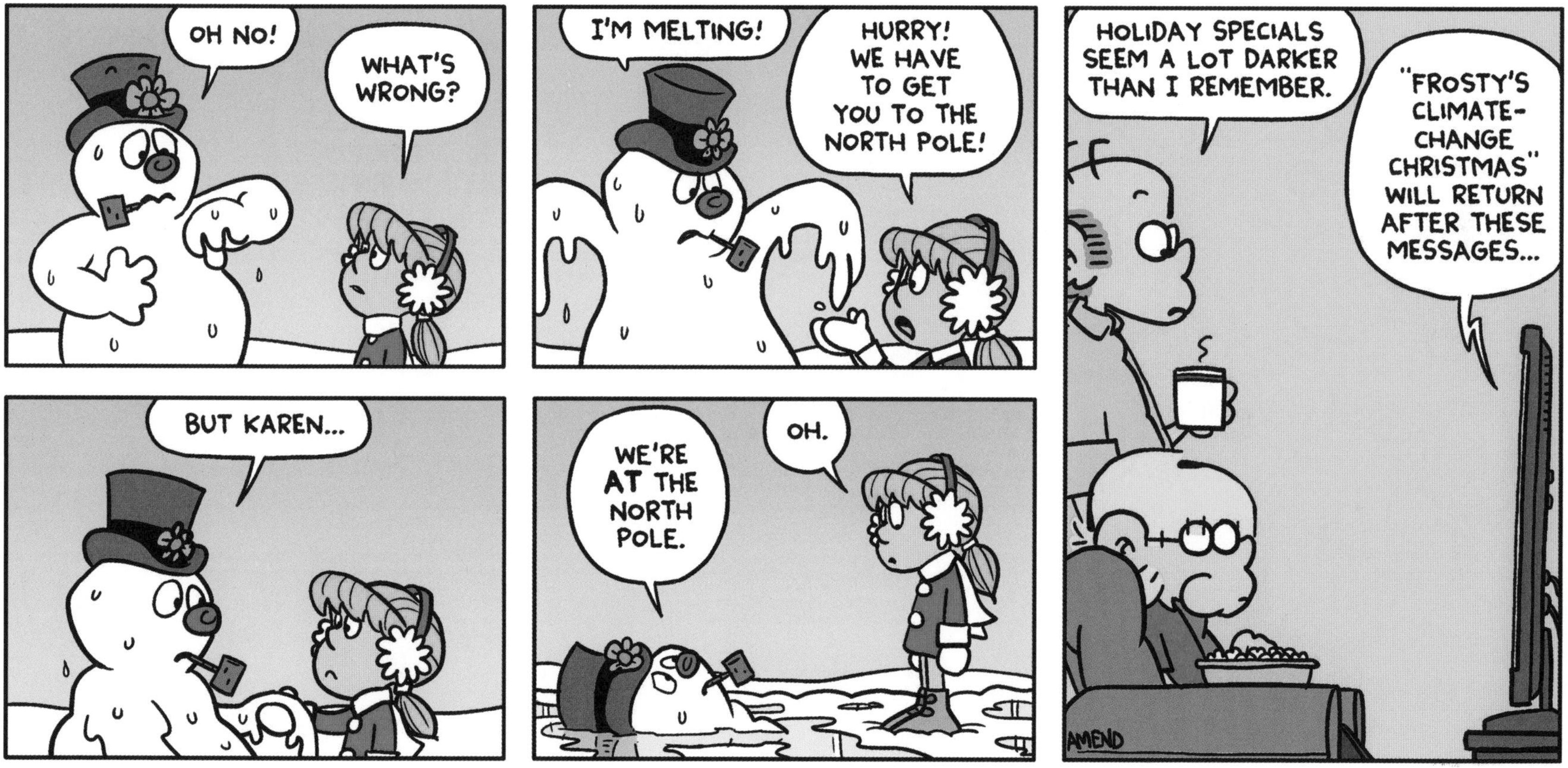
OH NO!
WHAT'S WRONG?
I'M MELTING!
HURRY! WE HAVE TO GET YOU TO THE NORTH POLE!
HOLIDAY SPECIALS SEEM A LOT DARKER THAN I REMEMBER.
"FROSTY'S CLIMATE-CHANGE CHRISTMAS" WILL RETURN AFTER THESE MESSAGES...
BUT KAREN...
WE'RE AT THE NORTH POLE.
OH.
AMEND

Sugar Cookies

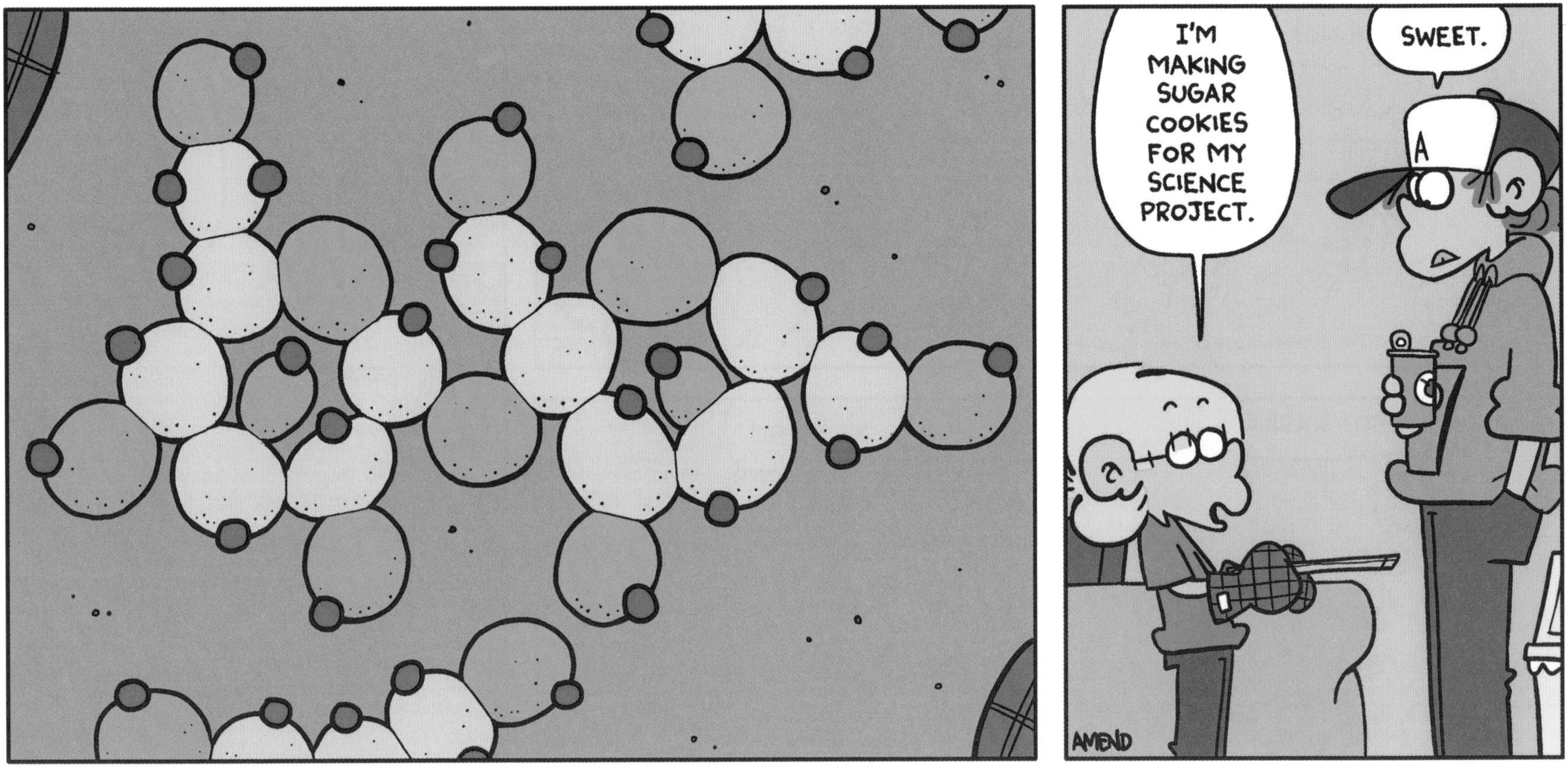
I'M MAKING SUGAR COOKIES FOR MY SCIENCE PROJECT.
SWEET.
A
AMEND

Holiday Stretch

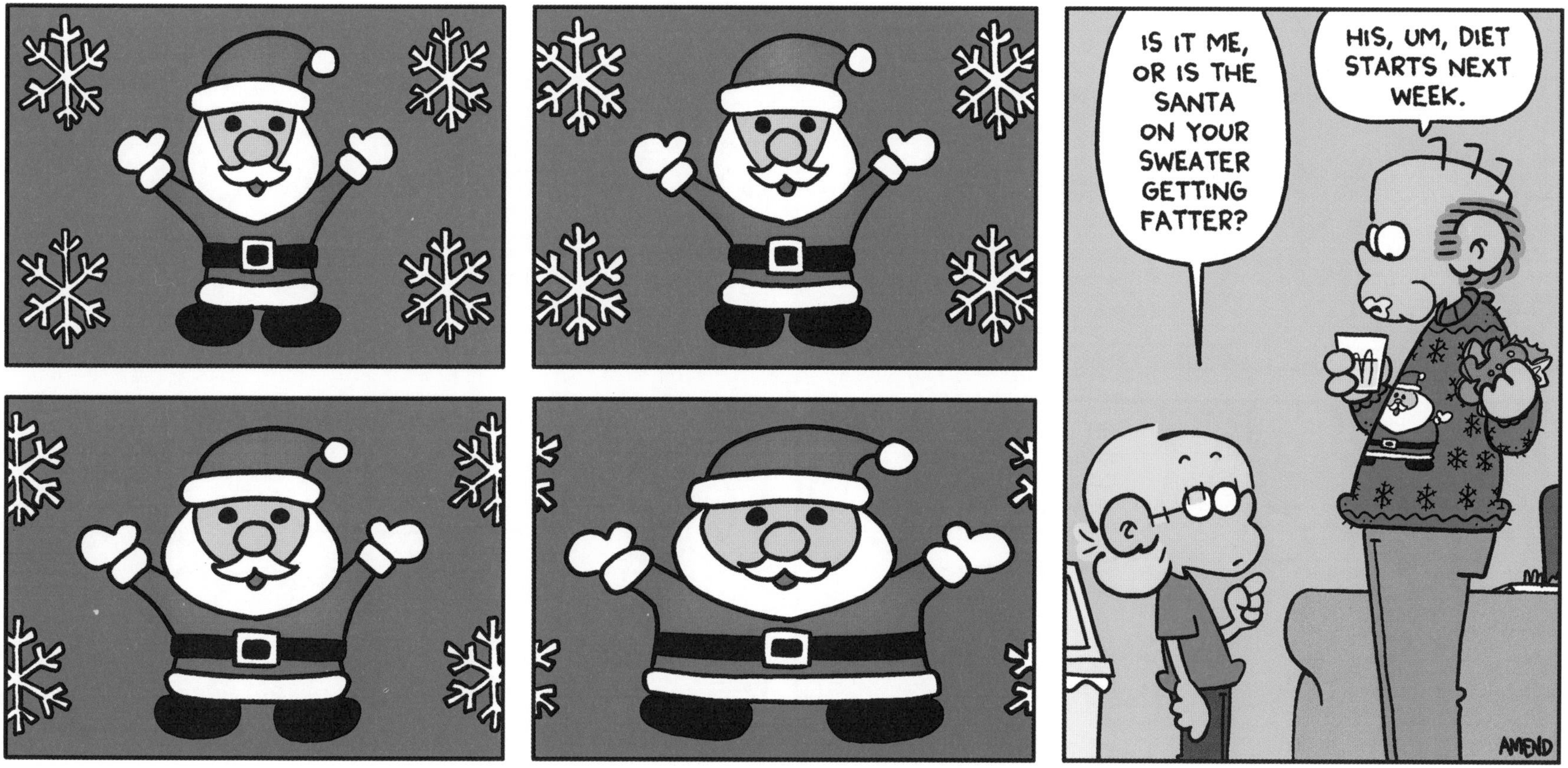
IS IT ME, OR IS THE SANTA ON YOUR SWEATER GETTING FATTER?
HIS, UM, DIET STARTS NEXT WEEK.
AMEND

Lost Chargers

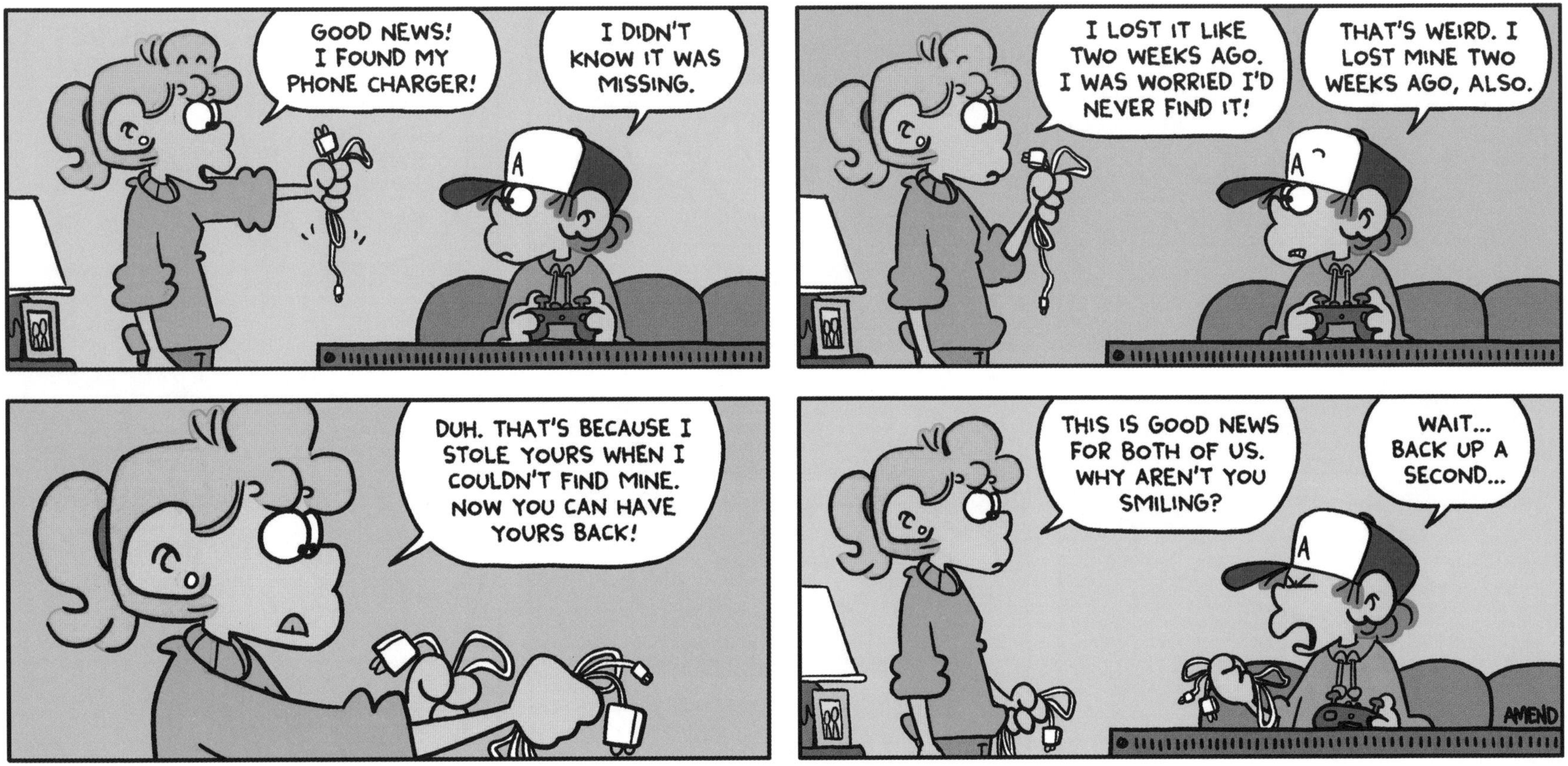
GOOD NEWS! I FOUND MY PHONE CHARGER!
I DIDN'T KNOW IT WAS MISSING.
I LOST IT LIKE TWO WEEKS AGO. I WAS WORRIED I'D NEVER FIND IT!
THAT'S WEIRD. I LOST MINE TWO WEEKS AGO, ALSO.
DUH. THAT'S BECAUSE I STOLE YOURS WHEN I COULDN'T FIND MINE. NOW YOU CAN HAVE YOURS BACK!
THIS IS GOOD NEWS FOR BOTH OF US. WHY AREN'T YOU SMILING?
WAIT... BACK UP A SECOND...
AMEND

Dressing for Winter

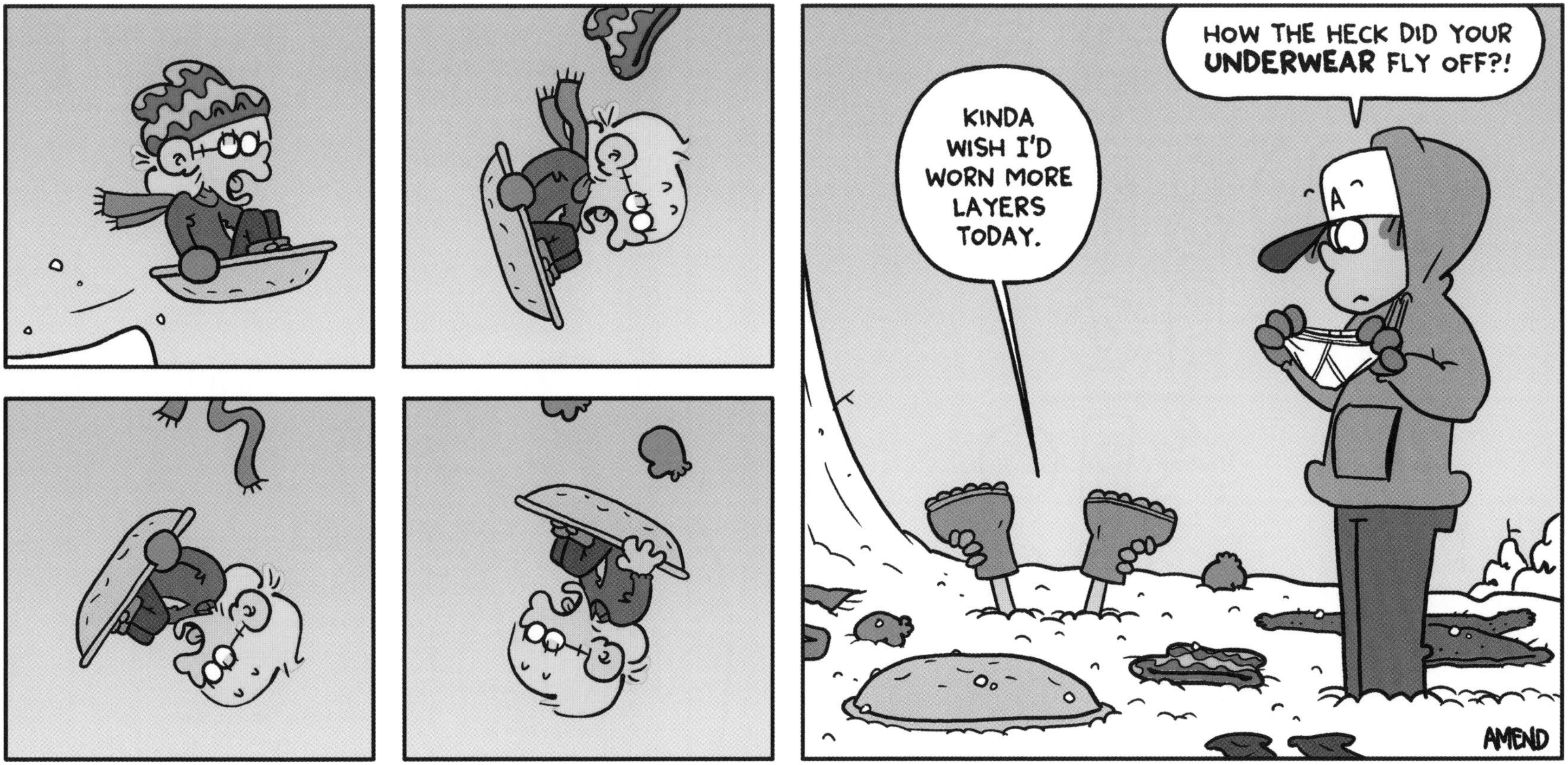
KINDA WISH I'D WORN MORE LAYERS TODAY.
HOW THE HECK DID YOUR **UNDERWEAR** FLY OFF?!
A
AMEND

Cell Division

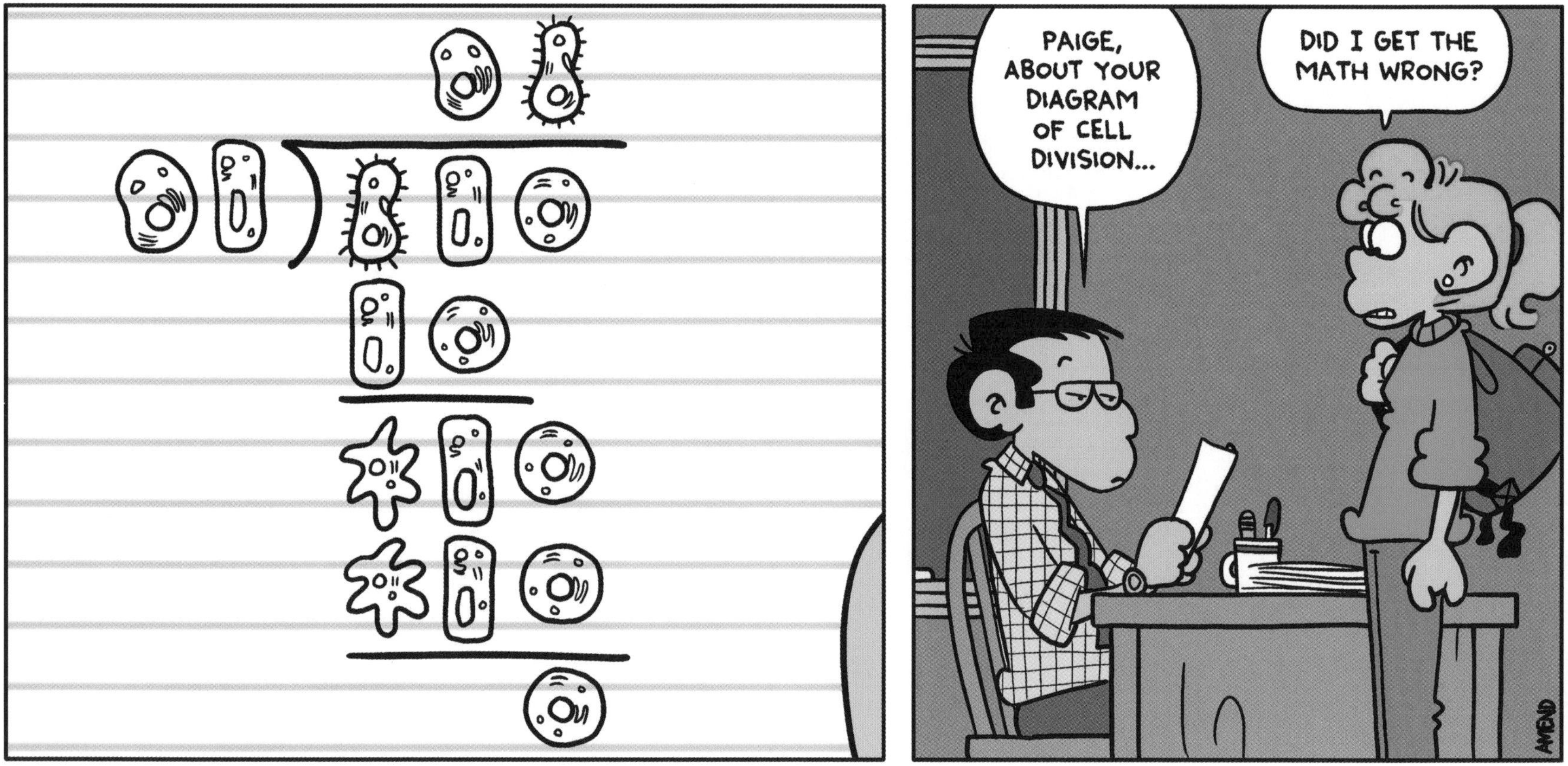
PAIGE, ABOUT YOUR DIAGRAM OF CELL DIVISION...
DID I GET THE MATH WRONG?
AMEND

Plow Boys

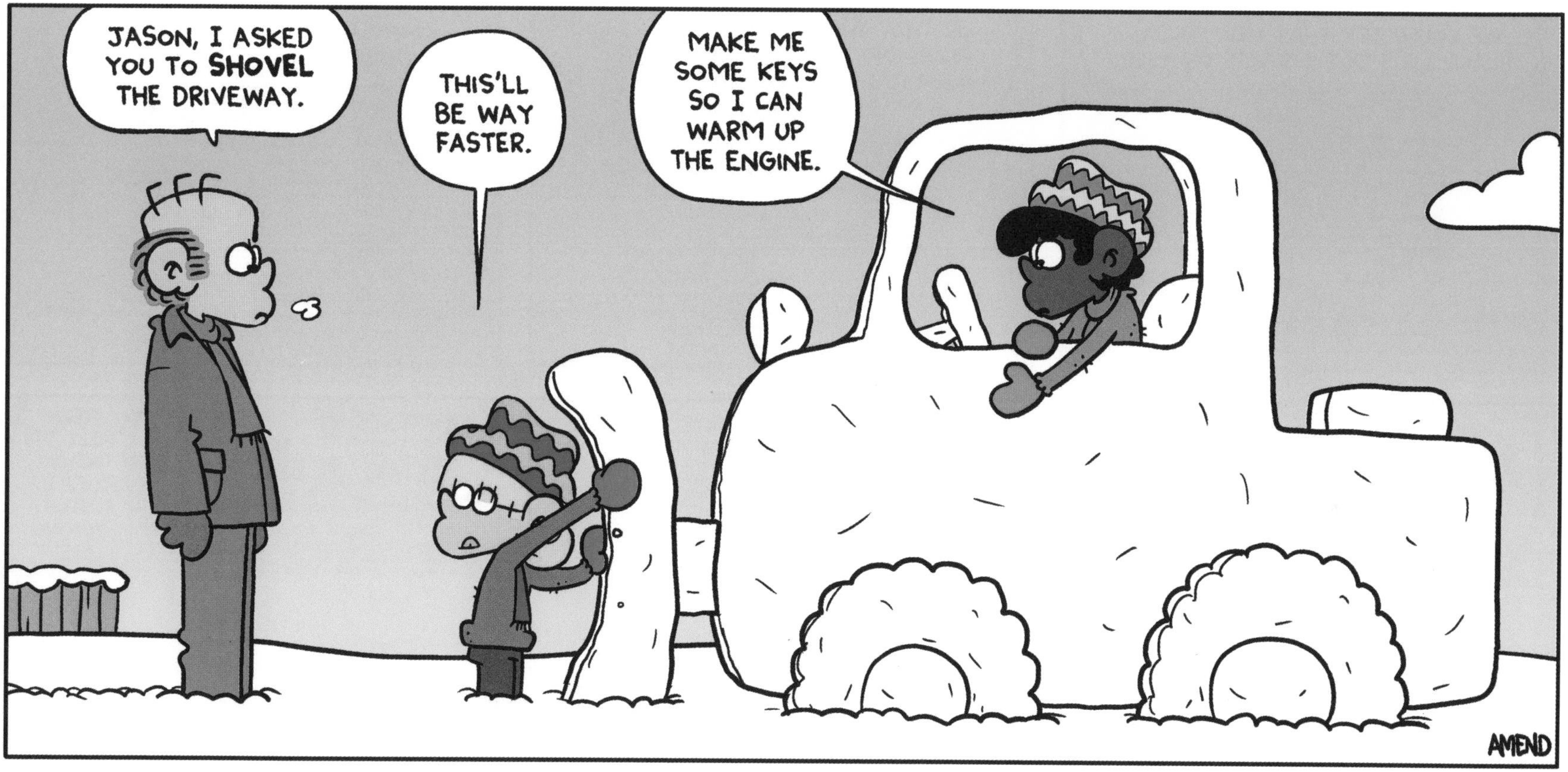
JASON, I ASKED YOU TO **SHOVEL** THE DRIVEWAY.
THIS'LL BE WAY FASTER.
MAKE ME SOME KEYS SO I CAN WARM UP THE ENGINE.
AMEND

Yelpings

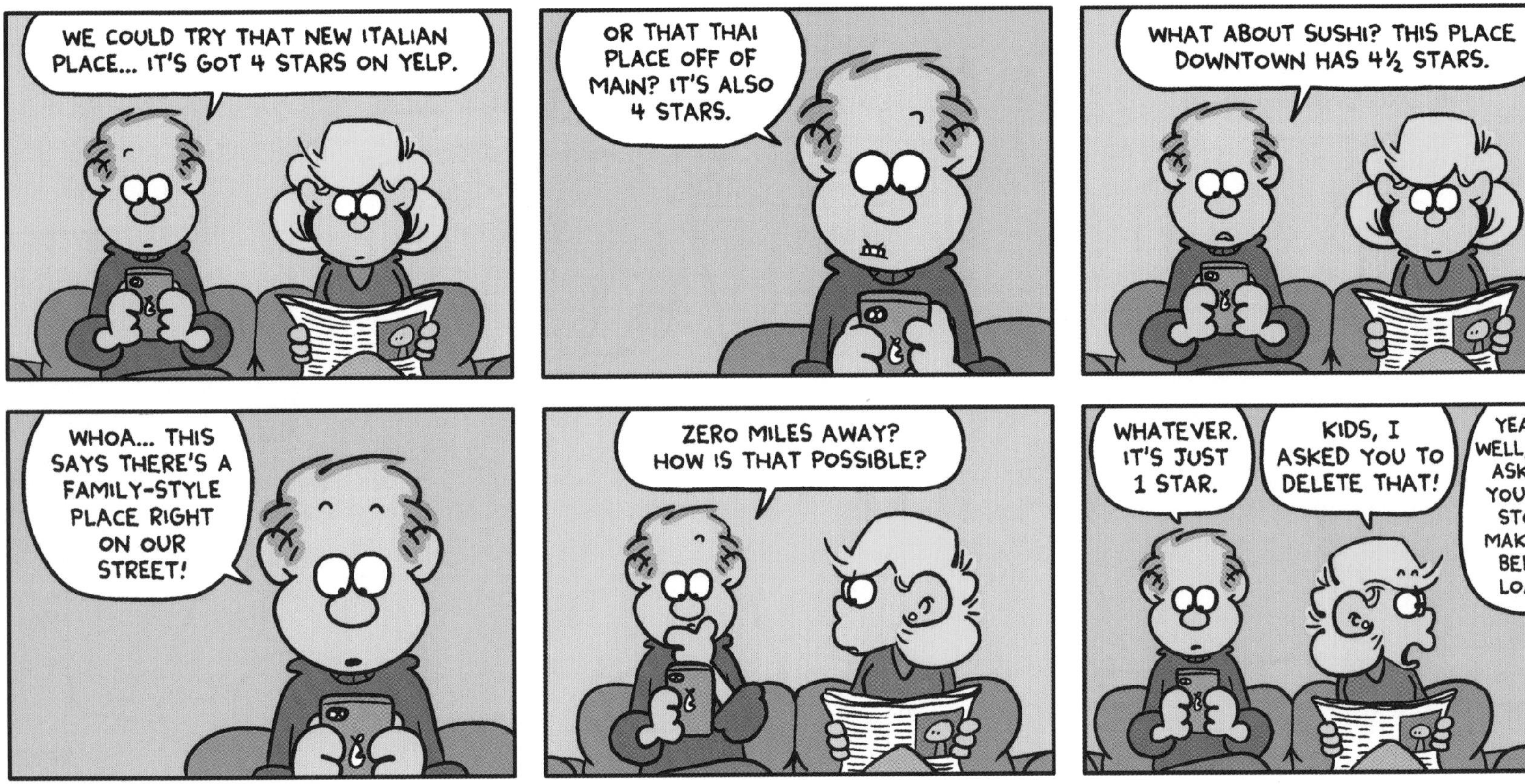
WE COULD TRY THAT NEW ITALIAN PLACE... IT'S GOT 4 STARS ON YELP.
OR THAT THAI PLACE OFF OF MAIN? IT'S ALSO 4 STARS.
WHAT ABOUT SUSHI? THIS PLACE DOWNTOWN HAS 4½ STARS.
WHOA... THIS SAYS THERE'S A FAMILY-STYLE PLACE RIGHT ON OUR STREET!
ZERO MILES AWAY? HOW IS THAT POSSIBLE?
WHATEVER. IT'S JUST 1 STAR.
KIDS, I ASKED YOU TO DELETE THAT!
YEAH, WELL, **WE** ASKED YOU TO STOP MAKING BEET-LOAF...
AMEND

Weighting Game

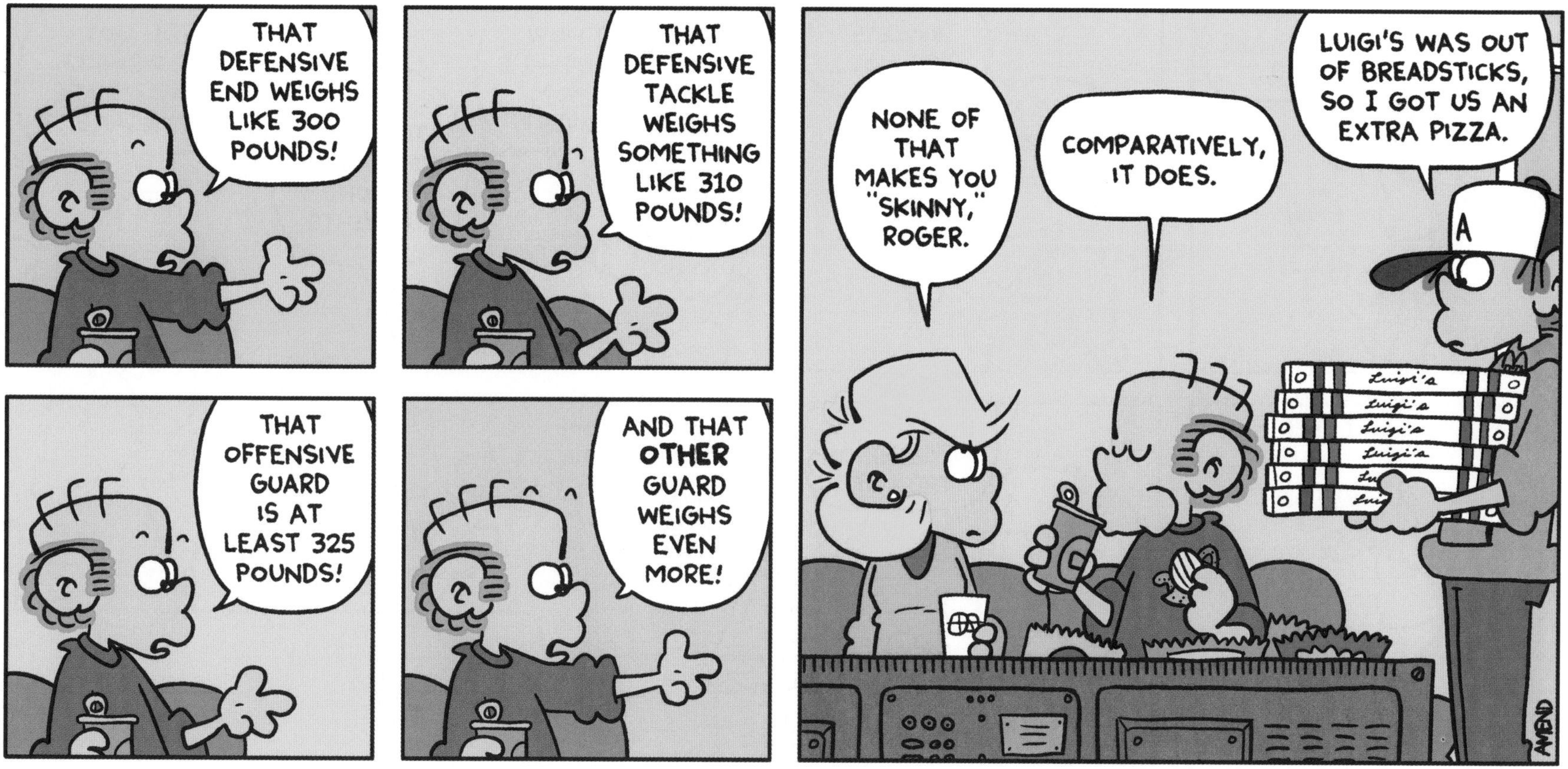
THAT DEFENSIVE END WEIGHS LIKE 300 POUNDS!
THAT DEFENSIVE TACKLE WEIGHS SOMETHING LIKE 310 POUNDS!
THAT OFFENSIVE GUARD IS AT LEAST 325 POUNDS!
AND THAT OTHER GUARD WEIGHS EVEN MORE!
NONE OF THAT MAKES YOU "SKINNY," ROGER.
COMPARATIVELY, IT DOES.
LUIGI'S WAS OUT OF BREADSTICKS, SO I GOT US AN EXTRA PIZZA.
AMEND

Violets Are Not

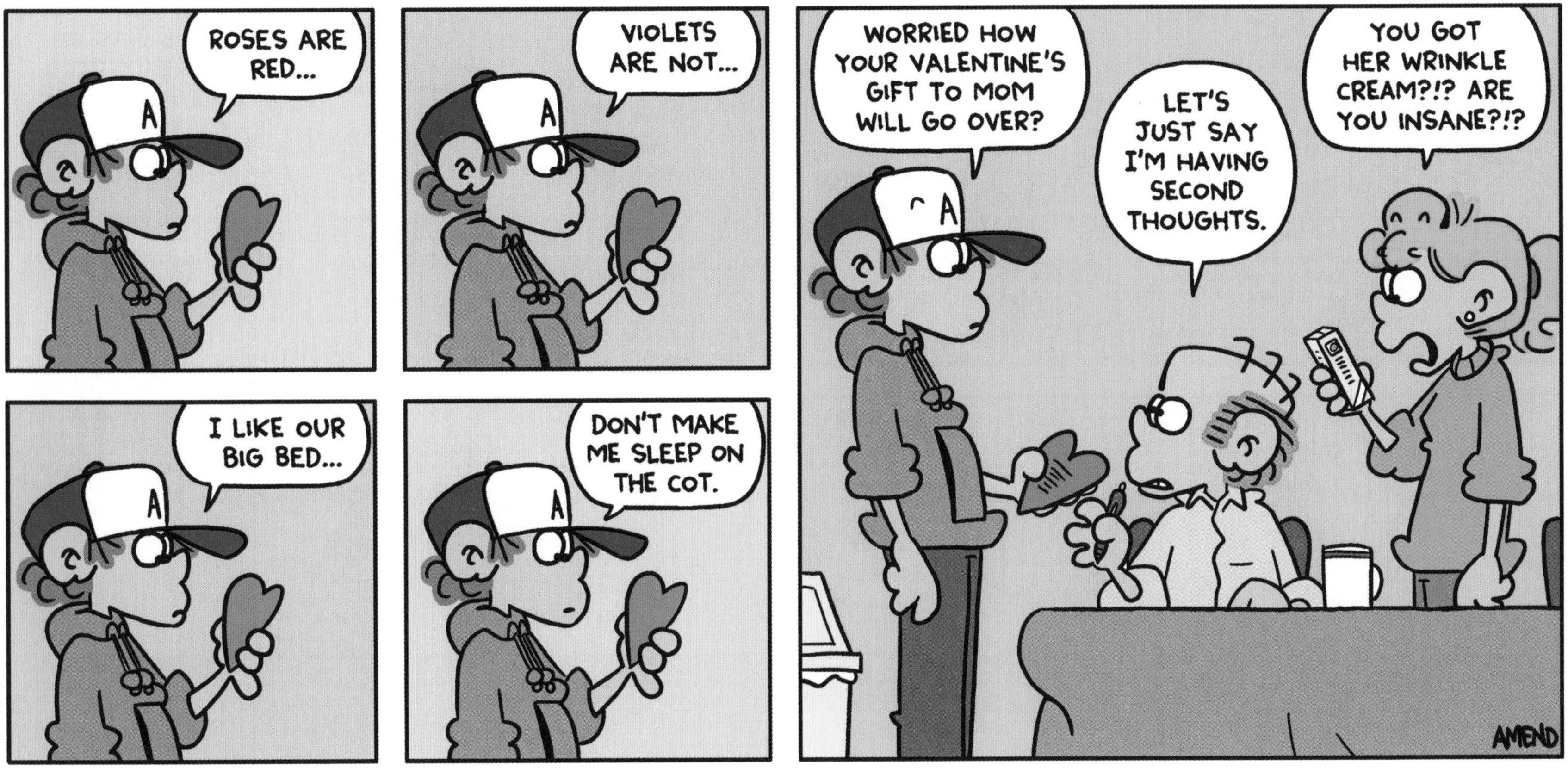
ROSES ARE RED...
VIOLETS ARE NOT...
I LIKE OUR BIG BED...
DON'T MAKE ME SLEEP ON THE COT.
WORRIED HOW YOUR VALENTINE'S GIFT TO MOM WILL GO OVER?
LET'S JUST SAY I'M HAVING SECOND THOUGHTS.
YOU GOT HER WRINKLE CREAM?!? ARE YOU INSANE?!?
AMEND

S.P.M.

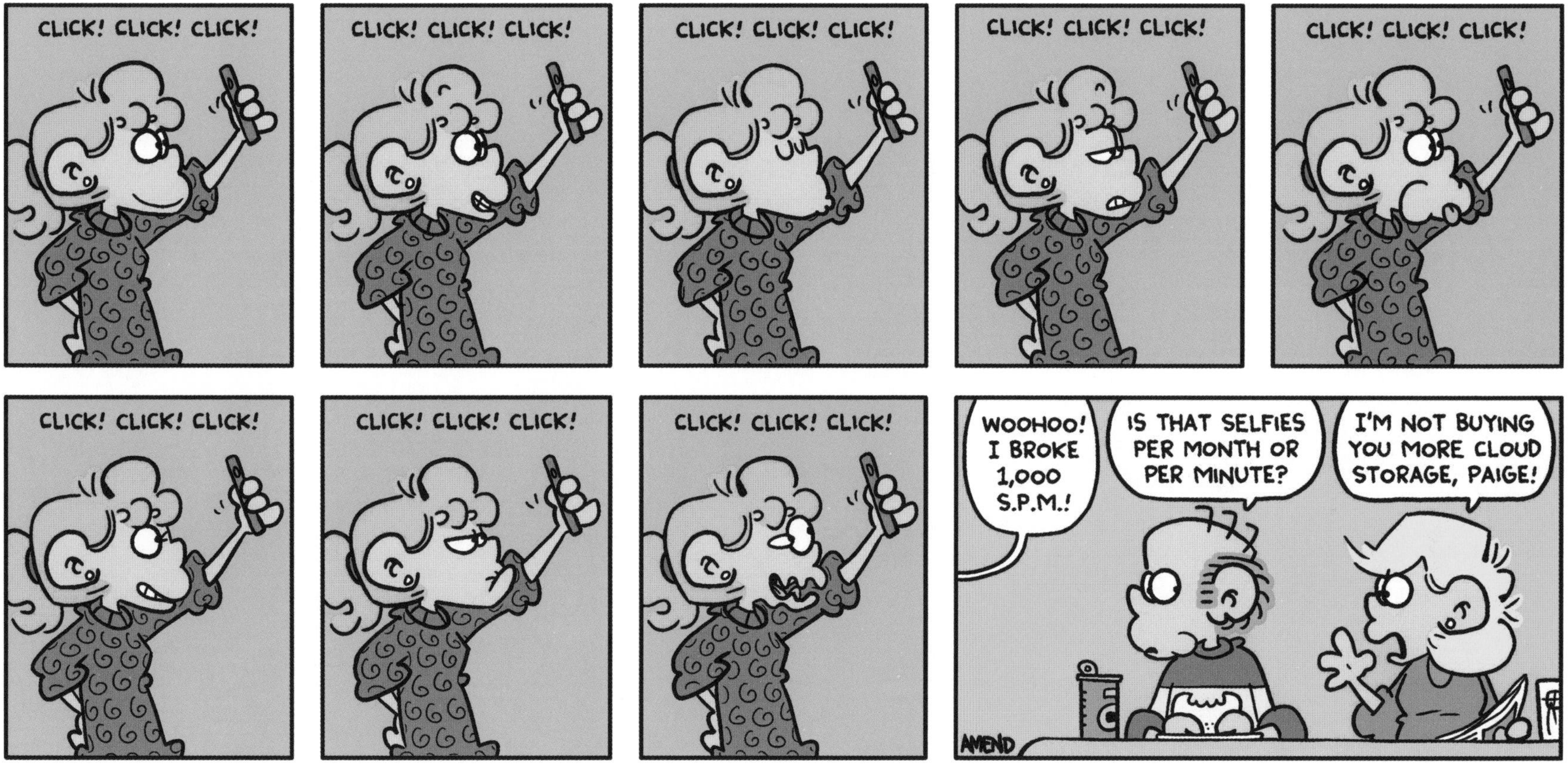
CLICK! CLICK! CLICK!
CLICK! CLICK! CLICK!
CLICK! CLICK! CLICK!
CLICK! CLICK! CLICK!
CLICK! CLICK! CLICK!
CLICK! CLICK! CLICK!
CLICK! CLICK! CLICK!
CLICK! CLICK! CLICK!
WOOHOO! I BROKE 1,000 S.P.M.!
IS THAT SELFIES PER MONTH OR PER MINUTE?
I'M NOT BUYING YOU MORE CLOUD STORAGE, PAIGE!
AMEND

Flossing

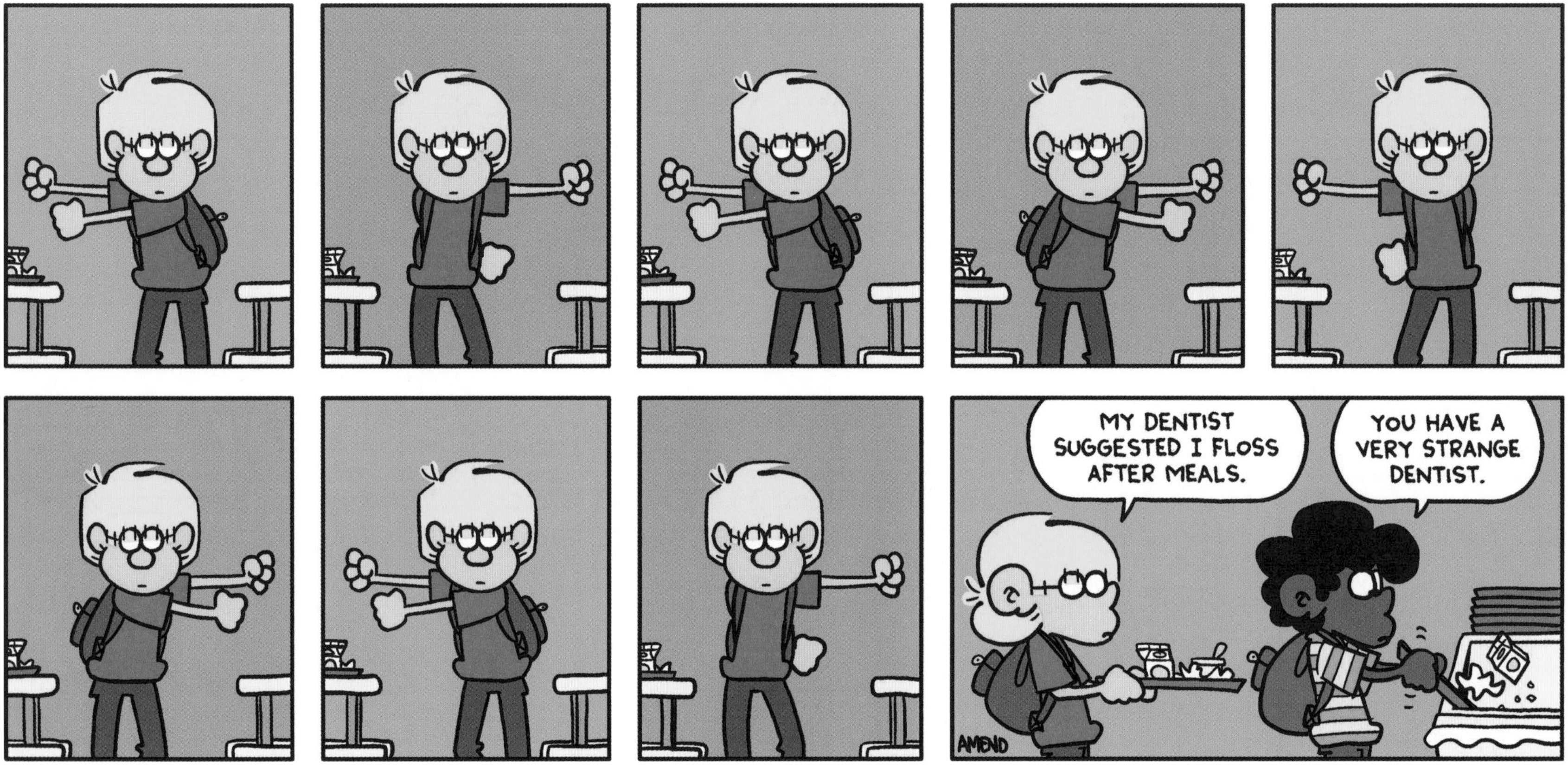
MY DENTIST SUGGESTED I FLOSS AFTER MEALS.
YOU HAVE A VERY STRANGE DENTIST.
AMEND

Mathzzz

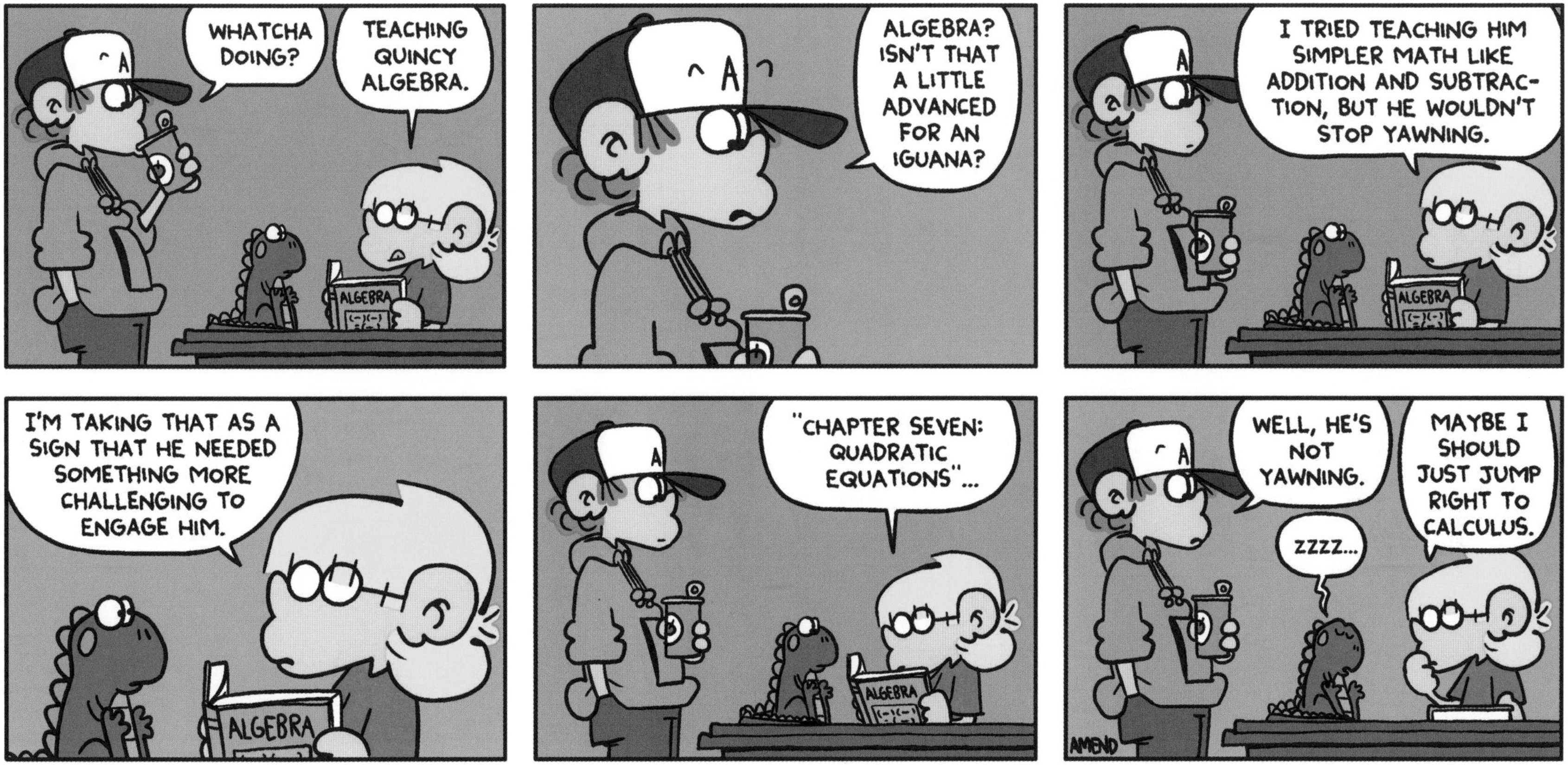
WHATCHA DOING?
TEACHING QUINCY ALGEBRA.
ALGEBRA
ALGEBRA? ISN'T THAT A LITTLE ADVANCED FOR AN IGUANA?
I TRIED TEACHING HIM SIMPLER MATH LIKE ADDITION AND SUBTRAC-TION, BUT HE WOULDN'T STOP YAWNING.
ALGEBRA
I'M TAKING THAT AS A SIGN THAT HE NEEDED SOMETHING MORE CHALLENGING TO ENGAGE HIM.
ALGEBRA
"CHAPTER SEVEN: QUADRATIC EQUATIONS"...
ALGEBRA
WELL, HE'S NOT YAWNING.
ZZZZ...
MAYBE I SHOULD JUST JUMP RIGHT TO CALCULUS.
AMEND

Let's Go!

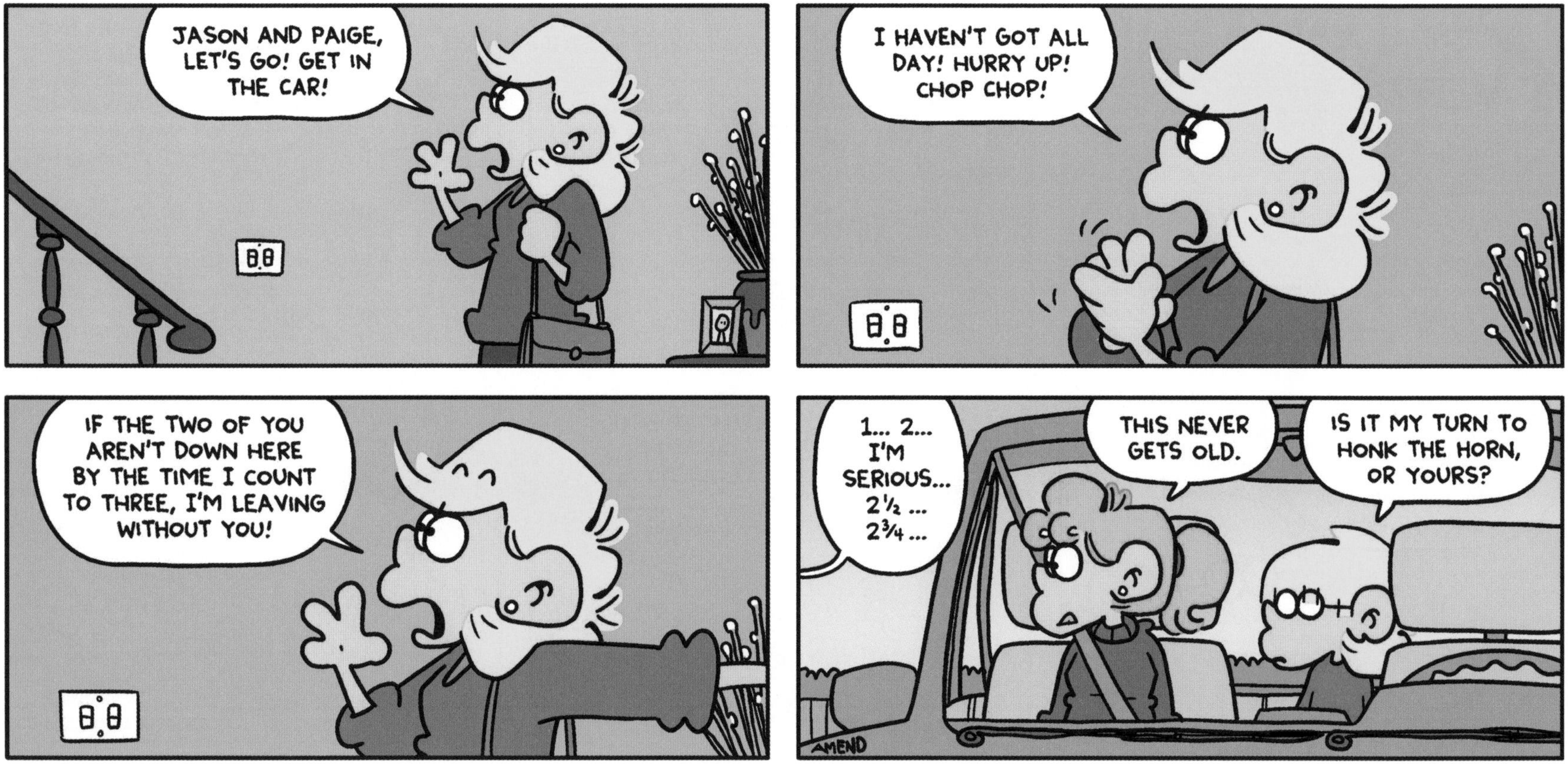
JASON AND PAIGE, LET'S GO! GET IN THE CAR!
I HAVEN'T GOT ALL DAY! HURRY UP! CHOP CHOP!
IF THE TWO OF YOU AREN'T DOWN HERE BY THE TIME I COUNT TO THREE, I'M LEAVING WITHOUT YOU!
1... 2... I'M SERIOUS... 2½ ... 2¾ ...
THIS NEVER GETS OLD.
IS IT MY TURN TO HONK THE HORN, OR YOURS?
AMEND

Fake Views

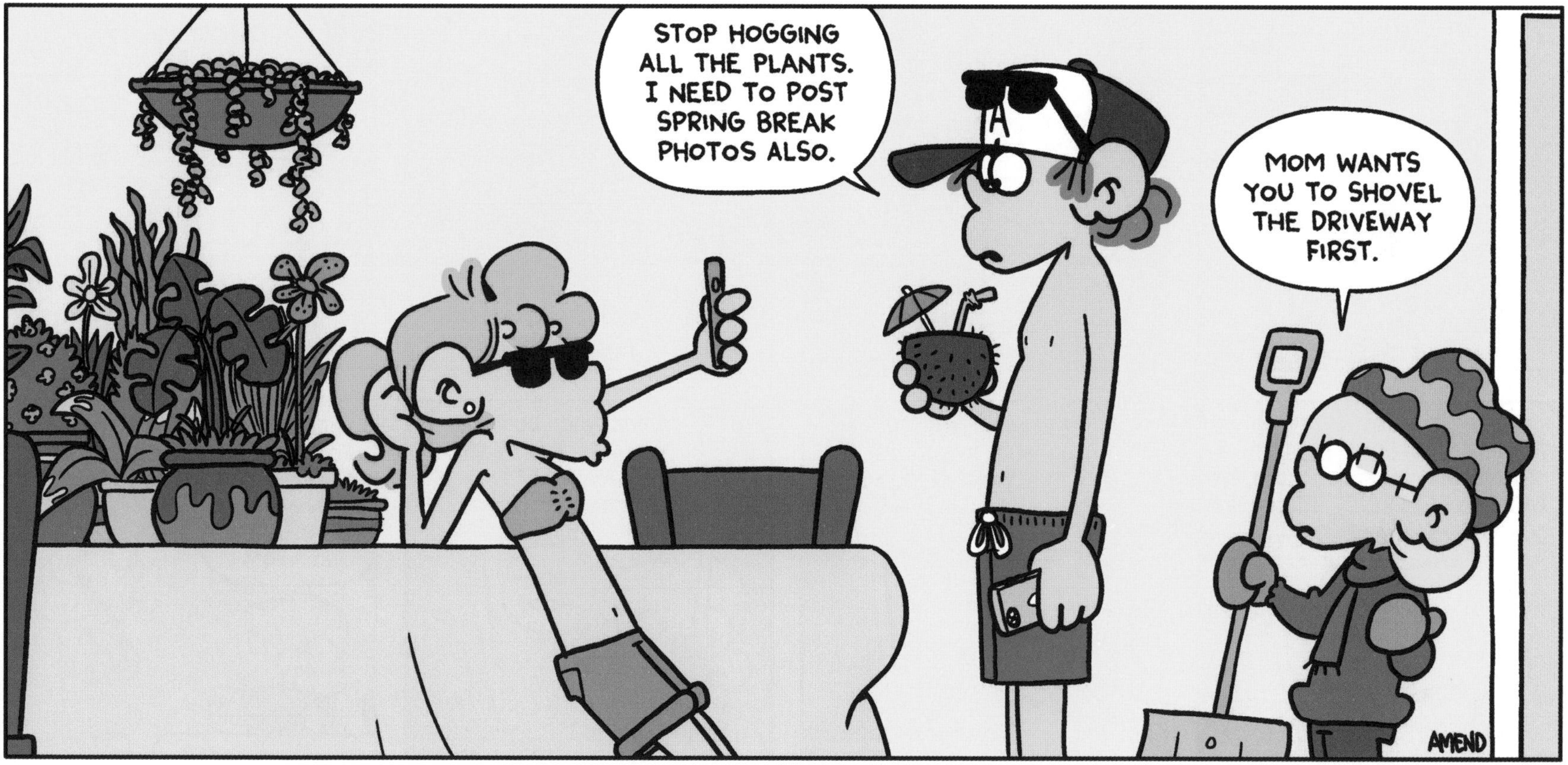
STOP HOGGING ALL THE PLANTS. I NEED TO POST SPRING BREAK PHOTOS ALSO.
MOM WANTS YOU TO SHOVEL THE DRIVEWAY FIRST.
AMEND

Dinner Disconnections

Lunch Encounters

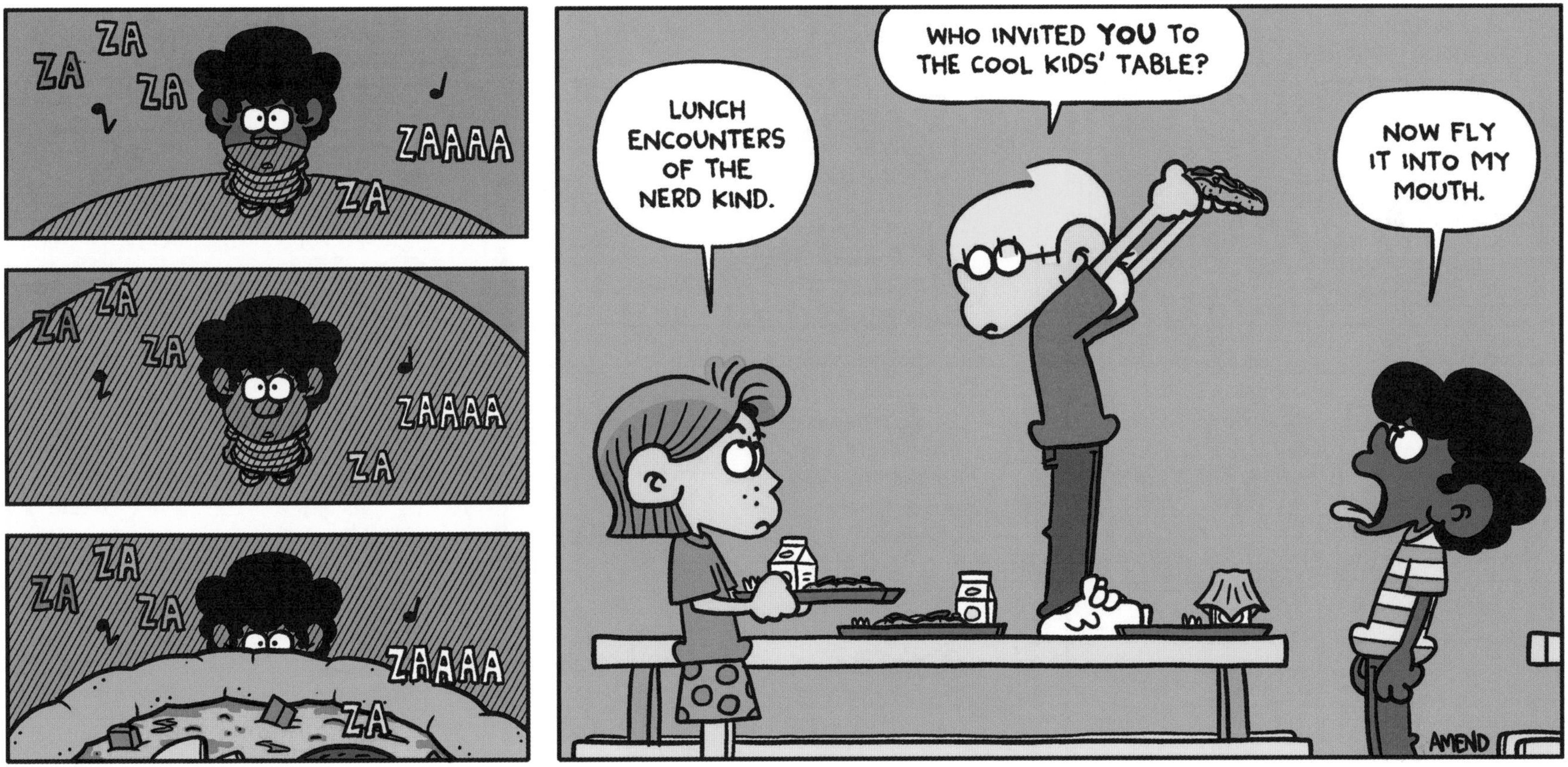
ZA ZA ZA ZAAAA ZA
ZA ZA ZA ZAAAA ZA
ZA ZA ZA ZAAAA ZA
LUNCH ENCOUNTERS OF THE NERD KIND.
WHO INVITED YOU TO THE COOL KIDS' TABLE?
NOW FLY IT INTO MY MOUTH.
AMEND

Brother Dearest

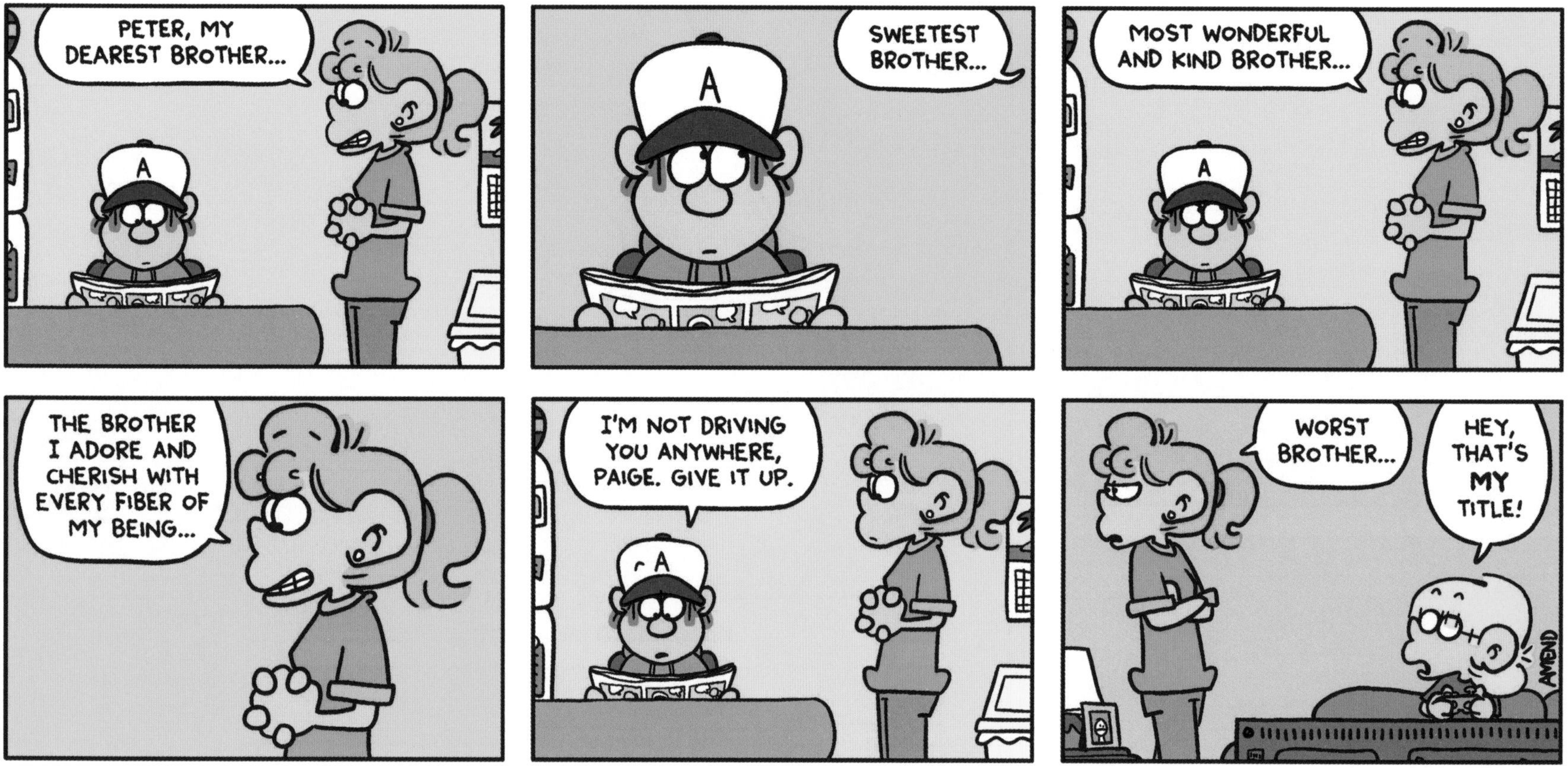
PETER, MY DEAREST BROTHER...
SWEETEST BROTHER...
MOST WONDERFUL AND KIND BROTHER...
THE BROTHER I ADORE AND CHERISH WITH EVERY FIBER OF MY BEING...
I'M NOT DRIVING YOU ANYWHERE, PAIGE. GIVE IT UP.
WORST BROTHER...
HEY, THAT'S MY TITLE!
AMEND

A Song of Mints and Fire

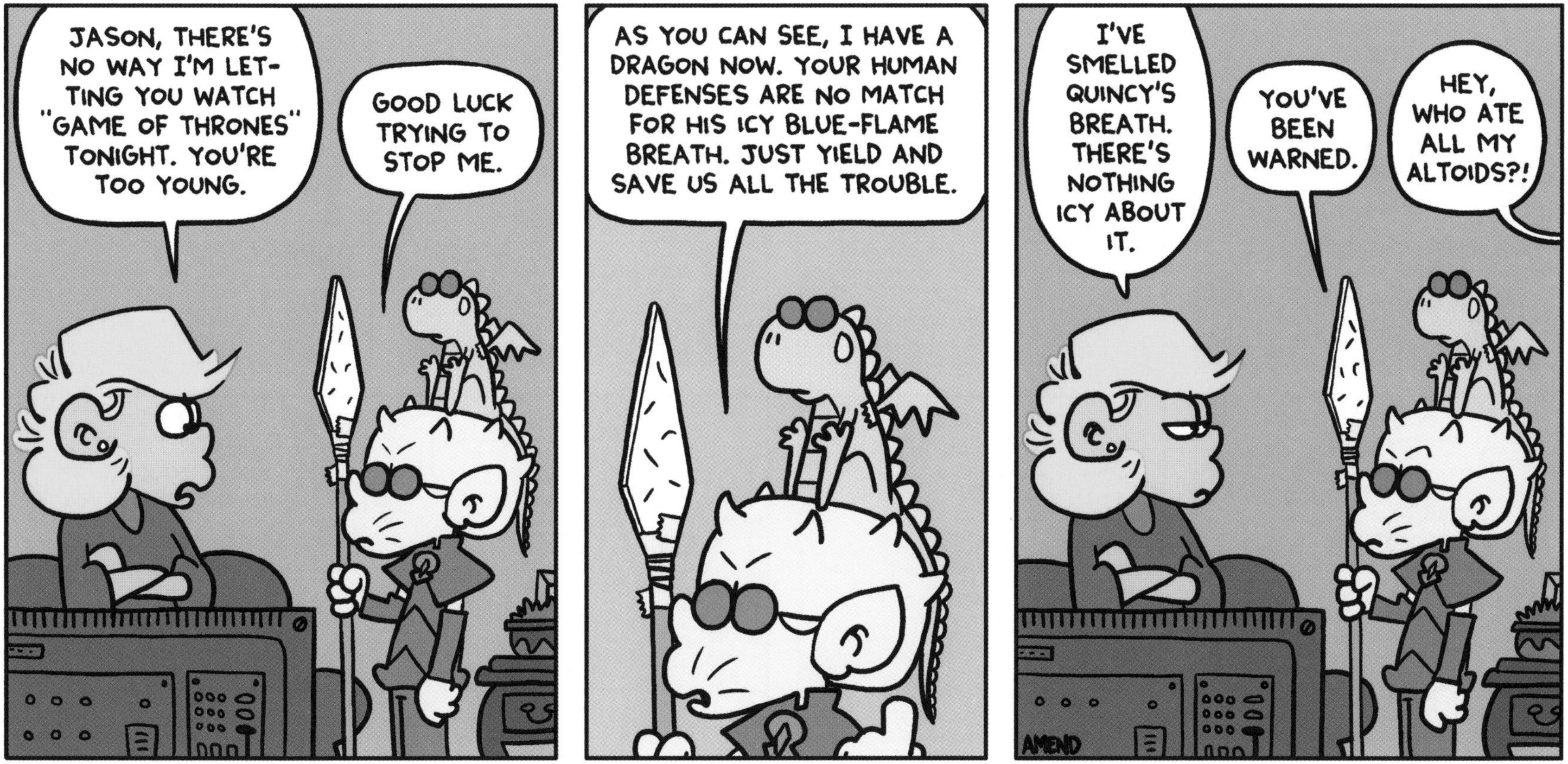
JASON, THERE'S NO WAY I'M LET-TING YOU WATCH "GAME OF THRONES" TONIGHT. YOU'RE TOO YOUNG.
GOOD LUCK TRYING TO STOP ME.
AS YOU CAN SEE, I HAVE A DRAGON NOW. YOUR HUMAN DEFENSES ARE NO MATCH FOR HIS ICY BLUE-FLAME BREATH. JUST YIELD AND SAVE US ALL THE TROUBLE.
I'VE SMELLED QUINCY'S BREATH. THERE'S NOTHING ICY ABOUT IT.
YOU'VE BEEN WARNED.
HEY, WHO ATE ALL MY ALTOIDS?!
AMEND

Infinity Beans

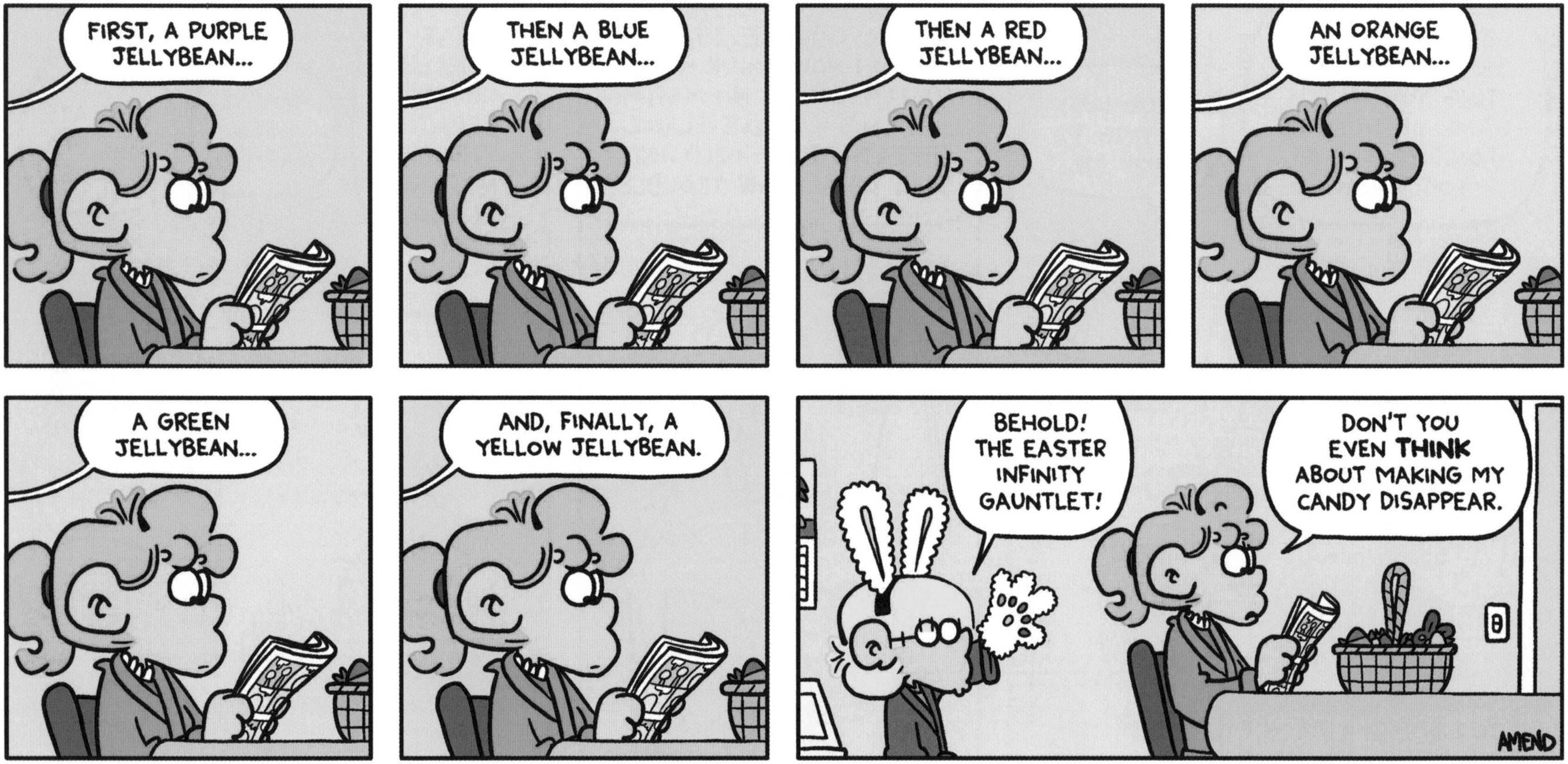
FIRST, A PURPLE JELLYBEAN...
THEN A BLUE JELLYBEAN...
THEN A RED JELLYBEAN...
AN ORANGE JELLYBEAN...
A GREEN JELLYBEAN...
AND, FINALLY, A YELLOW JELLYBEAN.
BEHOLD! THE EASTER INFINITY GAUNTLET!
DON'T YOU EVEN **THINK** ABOUT MAKING MY CANDY DISAPPEAR.
AMEND

Morton's Lottery

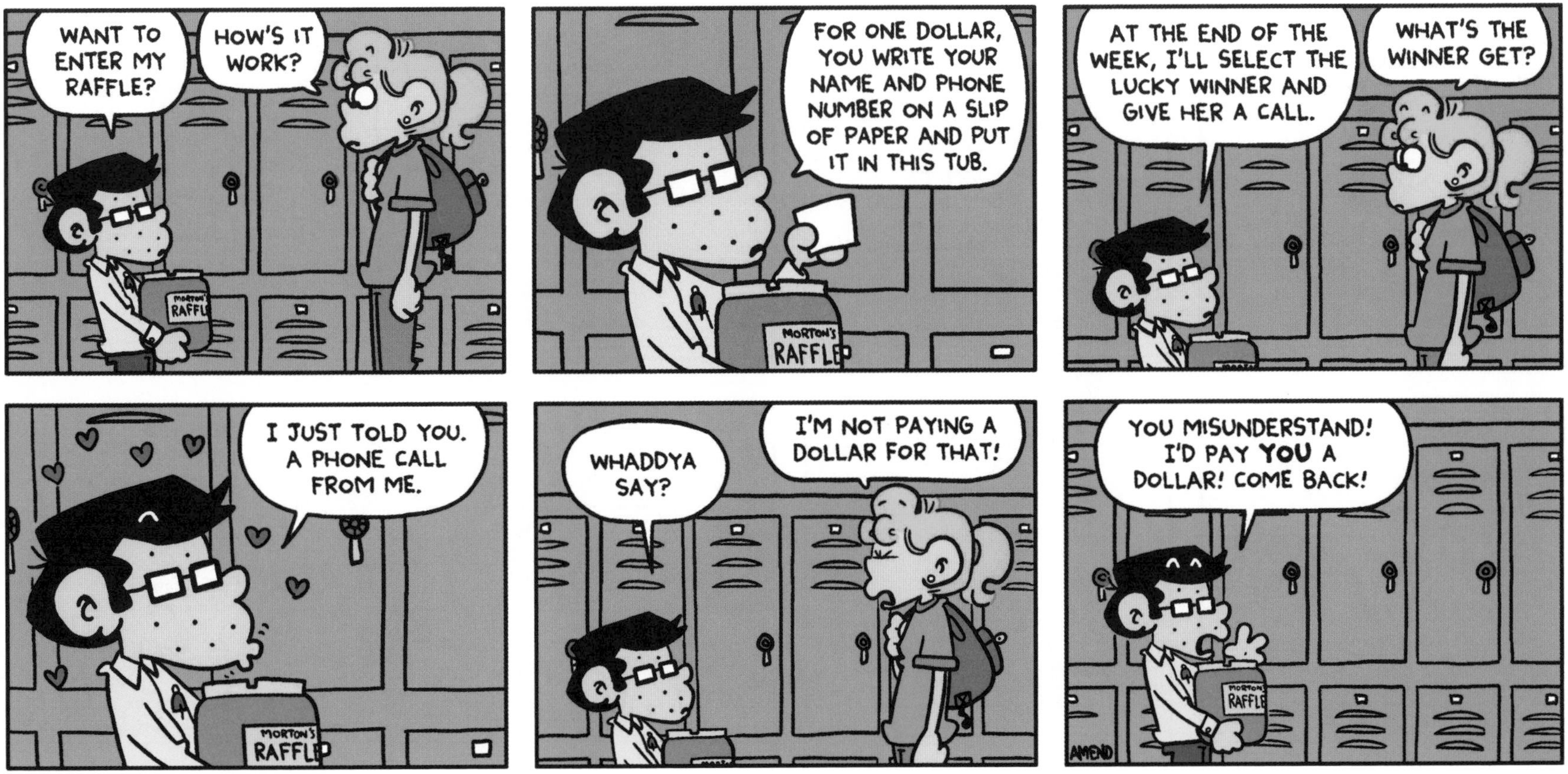
WANT TO ENTER MY RAFFLE?
HOW'S IT WORK?
MORTON'S RAFFLE
FOR ONE DOLLAR, YOU WRITE YOUR NAME AND PHONE NUMBER ON A SLIP OF PAPER AND PUT IT IN THIS TUB.
MORTON'S RAFFLE
AT THE END OF THE WEEK, I'LL SELECT THE LUCKY WINNER AND GIVE HER A CALL.
WHAT'S THE WINNER GET?
I JUST TOLD YOU. A PHONE CALL FROM ME.
MORTON'S RAFFLE
WHADDYA SAY?
I'M NOT PAYING A DOLLAR FOR THAT!
YOU MISUNDERSTAND! I'D PAY **YOU** A DOLLAR! COME BACK!
MORTON'S RAFFLE
AMEND

Mayo

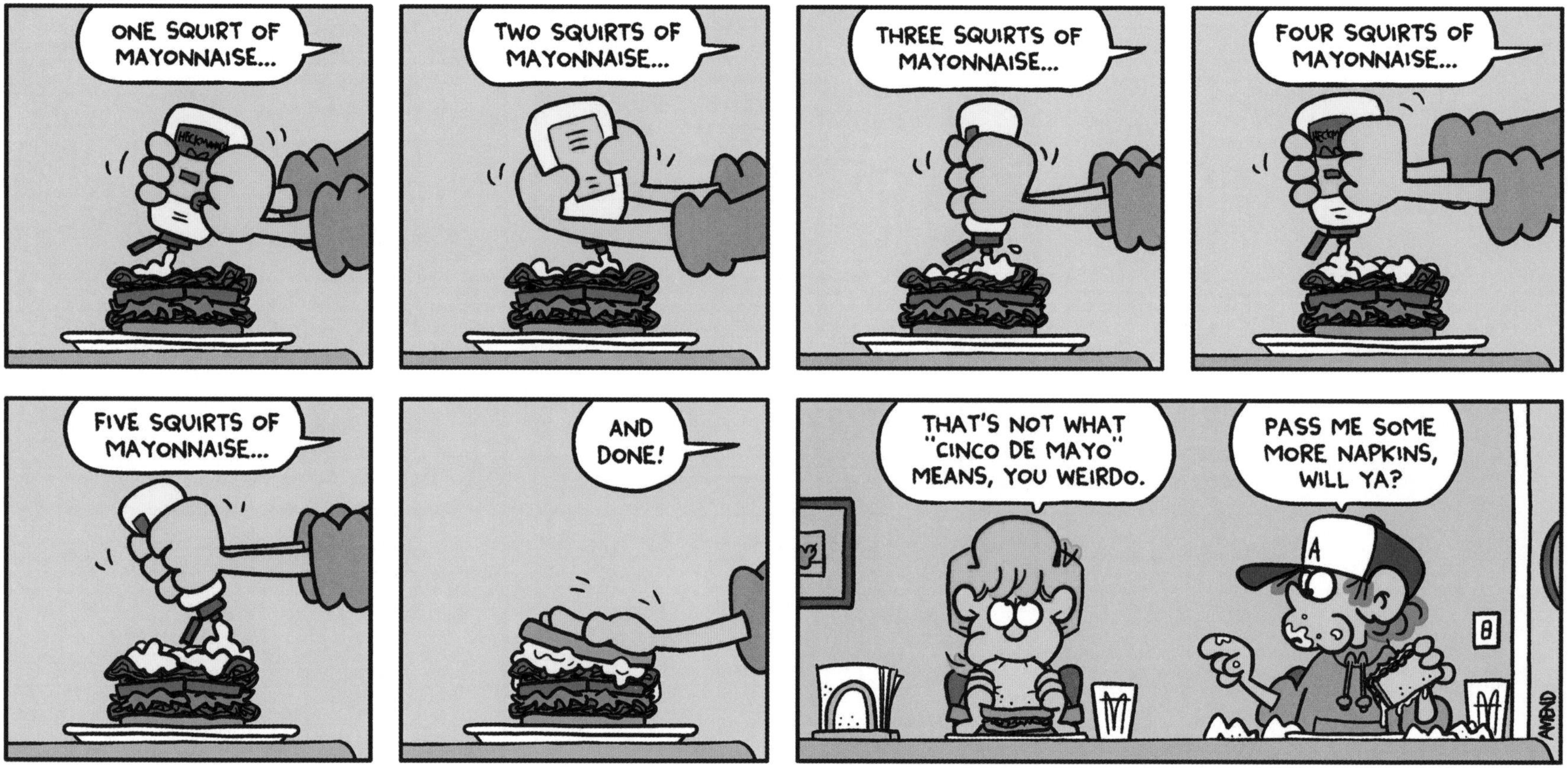
ONE SQUIRT OF MAYONNAISE...
TWO SQUIRTS OF MAYONNAISE...
THREE SQUIRTS OF MAYONNAISE...
FOUR SQUIRTS OF MAYONNAISE...
FIVE SQUIRTS OF MAYONNAISE...
AND DONE!
THAT'S NOT WHAT "CINCO DE MAYO" MEANS, YOU WEIRDO.
PASS ME SOME MORE NAPKINS, WILL YA?

Mudder's Day

Panel 1: Question: What's better than Mudder's Day...

Panel 2: Mugger's Day...

Panel 3: Mutterer's Day...

Grumble Grumble Grumble

Panel 4: And even Muppeter's Day...?

Panel 5: Answer: Why, it's... (drumroll)

Panel 6: $ $ $ $ $ $ $ $ $

Jason's Weekly Allowance Day!!!

Panel 7:

ALSO, MOTHER'S DAY.

NICE SAVE.

To Mom

AMEND

Study Aids

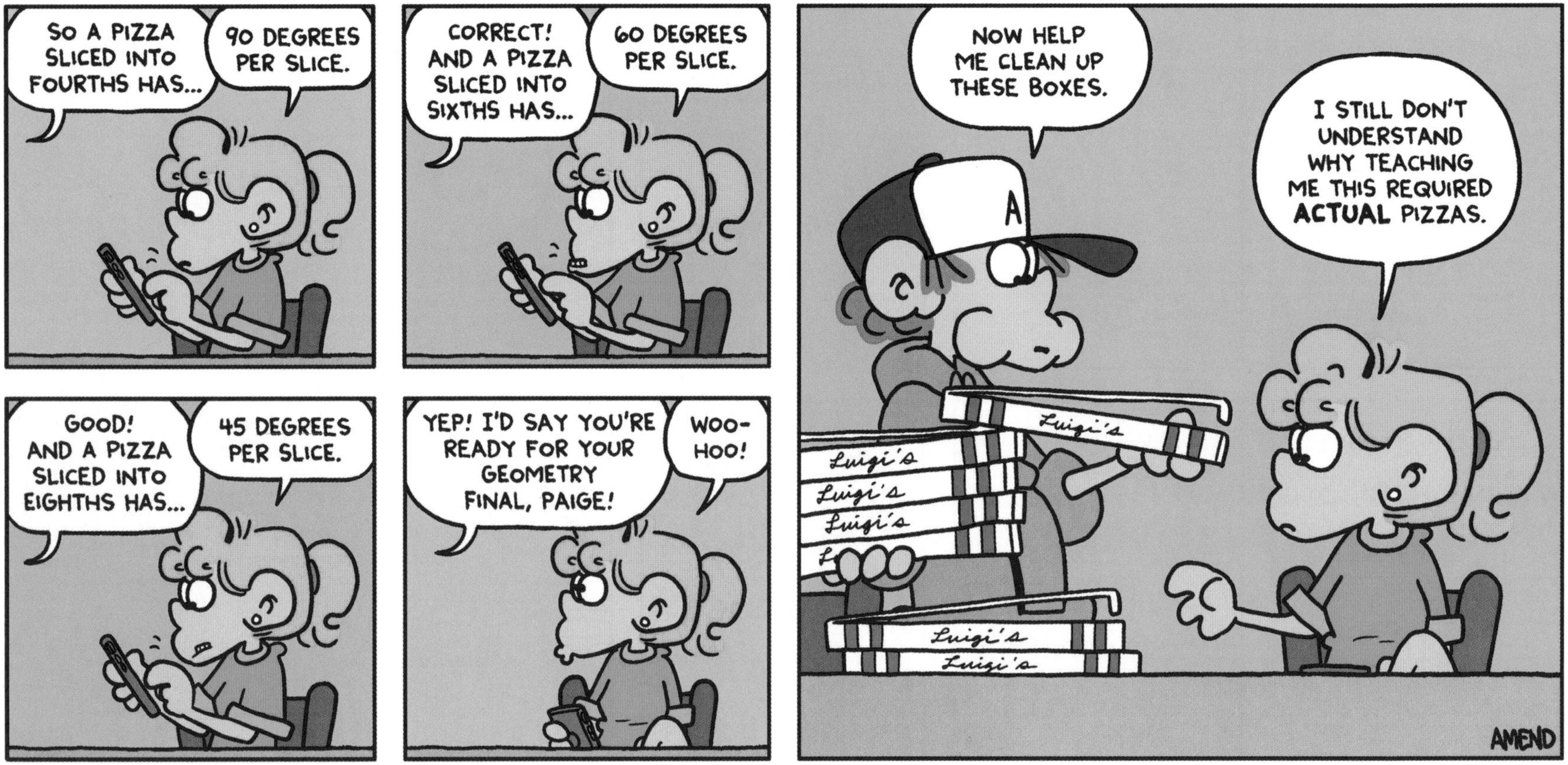
SO A PIZZA SLICED INTO FOURTHS HAS...
90 DEGREES PER SLICE.
CORRECT! AND A PIZZA SLICED INTO SIXTHS HAS...
60 DEGREES PER SLICE.
GOOD! AND A PIZZA SLICED INTO EIGHTHS HAS...
45 DEGREES PER SLICE.
YEP! I'D SAY YOU'RE READY FOR YOUR GEOMETRY FINAL, PAIGE!
WOO-HOO!
NOW HELP ME CLEAN UP THESE BOXES.
I STILL DON'T UNDERSTAND WHY TEACHING ME THIS REQUIRED ACTUAL PIZZAS.
AMEND

Goofy Eyes

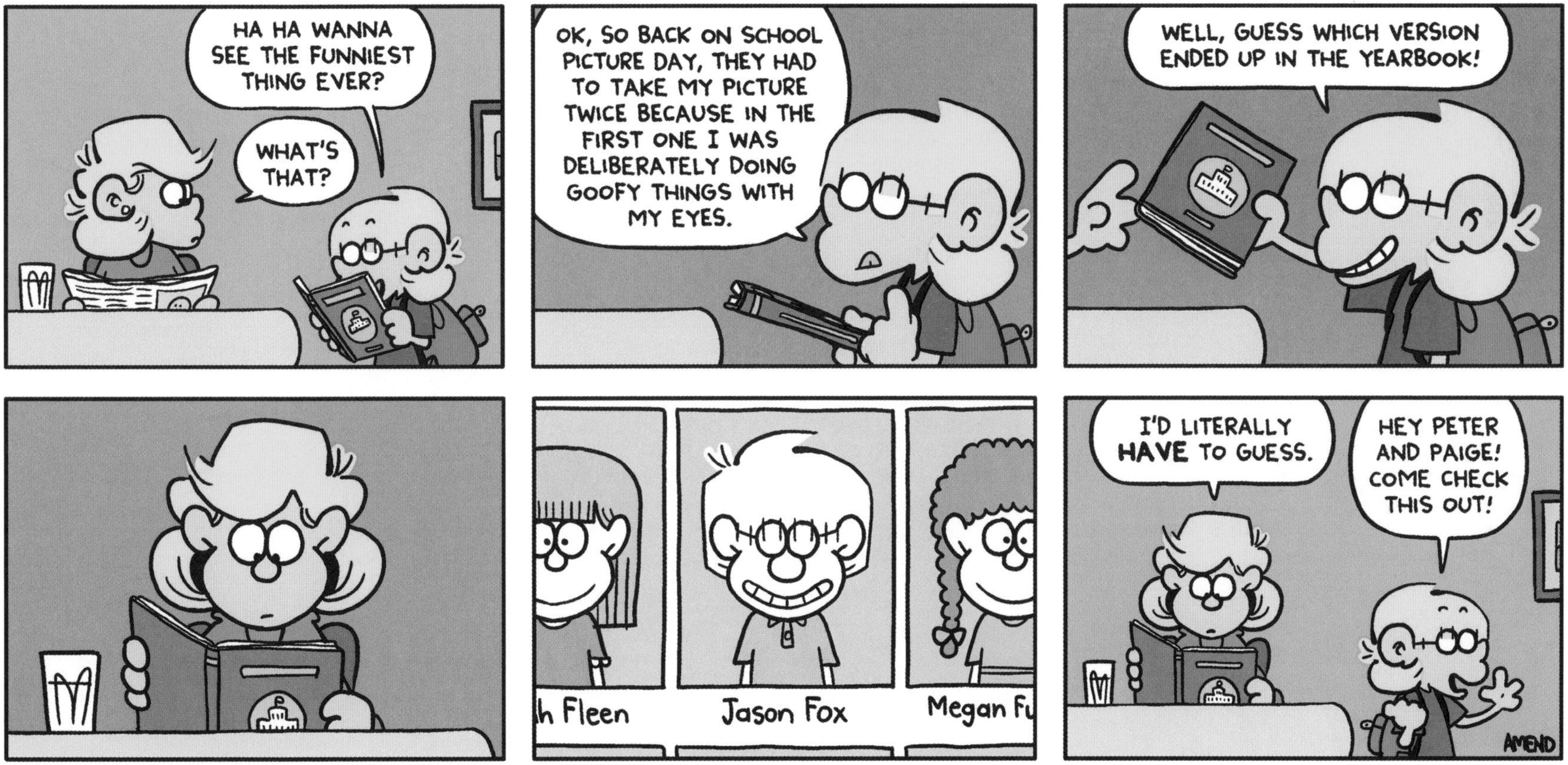

HA HA WANNA SEE THE FUNNIEST THING EVER?
WHAT'S THAT?
OK, SO BACK ON SCHOOL PICTURE DAY, THEY HAD TO TAKE MY PICTURE TWICE BECAUSE IN THE FIRST ONE I WAS DELIBERATELY DOING GOOFY THINGS WITH MY EYES.
WELL, GUESS WHICH VERSION ENDED UP IN THE YEARBOOK!
h Fleen
Jason Fox
Megan Fu
I'D LITERALLY **HAVE** TO GUESS.
HEY PETER AND PAIGE! COME CHECK THIS OUT!
AMEND

No Aimless Loafing

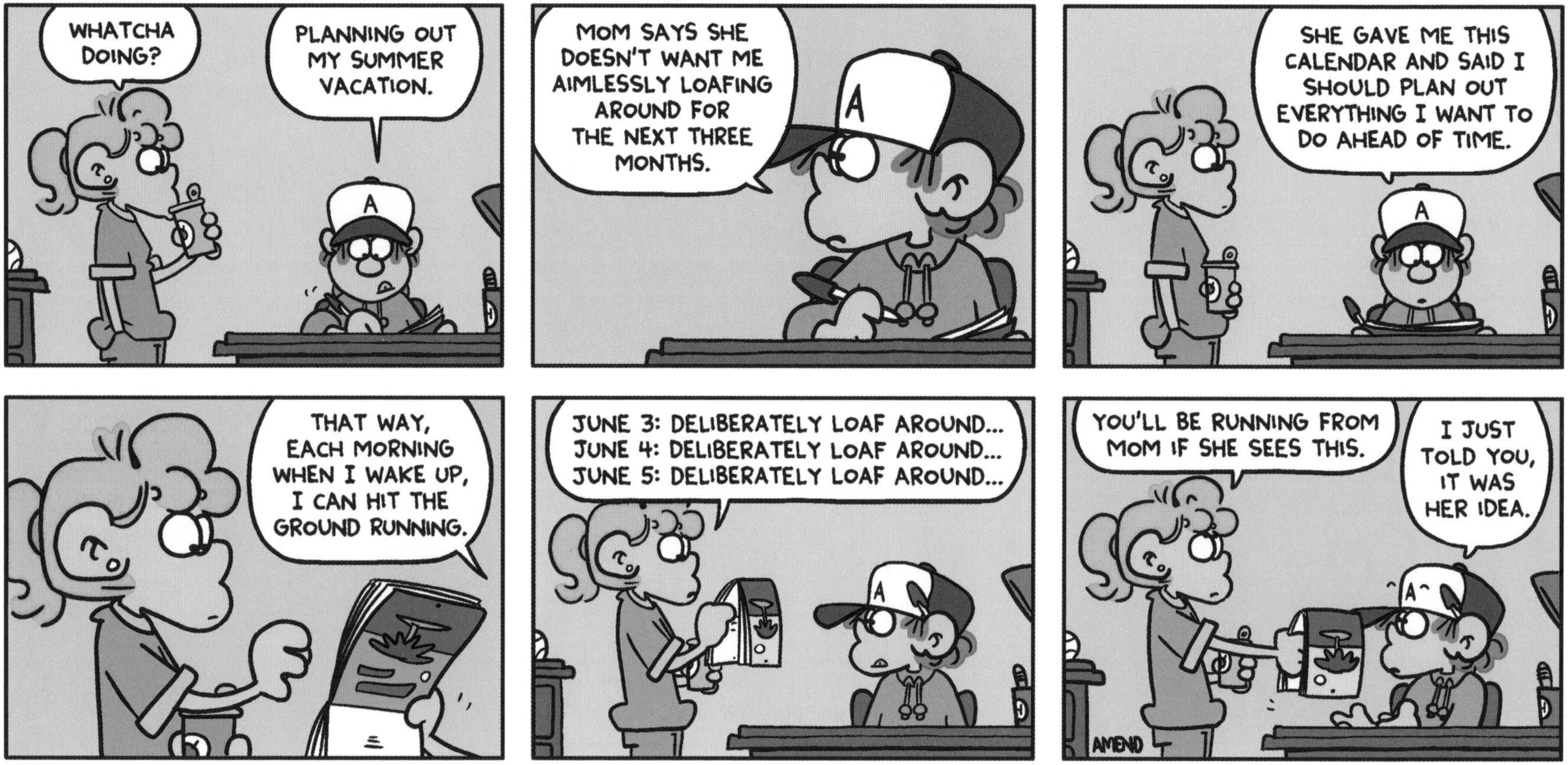
WHATCHA DOING?
PLANNING OUT MY SUMMER VACATION.
MOM SAYS SHE DOESN'T WANT ME AIMLESSLY LOAFING AROUND FOR THE NEXT THREE MONTHS.
SHE GAVE ME THIS CALENDAR AND SAID I SHOULD PLAN OUT EVERYTHING I WANT TO DO AHEAD OF TIME.
THAT WAY, EACH MORNING WHEN I WAKE UP, I CAN HIT THE GROUND RUNNING.
JUNE 3: DELIBERATELY LOAF AROUND... JUNE 4: DELIBERATELY LOAF AROUND... JUNE 5: DELIBERATELY LOAF AROUND...
YOU'LL BE RUNNING FROM MOM IF SHE SEES THIS.
I JUST TOLD YOU, IT WAS HER IDEA.
AMEND

Smart-Ass Phone

WHY ARE YOU RUNNING?

BECAUSE IT'S POURING RAIN!

IT IS?

DUH!

SORRY, I HADN'T NOTICED.

HOW COULD YOU NOT NOTICE?!

OH, WELL. WHAT'S A LITTLE MOISTURE, RIGHT?

WATERPROOF PHONES ARE GETTING COCKY, HAVE YOU NOTICED?

DO YOU NEED TO GO SEAL YOURSELF IN A BAG OF RICE FOR A FEW DAYS? I'LL WAIT.

AMEND

Happy Fat

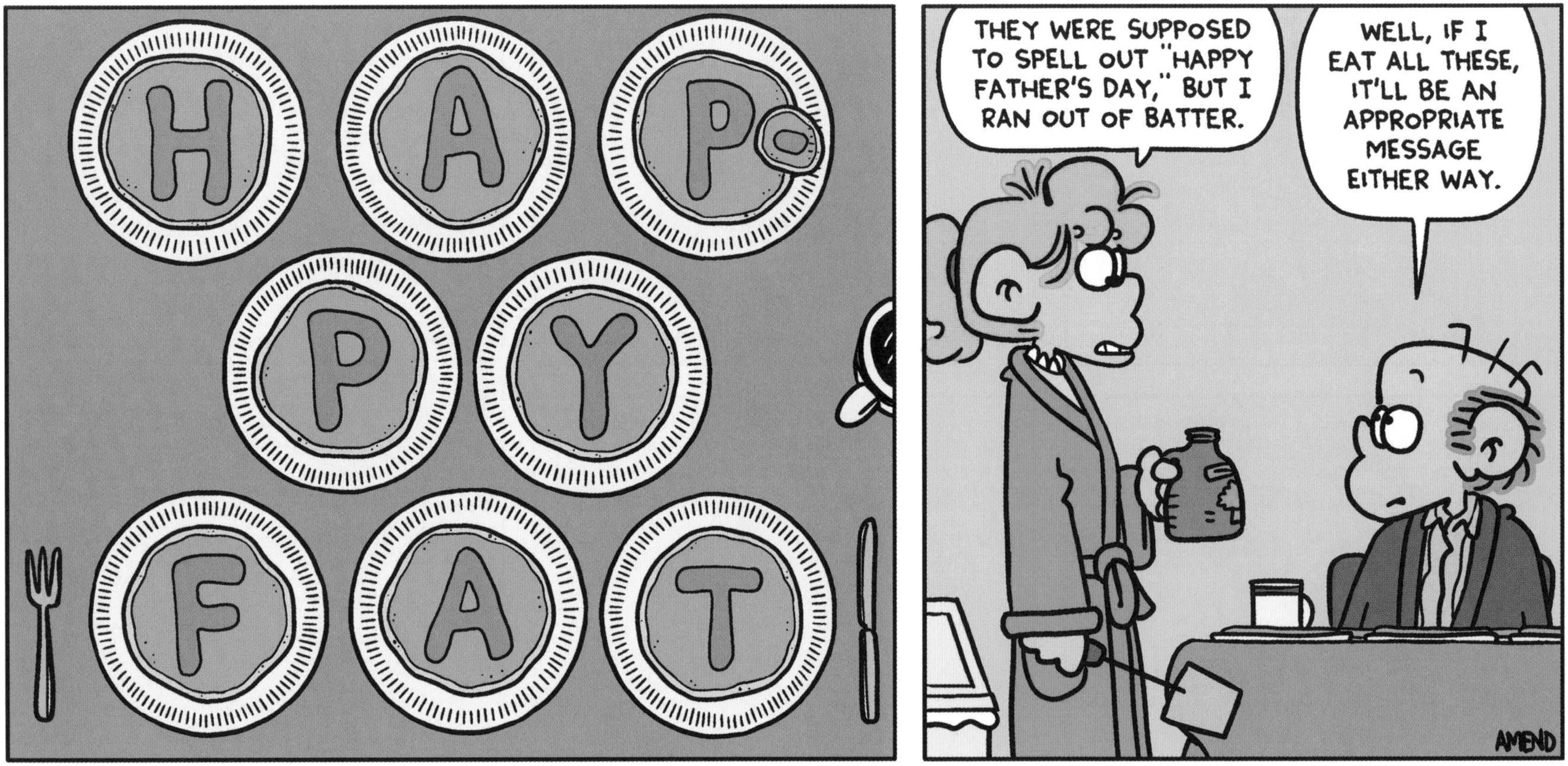
H A P P Y F A T
THEY WERE SUPPOSED TO SPELL OUT "HAPPY FATHER'S DAY," BUT I RAN OUT OF BATTER.
WELL, IF I EAT ALL THESE, IT'LL BE AN APPROPRIATE MESSAGE EITHER WAY.
AMEND

Playing Outside

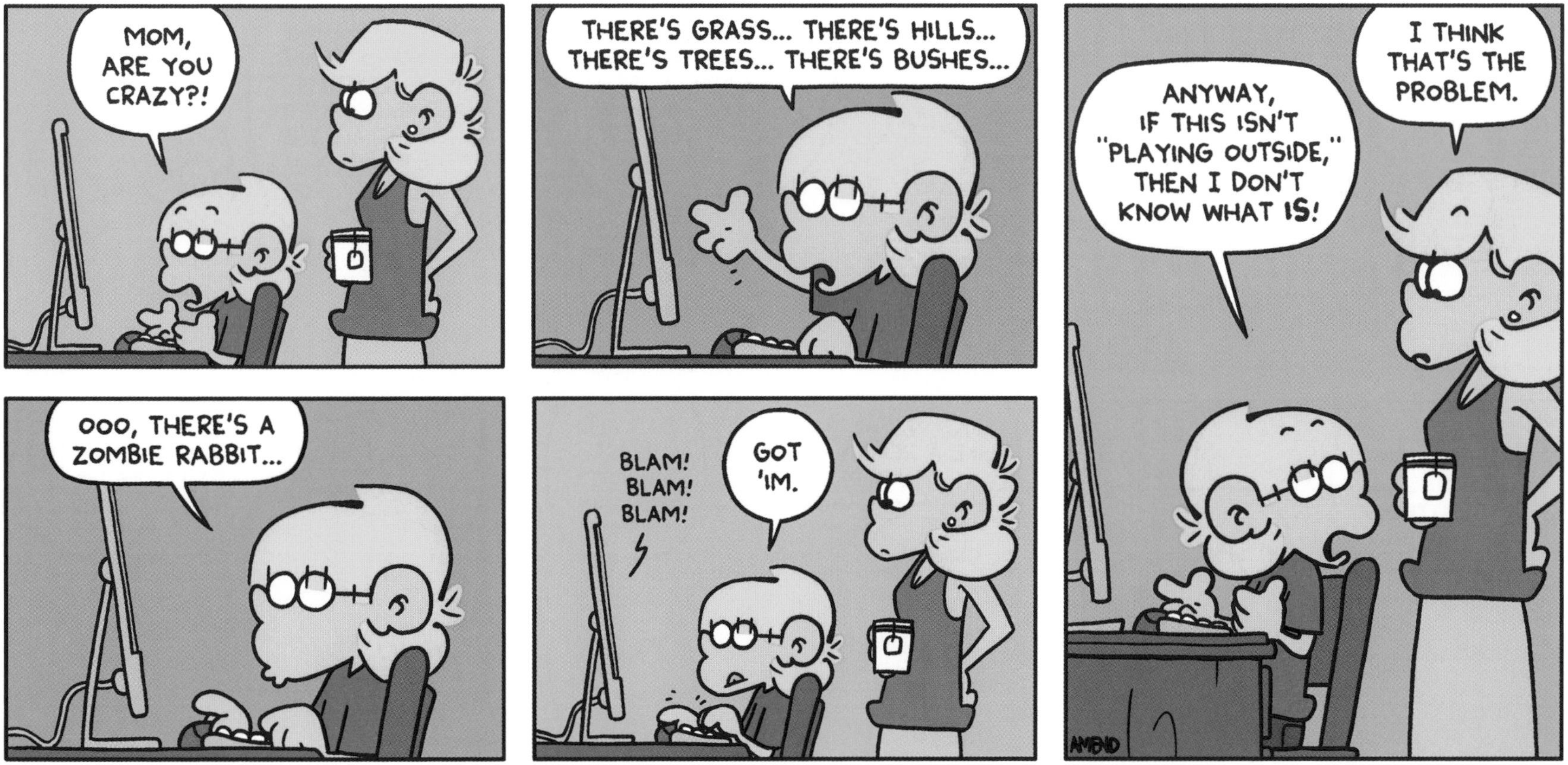
MOM, ARE YOU CRAZY?!
THERE'S GRASS... THERE'S HILLS... THERE'S TREES... THERE'S BUSHES...
OOO, THERE'S A ZOMBIE RABBIT...
BLAM! BLAM! BLAM!
GOT 'IM.
ANYWAY, IF THIS ISN'T "PLAYING OUTSIDE," THEN I DON'T KNOW WHAT IS!
I THINK THAT'S THE PROBLEM.
AMEND

Dog Day of Summer

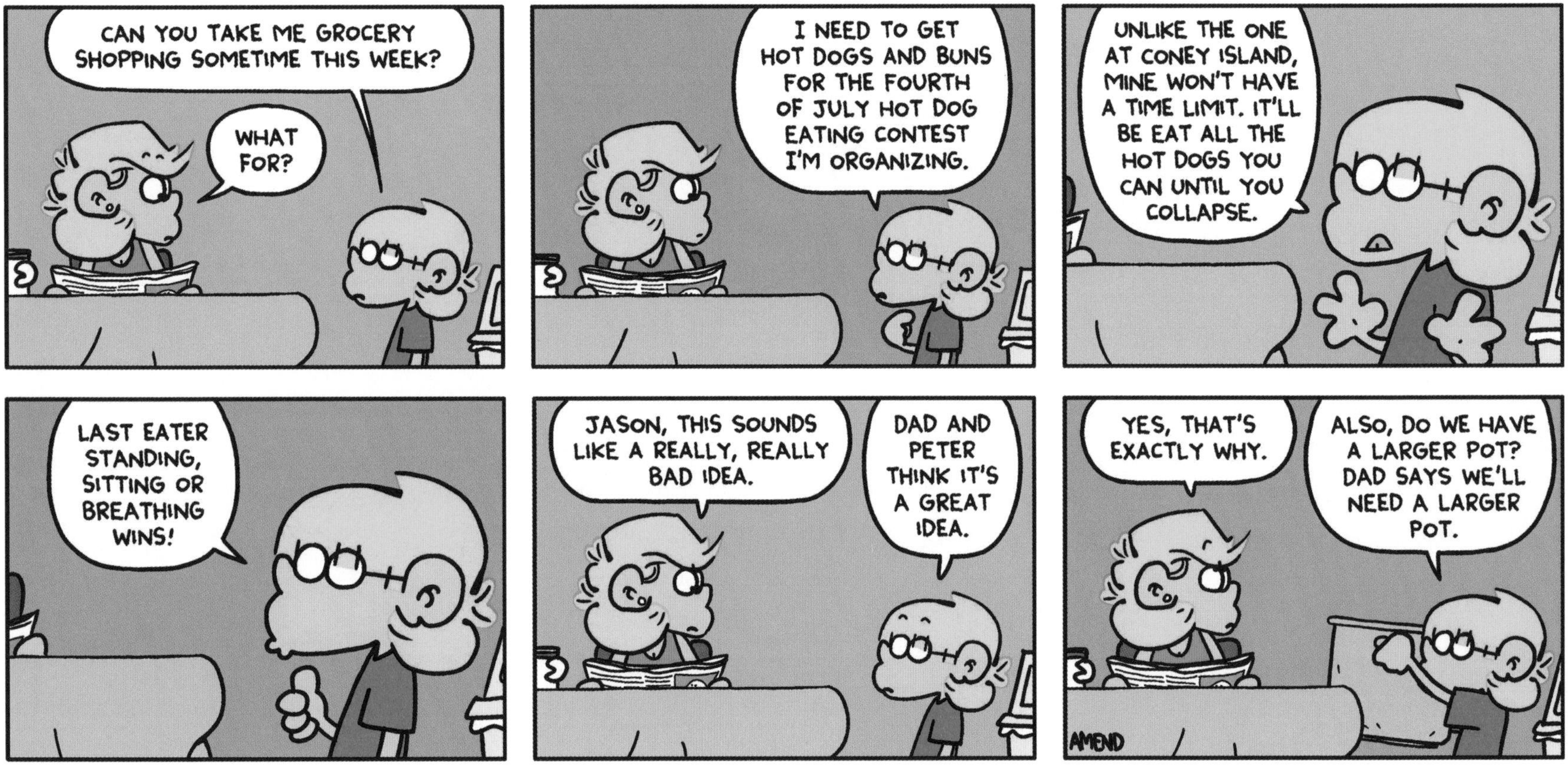
CAN YOU TAKE ME GROCERY SHOPPING SOMETIME THIS WEEK?
WHAT FOR?
I NEED TO GET HOT DOGS AND BUNS FOR THE FOURTH OF JULY HOT DOG EATING CONTEST I'M ORGANIZING.
UNLIKE THE ONE AT CONEY ISLAND, MINE WON'T HAVE A TIME LIMIT. IT'LL BE EAT ALL THE HOT DOGS YOU CAN UNTIL YOU COLLAPSE.
LAST EATER STANDING, SITTING OR BREATHING WINS!
JASON, THIS SOUNDS LIKE A REALLY, REALLY BAD IDEA.
DAD AND PETER THINK IT'S A GREAT IDEA.
YES, THAT'S EXACTLY WHY.
ALSO, DO WE HAVE A LARGER POT? DAD SAYS WE'LL NEED A LARGER POT.
AMEND

Moby Dad

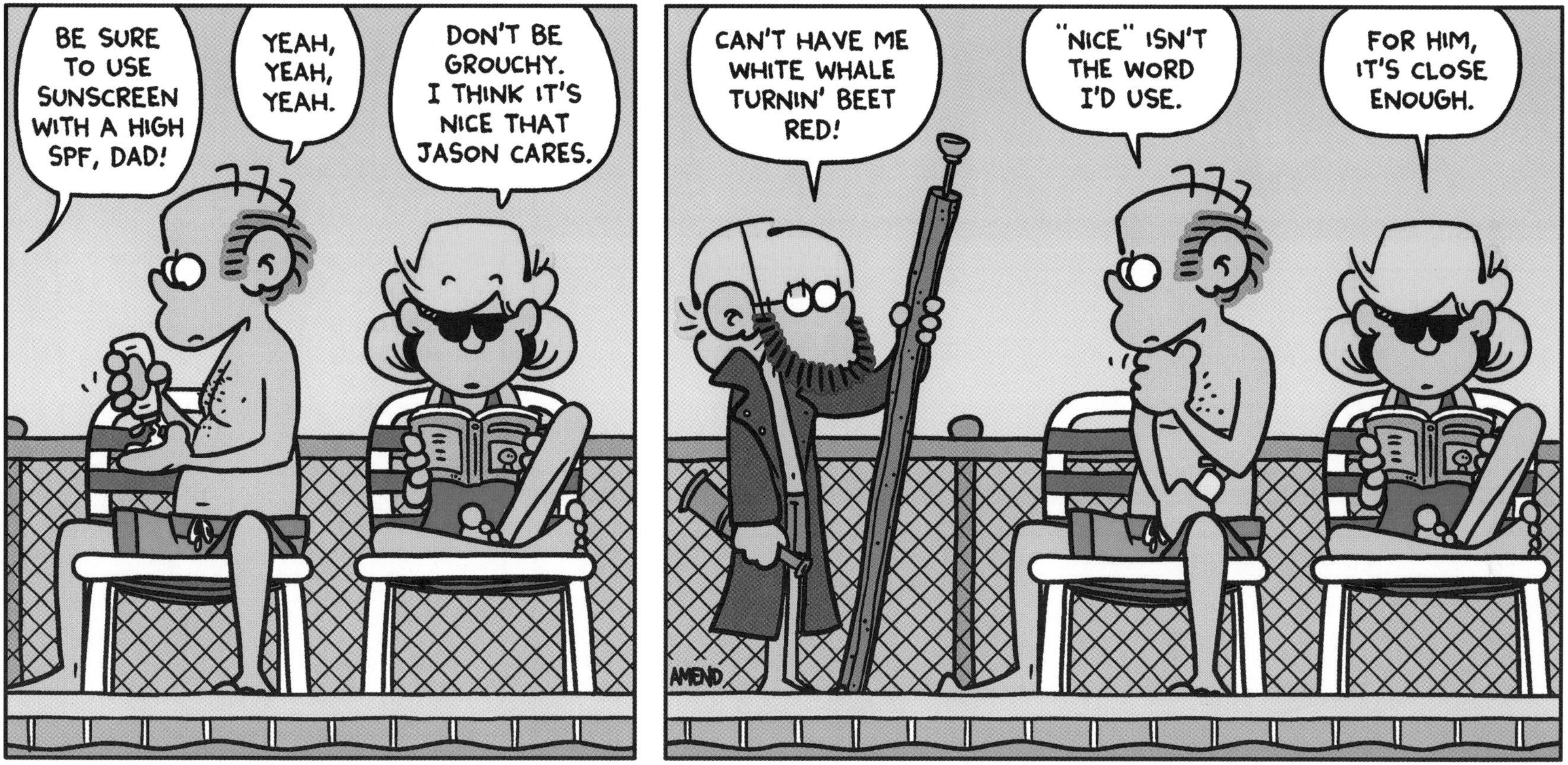

BE SURE TO USE SUNSCREEN WITH A HIGH SPF, DAD!
YEAH, YEAH, YEAH.
DON'T BE GROUCHY. I THINK IT'S NICE THAT JASON CARES.
CAN'T HAVE ME WHITE WHALE TURNIN' BEET RED!
"NICE" ISN'T THE WORD I'D USE.
FOR HIM, IT'S CLOSE ENOUGH.
AMEND

Wind Hog

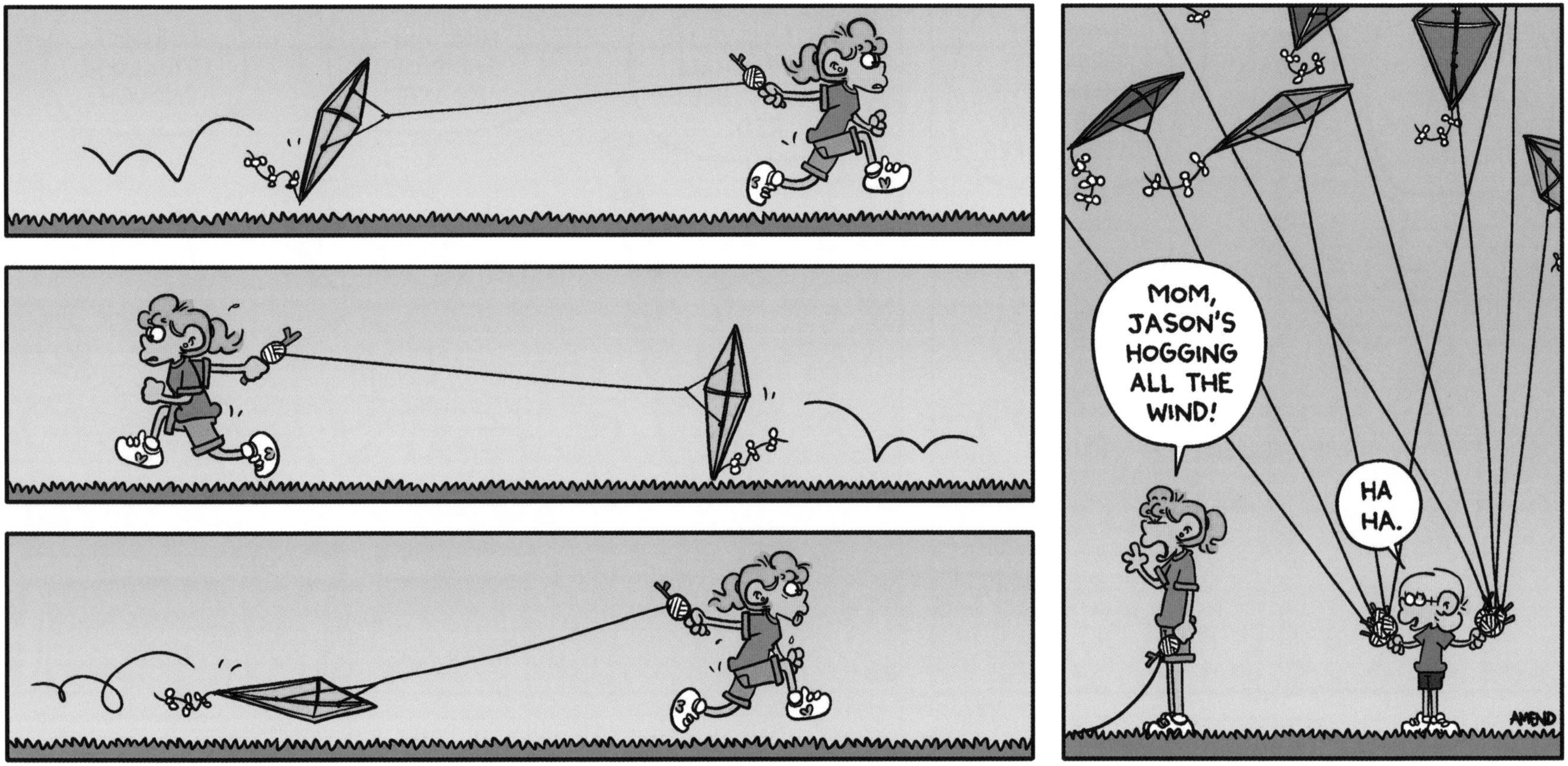
MOM, JASON'S HOGGING ALL THE WIND!
HA HA.
AMEND

Green Thumb

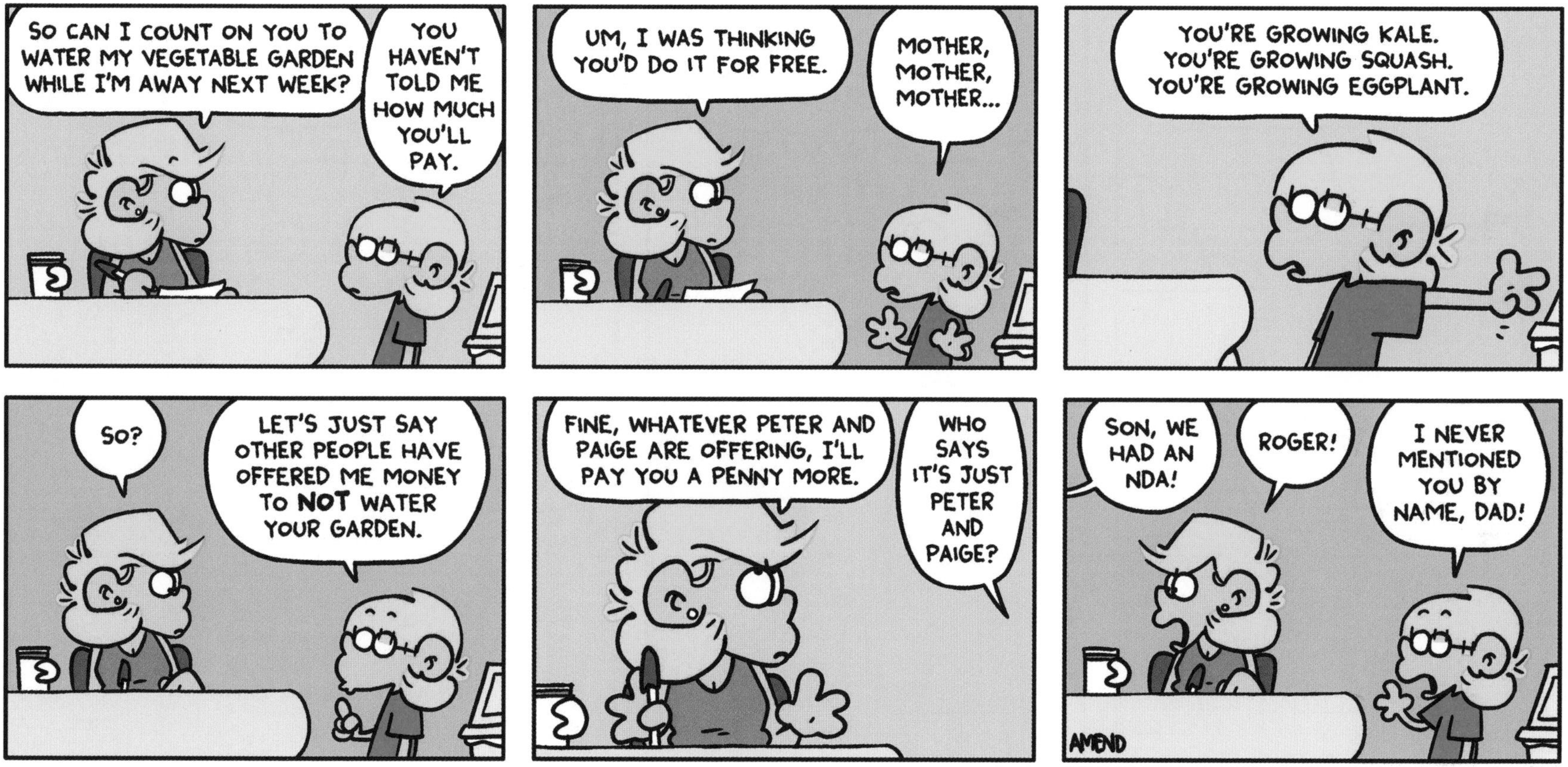
SO CAN I COUNT ON YOU TO WATER MY VEGETABLE GARDEN WHILE I'M AWAY NEXT WEEK?
YOU HAVEN'T TOLD ME HOW MUCH YOU'LL PAY.
UM, I WAS THINKING YOU'D DO IT FOR FREE.
MOTHER, MOTHER, MOTHER...
YOU'RE GROWING KALE. YOU'RE GROWING SQUASH. YOU'RE GROWING EGGPLANT.
SO?
LET'S JUST SAY OTHER PEOPLE HAVE OFFERED ME MONEY TO **NOT** WATER YOUR GARDEN.
FINE, WHATEVER PETER AND PAIGE ARE OFFERING, I'LL PAY YOU A PENNY MORE.
WHO SAYS IT'S JUST PETER AND PAIGE?
SON, WE HAD AN NDA!
ROGER!
I NEVER MENTIONED YOU BY NAME, DAD!
AMEND

Other Options

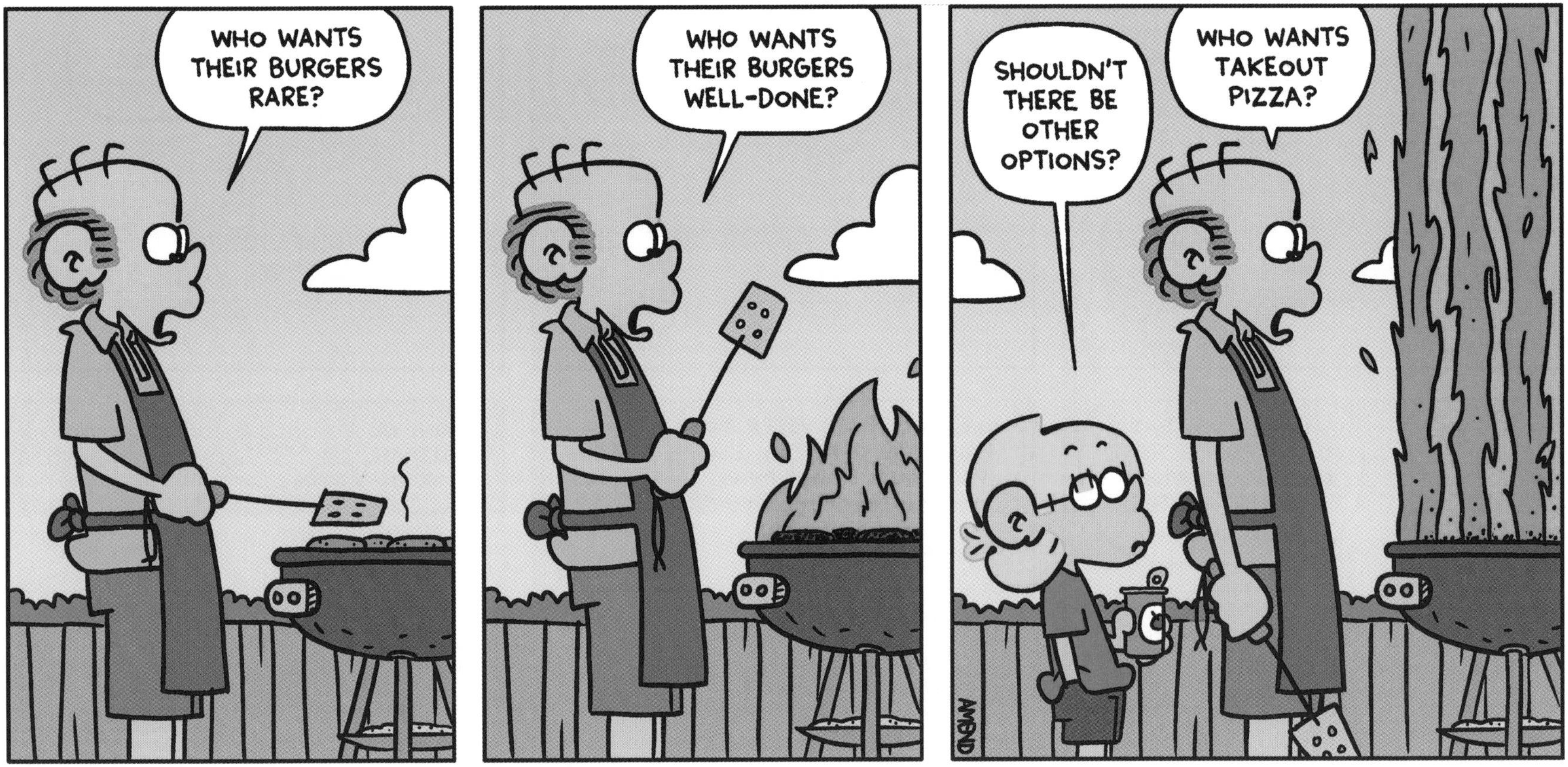
WHO WANTS THEIR BURGERS RARE?
WHO WANTS THEIR BURGERS WELL-DONE?
SHOULDN'T THERE BE OTHER OPTIONS?
WHO WANTS TAKEOUT PIZZA?

Wish Fulfillment

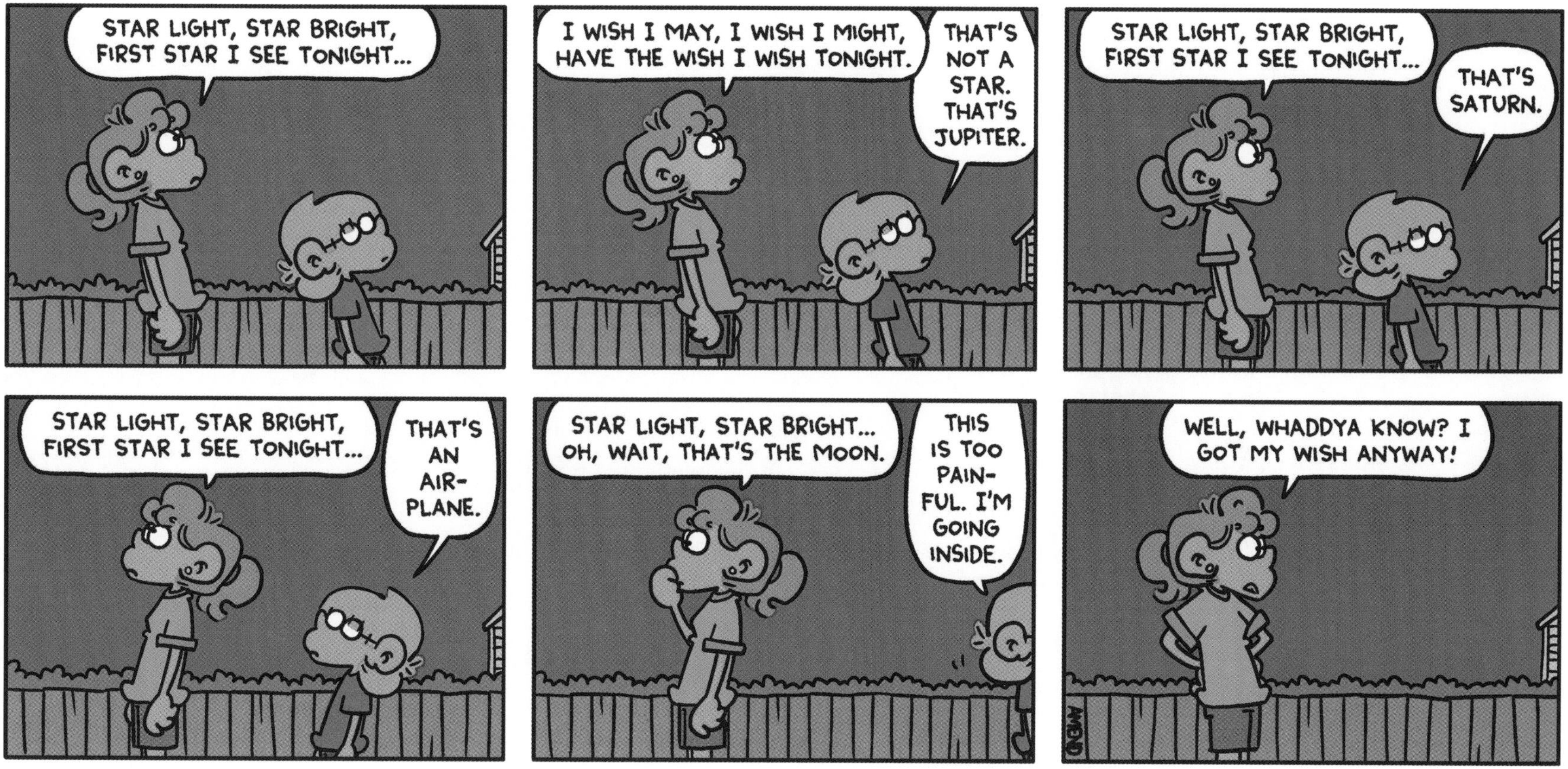
STAR LIGHT, STAR BRIGHT, FIRST STAR I SEE TONIGHT...
I WISH I MAY, I WISH I MIGHT, HAVE THE WISH I WISH TONIGHT.
THAT'S NOT A STAR. THAT'S JUPITER.
STAR LIGHT, STAR BRIGHT, FIRST STAR I SEE TONIGHT...
THAT'S SATURN.
STAR LIGHT, STAR BRIGHT, FIRST STAR I SEE TONIGHT...
THAT'S AN AIR-PLANE.
STAR LIGHT, STAR BRIGHT... OH, WAIT, THAT'S THE MOON.
THIS IS TOO PAIN-FUL. I'M GOING INSIDE.
WELL, WHADDYA KNOW? I GOT MY WISH ANYWAY!

Mostmallows

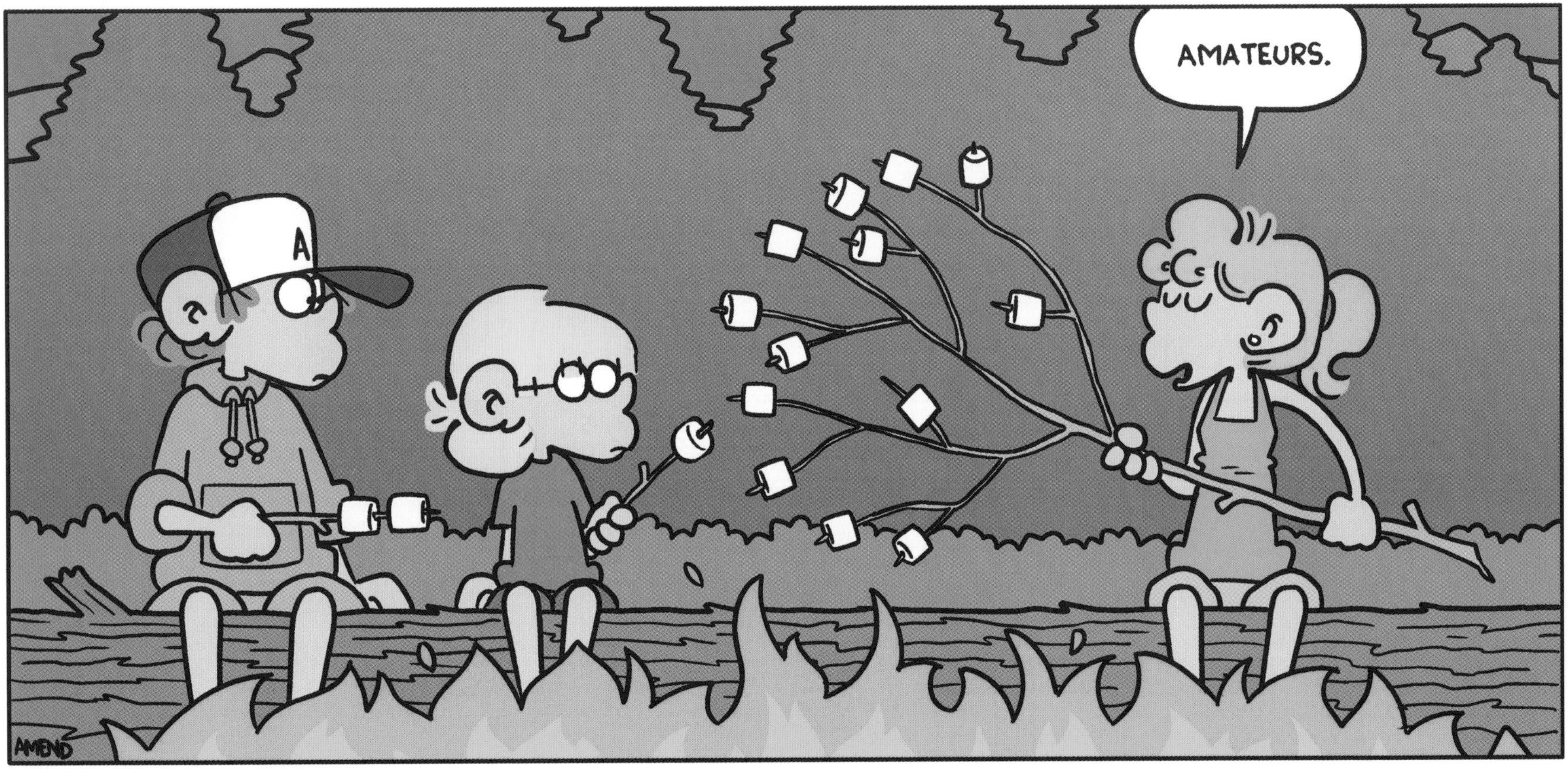

A
AMATEURS.
AMEND

Pack to School

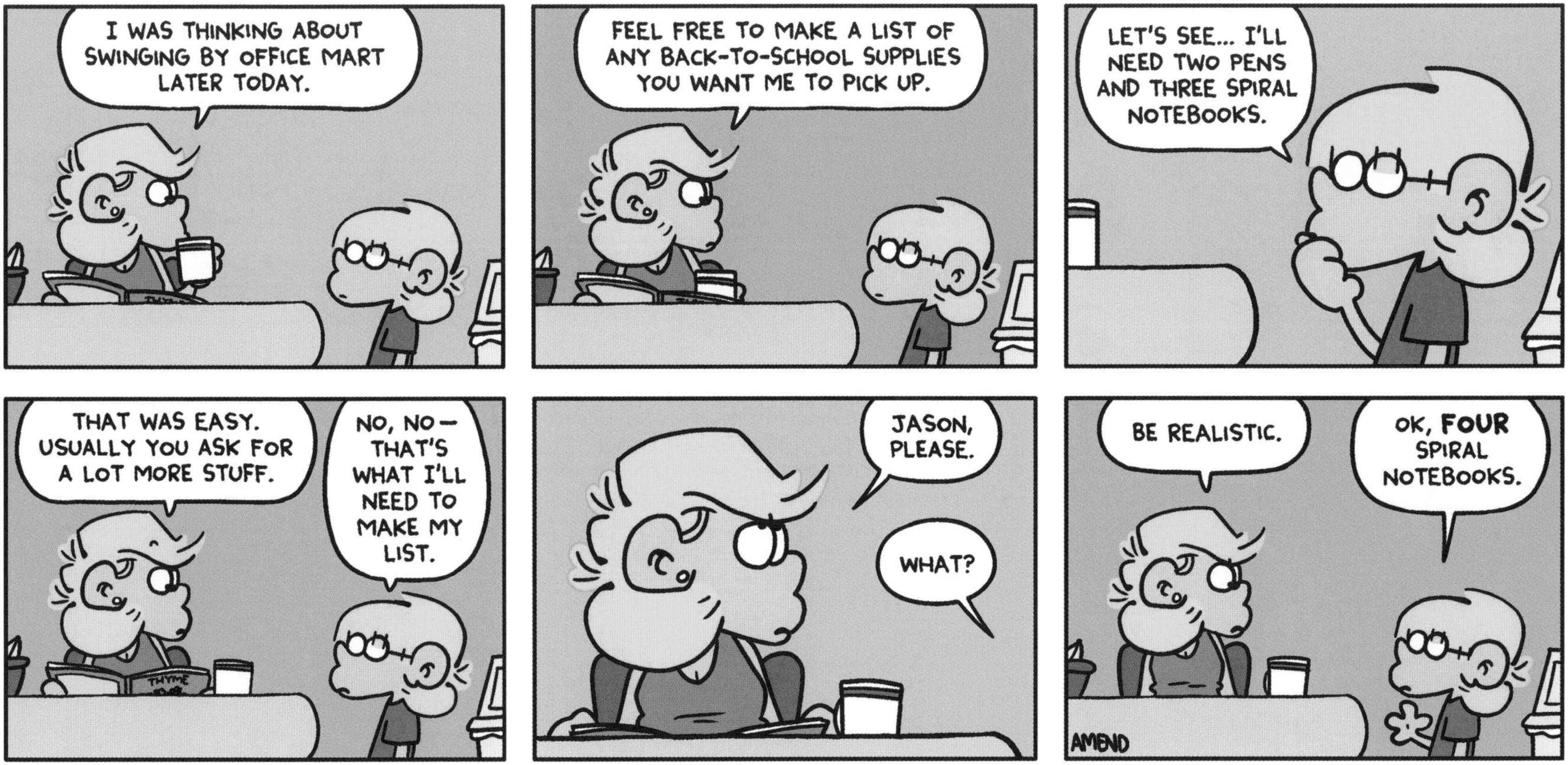
I WAS THINKING ABOUT SWINGING BY OFFICE MART LATER TODAY.
FEEL FREE TO MAKE A LIST OF ANY BACK-TO-SCHOOL SUPPLIES YOU WANT ME TO PICK UP.
LET'S SEE... I'LL NEED TWO PENS AND THREE SPIRAL NOTEBOOKS.
THAT WAS EASY. USUALLY YOU ASK FOR A LOT MORE STUFF.
NO, NO— THAT'S WHAT I'LL NEED TO MAKE MY LIST.
JASON, PLEASE.
WHAT?
BE REALISTIC.
OK, **FOUR** SPIRAL NOTEBOOKS.
AMEND

Locker Hurt

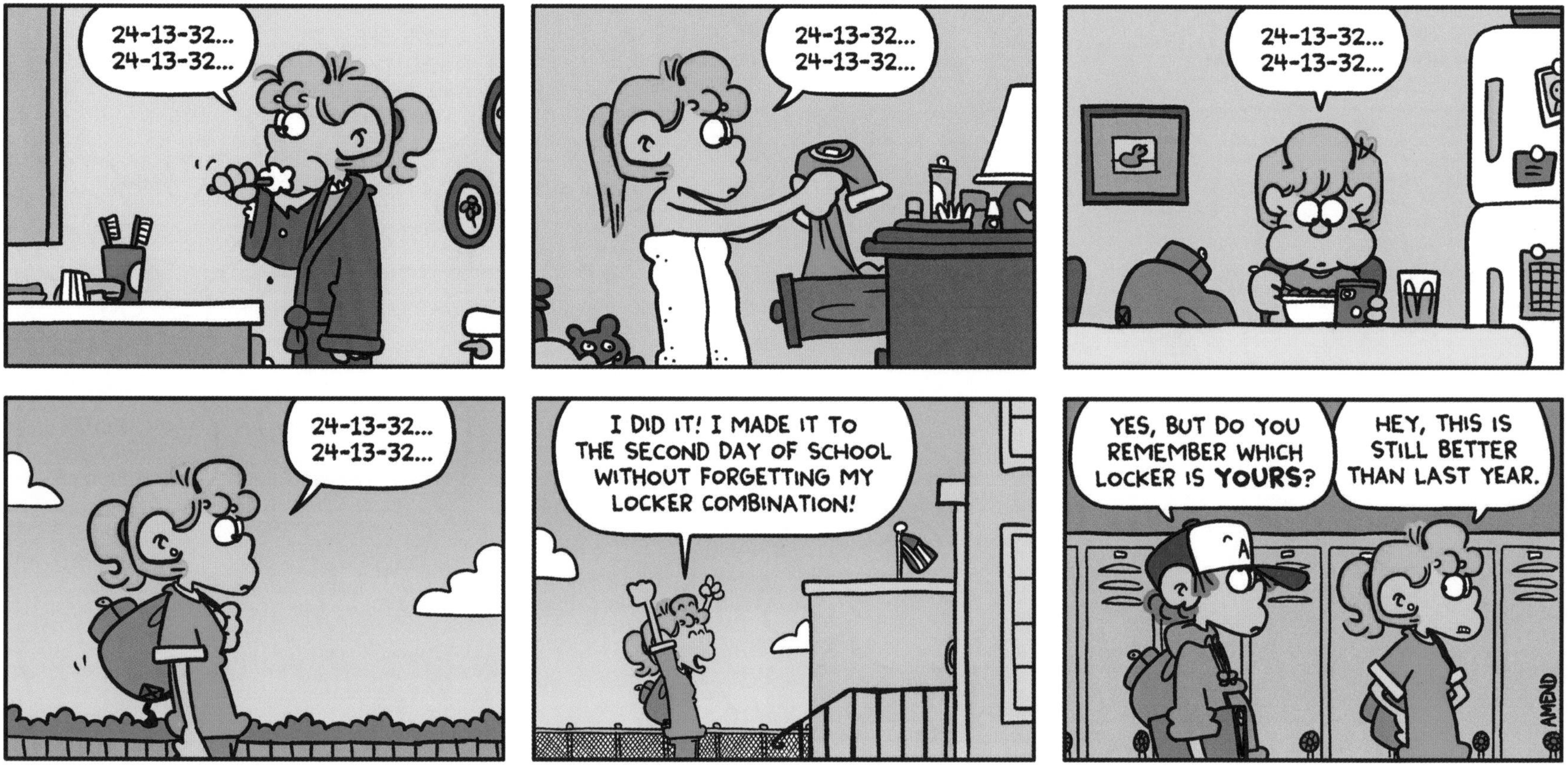
24-13-32...
24-13-32...
24-13-32...
24-13-32...
24-13-32...
24-13-32...
24-13-32...
24-13-32...
I DID IT! I MADE IT TO THE SECOND DAY OF SCHOOL WITHOUT FORGETTING MY LOCKER COMBINATION!
YES, BUT DO YOU REMEMBER WHICH LOCKER IS YOURS?
HEY, THIS IS STILL BETTER THAN LAST YEAR.
AMEND

Classic Jason

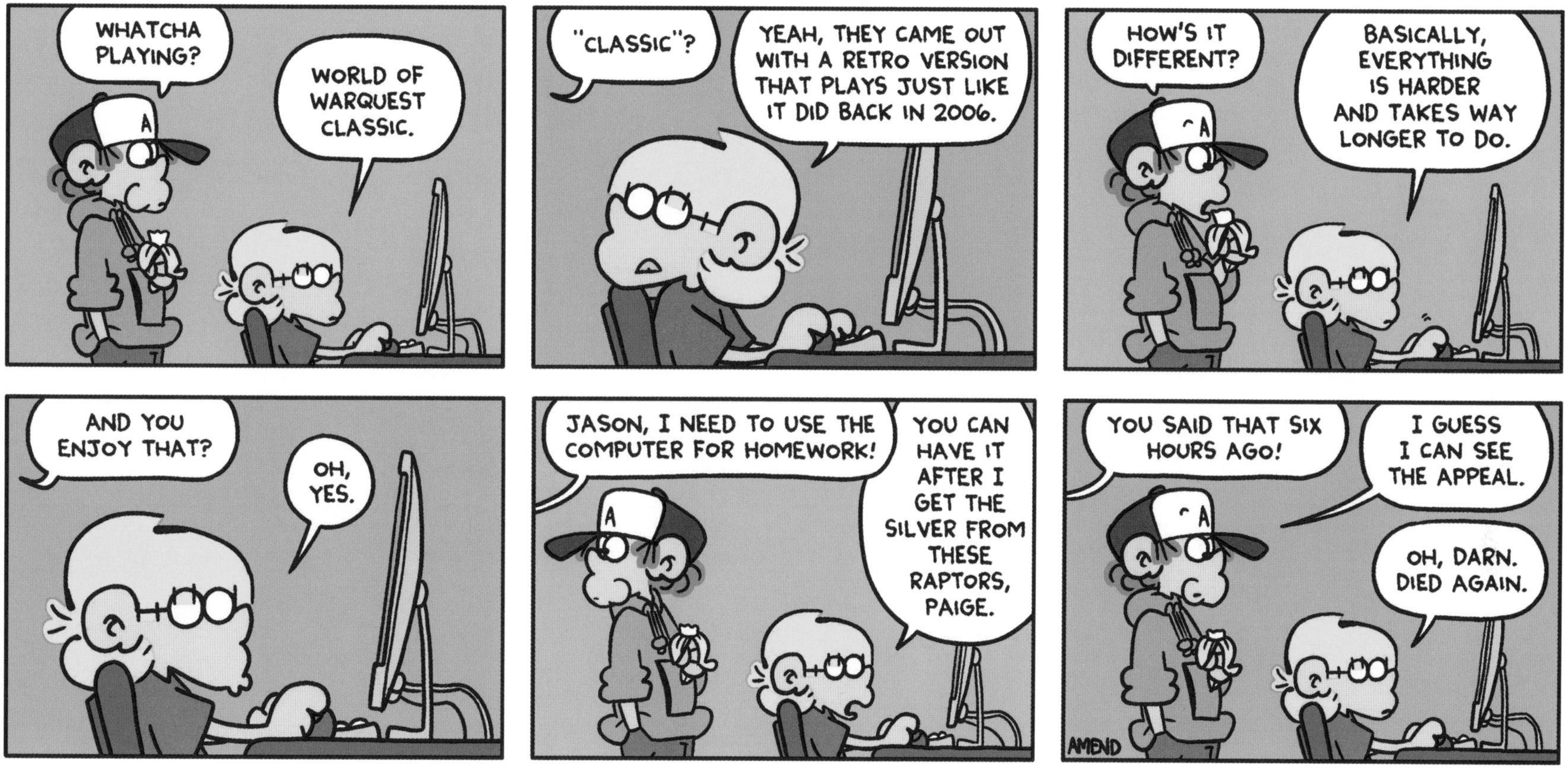
WHATCHA PLAYING?
WORLD OF WARQUEST CLASSIC.
"CLASSIC"?
YEAH, THEY CAME OUT WITH A RETRO VERSION THAT PLAYS JUST LIKE IT DID BACK IN 2006.
HOW'S IT DIFFERENT?
BASICALLY, EVERYTHING IS HARDER AND TAKES WAY LONGER TO DO.
AND YOU ENJOY THAT?
OH, YES.
JASON, I NEED TO USE THE COMPUTER FOR HOMEWORK!
YOU CAN HAVE IT AFTER I GET THE SILVER FROM THESE RAPTORS, PAIGE.
YOU SAID THAT SIX HOURS AGO!
I GUESS I CAN SEE THE APPEAL.
OH, DARN. DIED AGAIN.
AMEND

Poser

DO YOU THINK THERE'LL EVER COME A DAY, LIKE IN "WESTWORLD" OR "TERMINATOR," WHERE YOU COULD HAVE KILLER ROBOTS POSING AS NORMAL HUMAN BEINGS?
* BEEP * PARSING QUERY...
CHECKING LANGUAGE DATASET...
GENERATING OPTIMAL RESPONSE...
NO, BROTHER. YOU HAVE NOTHING TO WORRY ABOUT. SLEEP WELL TONIGHT.
NOTE, I SAID **NORMAL** HUMAN BEINGS.
* BEEP * PARSING SARCASM...
AMEND

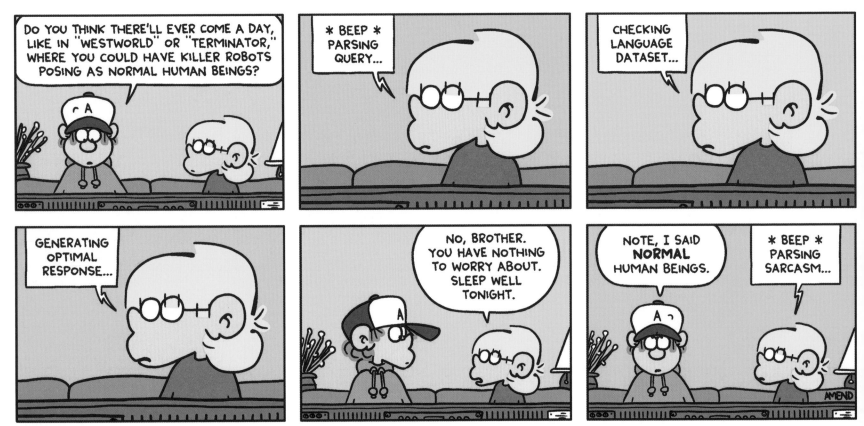

Coverup

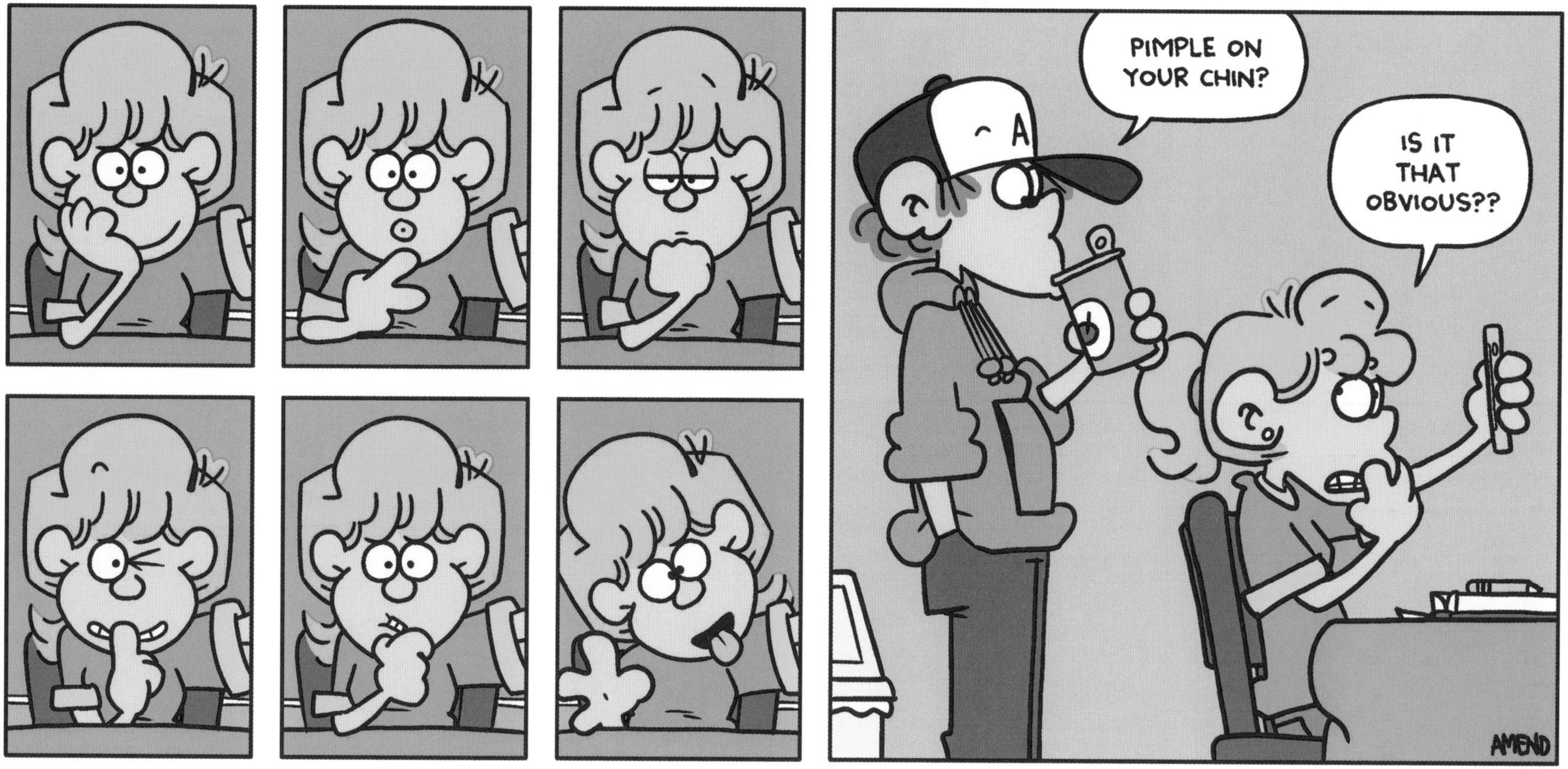

PIMPLE ON YOUR CHIN?
IS IT THAT OBVIOUS??
AMEND

Capital Punishment

Panel 1: AS YOU ENTER THE DUNGEON, YOU SEE BEFORE YOU AN ELDERLY WOMAN.

Panel 2: SHE SAYS THAT IN ORDER TO PASS, YOU MUST ANSWER HER QUESTIONS CORRECTLY. ARE YOU READY? — YES.

Panel 3: "WHAT IS THE CAPITAL OF MICHIGAN?" — LANSING.

Panel 4: "WHAT IS THE CAPITAL OF NEVADA?" — CARSON CITY.

Panel 5: "WHAT IS THE CAPITAL OF PENNSYLVANIA?" — PHILA-DELPHIA?

Panel 6: WRONG! SHE SHAPE-SHIFTS INTO A DEMON, PLUNGES A FIST INTO YOUR CHEST AND RIPS OUT YOUR HEART! — OUCH.

Panel 7: ABOUT THE WAY YOU TWO STUDY FOR TESTS... — IT HELPS US GET EXTRA-MOTIVATED. — YOU SEE BEFORE YOU AN ELDERLY WOMAN...

Loopy Physics

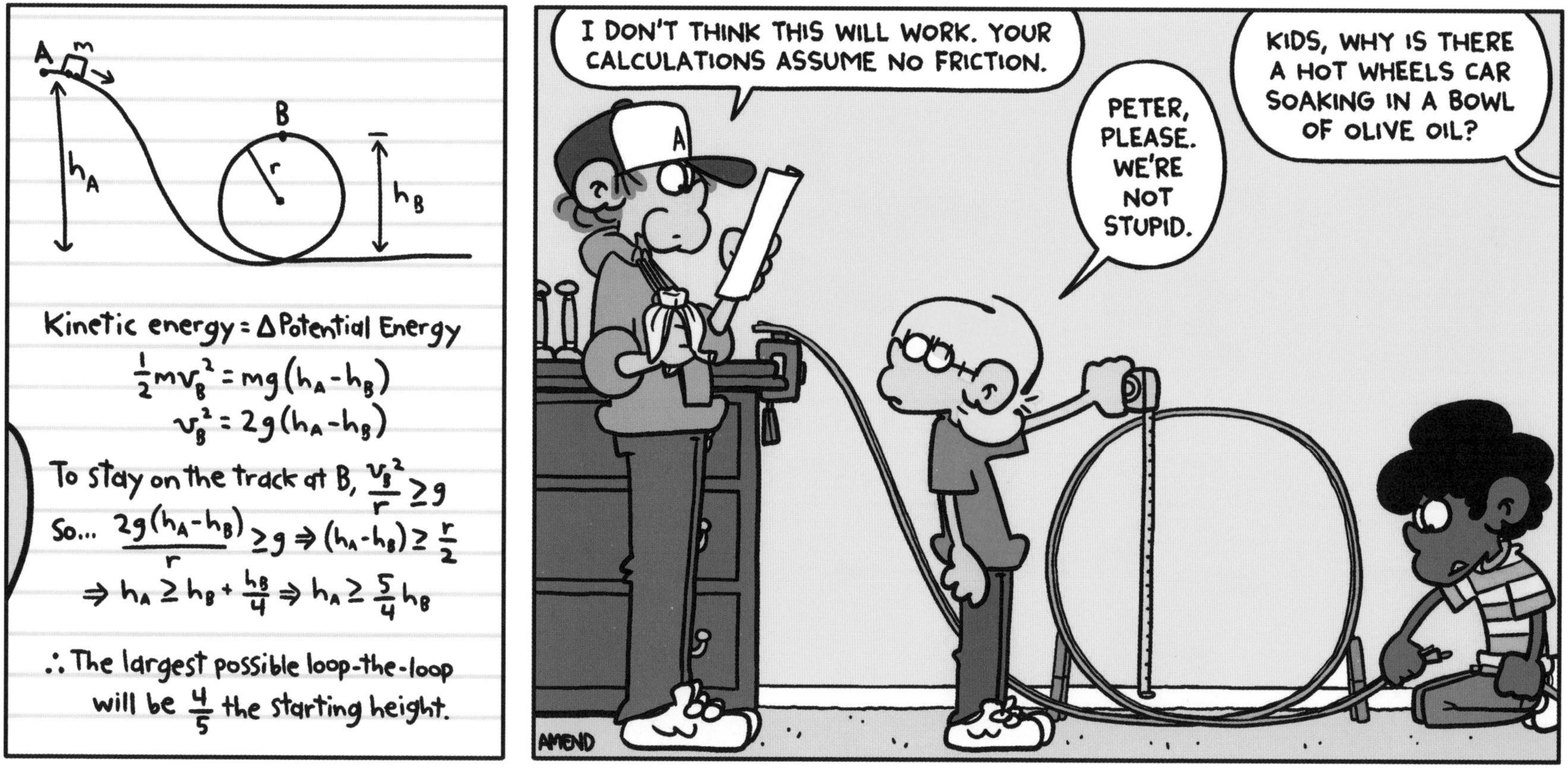
A
m
B
r
h_A
h_B
Kinetic energy = ΔPotential Energy
$\frac{1}{2}mv_B^2 = mg(h_A - h_B)$
$v_B^2 = 2g(h_A - h_B)$
To stay on the track at B, $\frac{v_B^2}{r} \geq g$
So... $\frac{2g(h_A - h_B)}{r} \geq g \Rightarrow (h_A - h_B) \geq \frac{r}{2}$
$\Rightarrow h_A \geq h_B + \frac{h_B}{4} \Rightarrow h_A \geq \frac{5}{4} h_B$
∴ The largest possible loop-the-loop will be $\frac{4}{5}$ the starting height.
I DON'T THINK THIS WILL WORK. YOUR CALCULATIONS ASSUME NO FRICTION.
PETER, PLEASE. WE'RE NOT STUPID.
KIDS, WHY IS THERE A HOT WHEELS CAR SOAKING IN A BOWL OF OLIVE OIL?
A
AMEND

Yoctoback

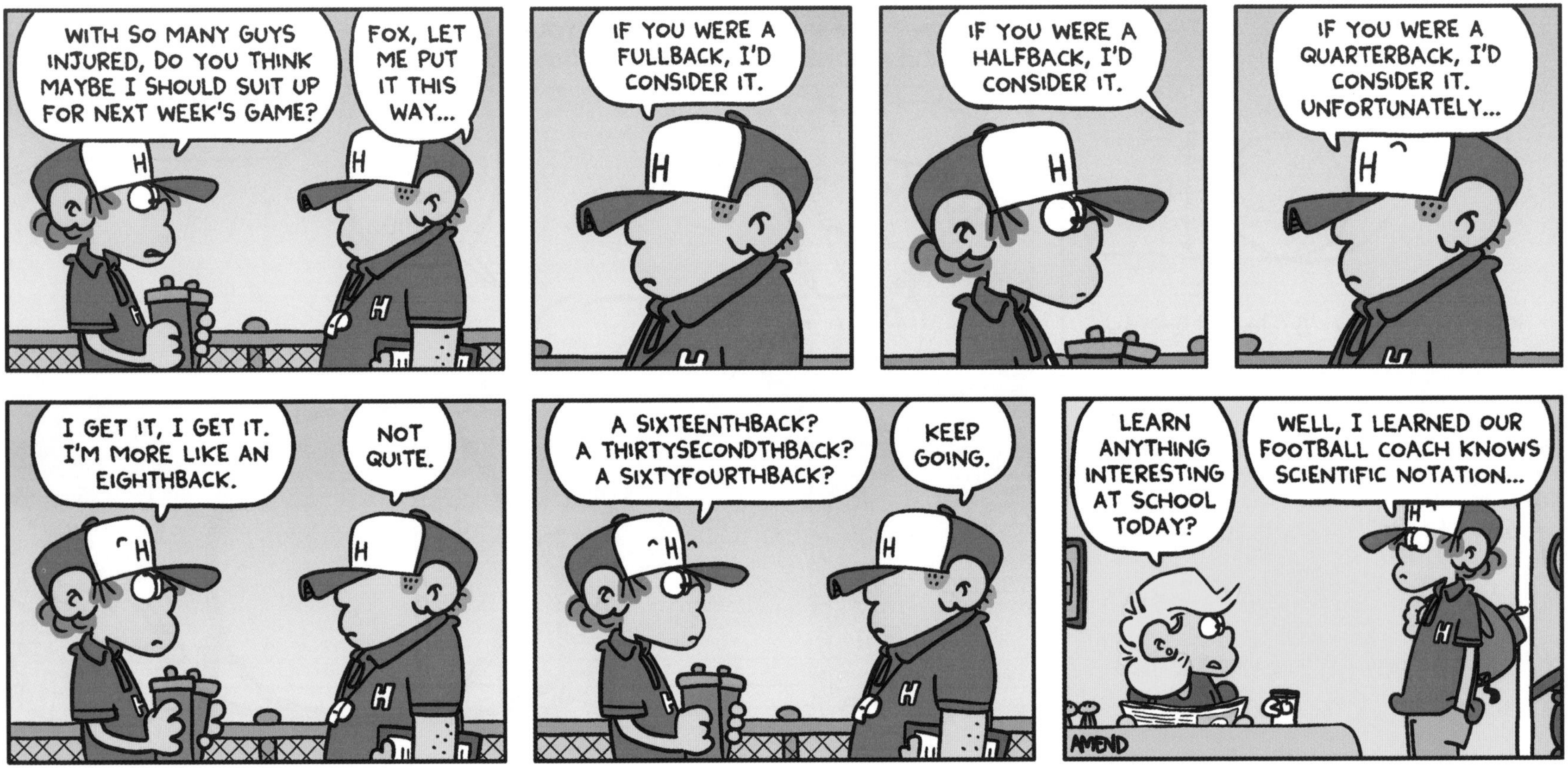

WITH SO MANY GUYS INJURED, DO YOU THINK MAYBE I SHOULD SUIT UP FOR NEXT WEEK'S GAME?
FOX, LET ME PUT IT THIS WAY...
IF YOU WERE A FULLBACK, I'D CONSIDER IT.
IF YOU WERE A HALFBACK, I'D CONSIDER IT.
IF YOU WERE A QUARTERBACK, I'D CONSIDER IT. UNFORTUNATELY...
I GET IT, I GET IT. I'M MORE LIKE AN EIGHTHBACK.
NOT QUITE.
A SIXTEENTHBACK? A THIRTYSECONDTHBACK? A SIXTYFOURTHBACK?
KEEP GOING.
LEARN ANYTHING INTERESTING AT SCHOOL TODAY?
WELL, I LEARNED OUR FOOTBALL COACH KNOWS SCIENTIFIC NOTATION...
AMEND

The Turkey Club

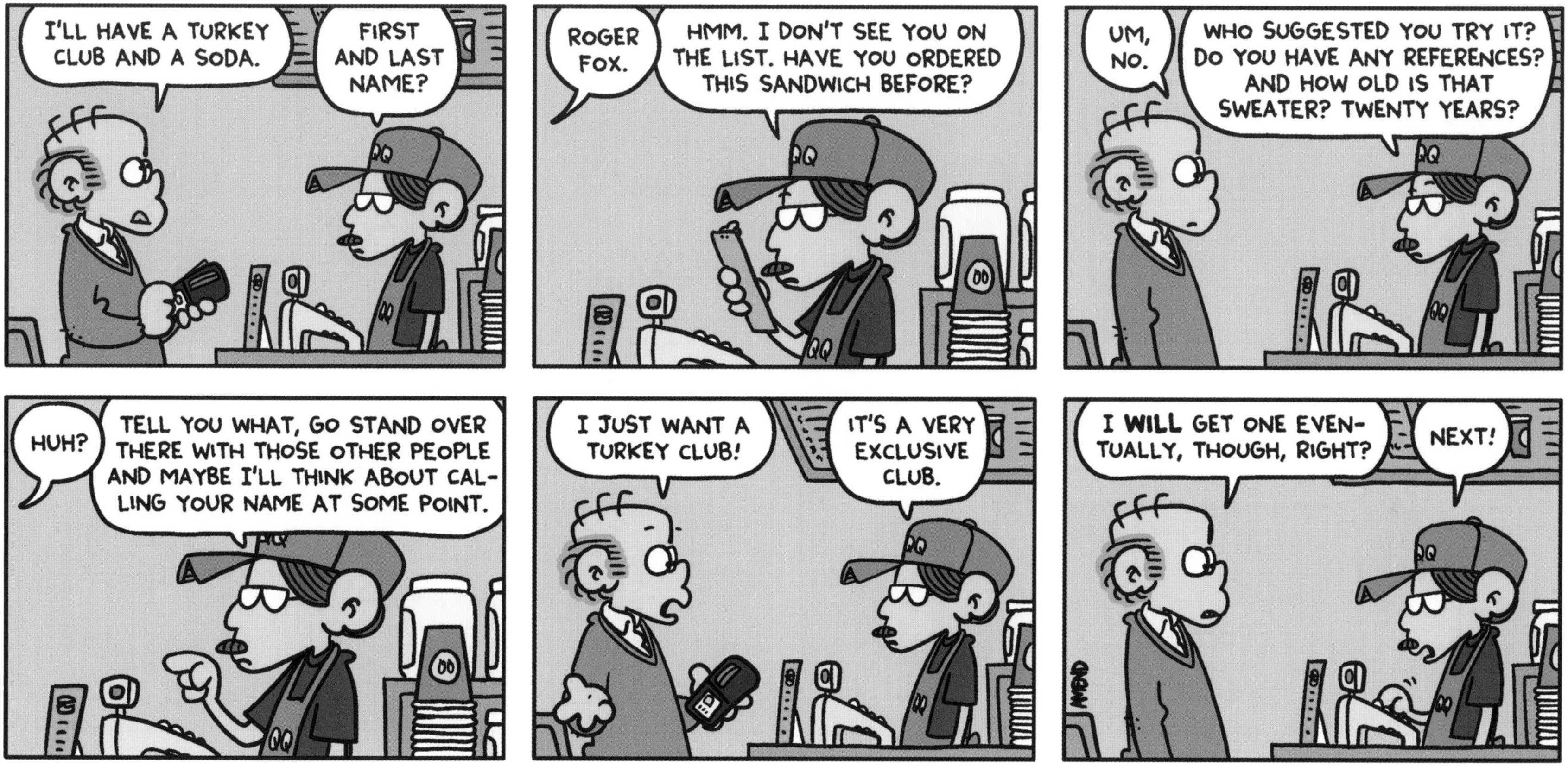
I'LL HAVE A TURKEY CLUB AND A SODA.
FIRST AND LAST NAME?
ROGER FOX.
HMM. I DON'T SEE YOU ON THE LIST. HAVE YOU ORDERED THIS SANDWICH BEFORE?
UM, NO.
WHO SUGGESTED YOU TRY IT? DO YOU HAVE ANY REFERENCES? AND HOW OLD IS THAT SWEATER? TWENTY YEARS?
HUH?
TELL YOU WHAT, GO STAND OVER THERE WITH THOSE OTHER PEOPLE AND MAYBE I'LL THINK ABOUT CALLING YOUR NAME AT SOME POINT.
I JUST WANT A TURKEY CLUB!
IT'S A VERY EXCLUSIVE CLUB.
I **WILL** GET ONE EVENTUALLY, THOUGH, RIGHT?
NEXT!

J&PB

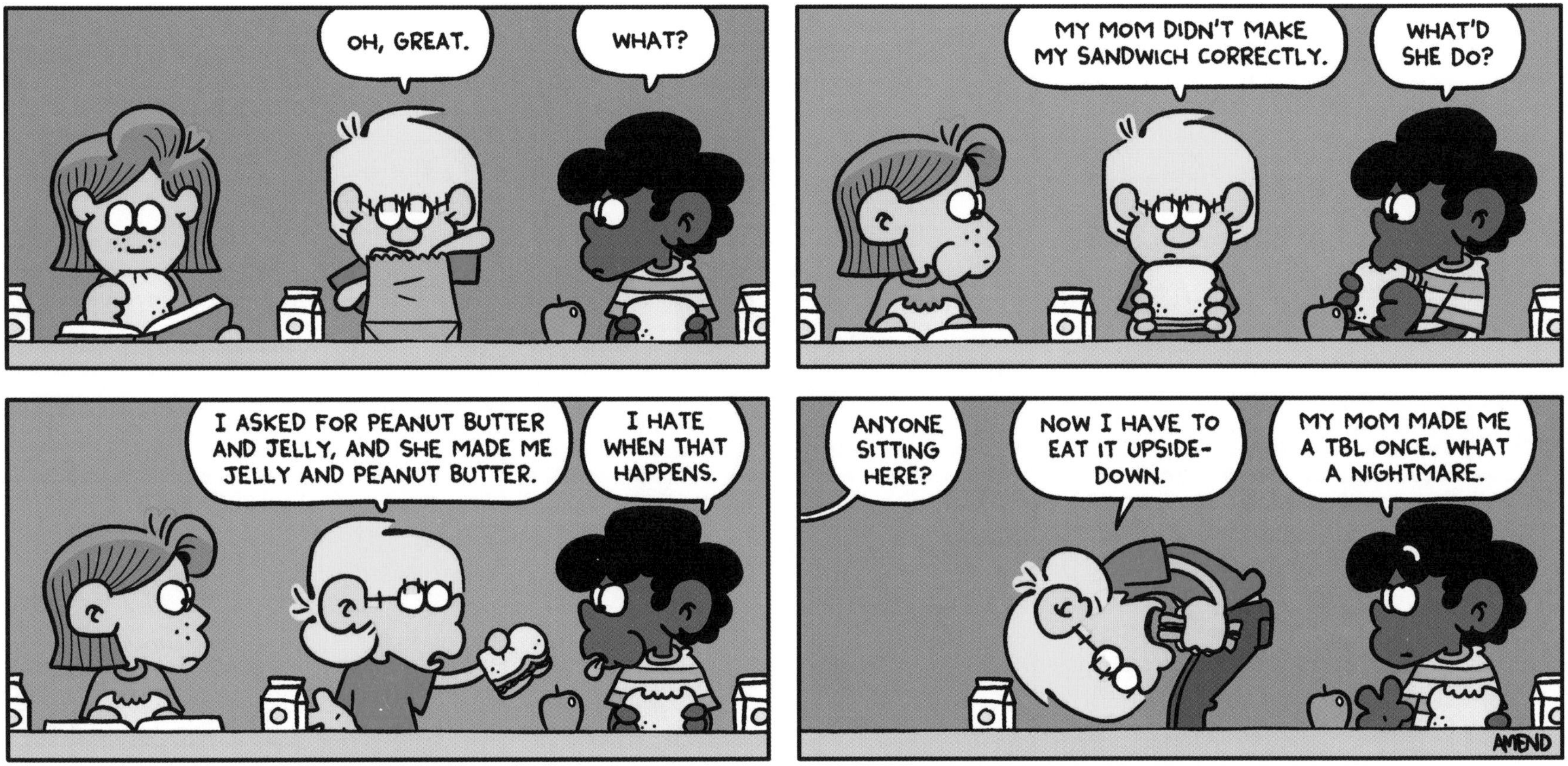

OH, GREAT.
WHAT?
MY MOM DIDN'T MAKE MY SANDWICH CORRECTLY.
WHAT'D SHE DO?
I ASKED FOR PEANUT BUTTER AND JELLY, AND SHE MADE ME JELLY AND PEANUT BUTTER.
I HATE WHEN THAT HAPPENS.
ANYONE SITTING HERE?
NOW I HAVE TO EAT IT UPSIDE-DOWN.
MY MOM MADE ME A TBL ONCE. WHAT A NIGHTMARE.
AMEND

Scaled Silly

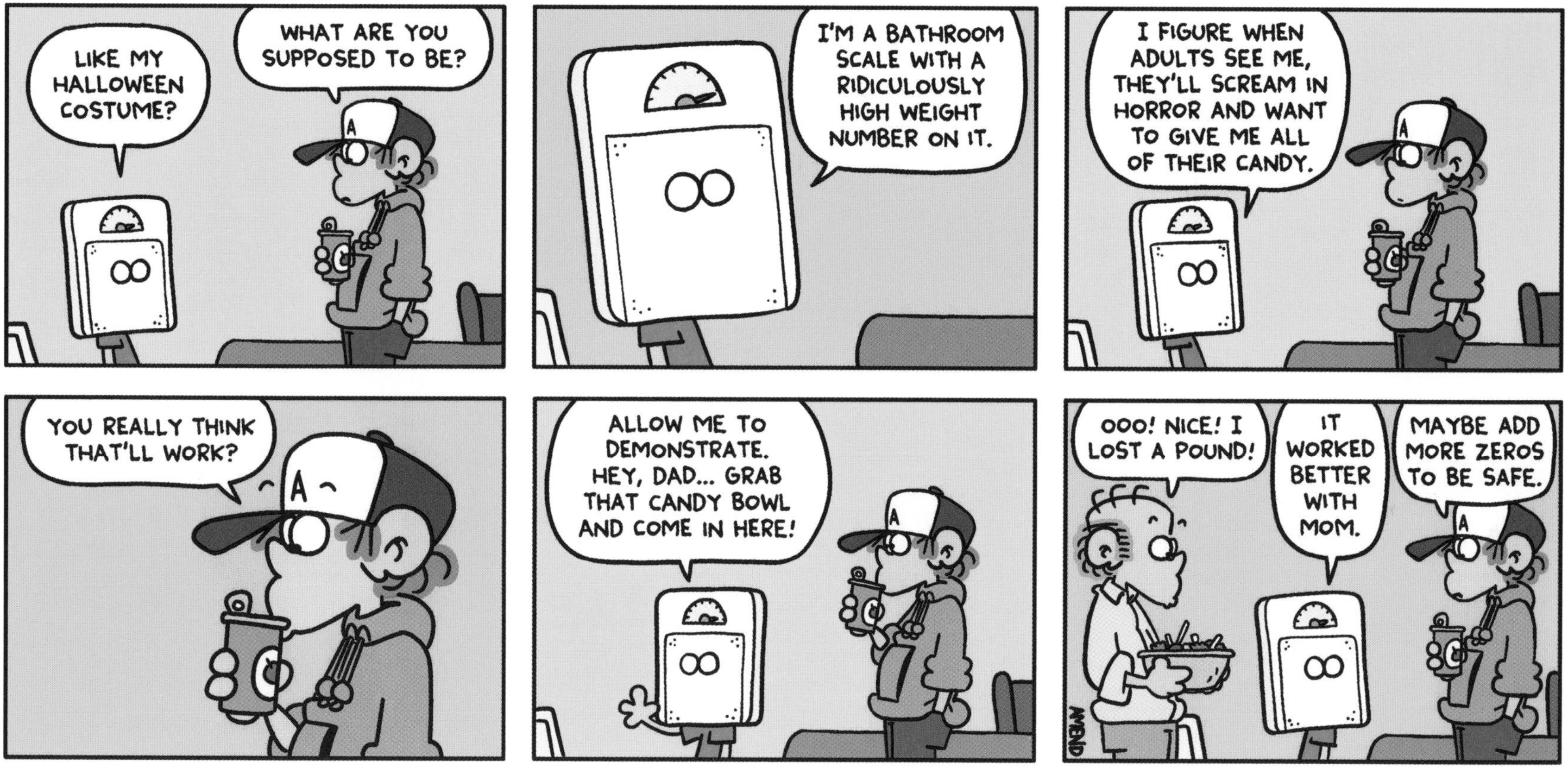
LIKE MY HALLOWEEN COSTUME?
WHAT ARE YOU SUPPOSED TO BE?
I'M A BATHROOM SCALE WITH A RIDICULOUSLY HIGH WEIGHT NUMBER ON IT.
I FIGURE WHEN ADULTS SEE ME, THEY'LL SCREAM IN HORROR AND WANT TO GIVE ME ALL OF THEIR CANDY.
YOU REALLY THINK THAT'LL WORK?
ALLOW ME TO DEMONSTRATE. HEY, DAD... GRAB THAT CANDY BOWL AND COME IN HERE!
OOO! NICE! I LOST A POUND!
IT WORKED BETTER WITH MOM.
MAYBE ADD MORE ZEROS TO BE SAFE.
AMEND

Yardly Working

THANK YOU, LITTLE LEAF, FOR ALL YOU'VE GIVEN US...

OXYGEN TO BREATHE...

SHADE IN THE SUMMER...

PRETTY COLORS IN THE FALL...

I'LL MISS YOU.

THANK YOU, LITTLE LEAF...

FYI, DAD'S PAYING US BY THE BAG, NOT BY THE HOUR.

SHEESH, **NOW** YOU TELL ME!

Roughage

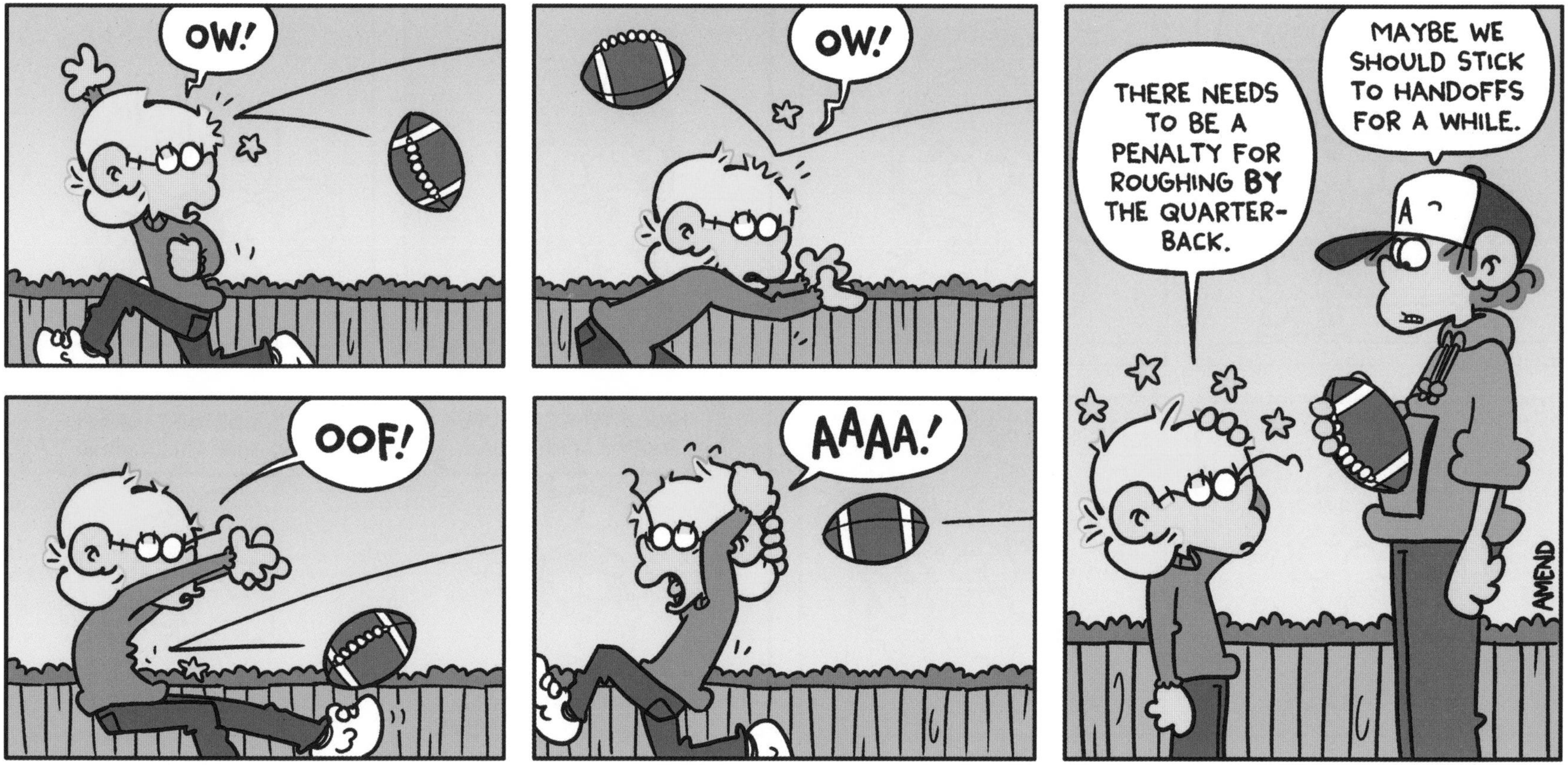
OW!
OW!
OOF!
AAAA!
THERE NEEDS TO BE A PENALTY FOR ROUGHING BY THE QUARTER-BACK.
MAYBE WE SHOULD STICK TO HANDOFFS FOR A WHILE.
AMEND

Hot or Not?

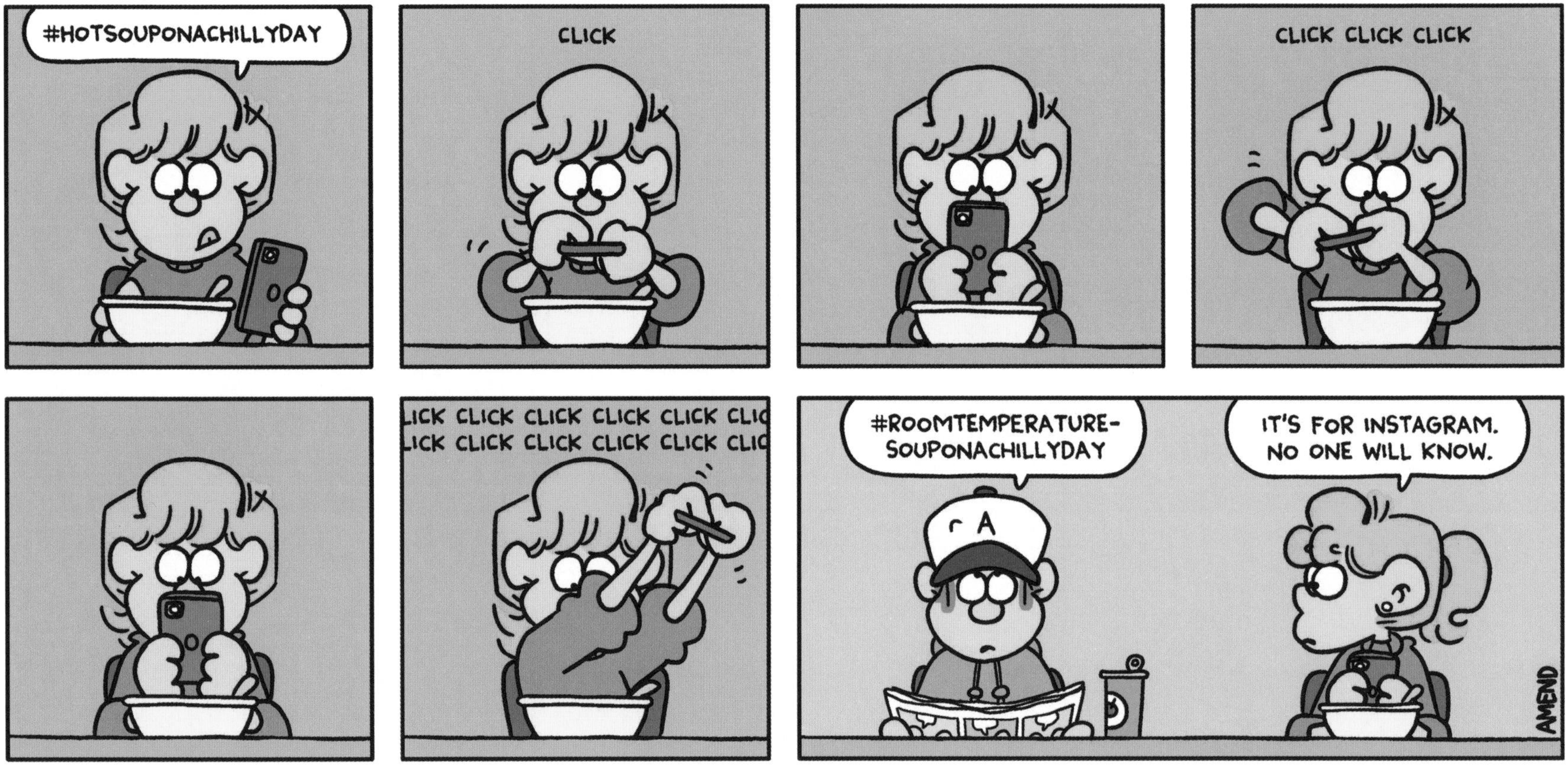
#HOTSOUPONACHILLYDAY
CLICK
CLICK CLICK CLICK
LICK CLICK CLICK CLICK CLICK CLIC
LICK CLICK CLICK CLICK CLICK CLIC
#ROOMTEMPERATURE-SOUPONACHILLYDAY
IT'S FOR INSTAGRAM. NO ONE WILL KNOW.
AMEND

Giving Thanks

Panel 1:
DOING HOMEWORK?

YEAH. FOR THANKSGIVING MY TEACHER WANTS US TO LIST TEN THINGS WE'RE THANKFUL FOR.

Panel 2:
I CAME UP WITH NINE, BUT I'M STUCK ON THE LAST ONE.

Panel 3:
OH, SPEAKING OF THANKSGIVING, I HAVE SOME BAD NEWS.

Panel 4:
HOLISTIC FOODS WAS ALL OUT OF PICKLED ALFALFA SPROUTS. I'M NOT GOING TO BE ABLE TO MAKE MY FAMOUS TURKEY STUFFING THIS YEAR.

Panel 5:
SO, BACK TO YOUR HOMEWORK...

Panel 6:
YOU NEED TO THINK UP ONE MORE THING YOU'RE THANKFUL FOR?

NOPE. ALL DONE.

Root Beer

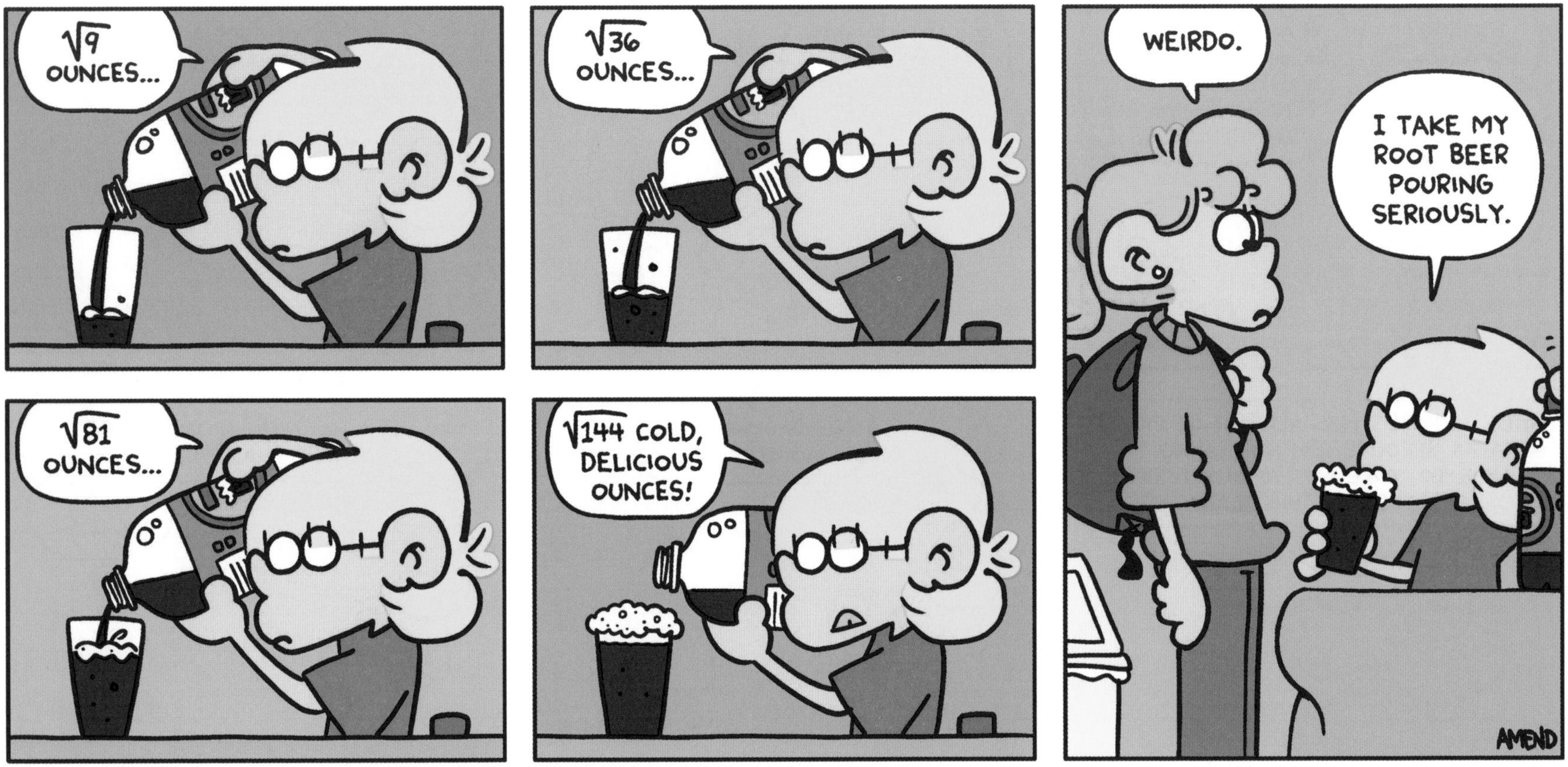

√9 OUNCES...
√36 OUNCES...
√81 OUNCES...
√144 COLD, DELICIOUS OUNCES!
WEIRDO.
I TAKE MY ROOT BEER POURING SERIOUSLY.
AMEND

Not a Smidge

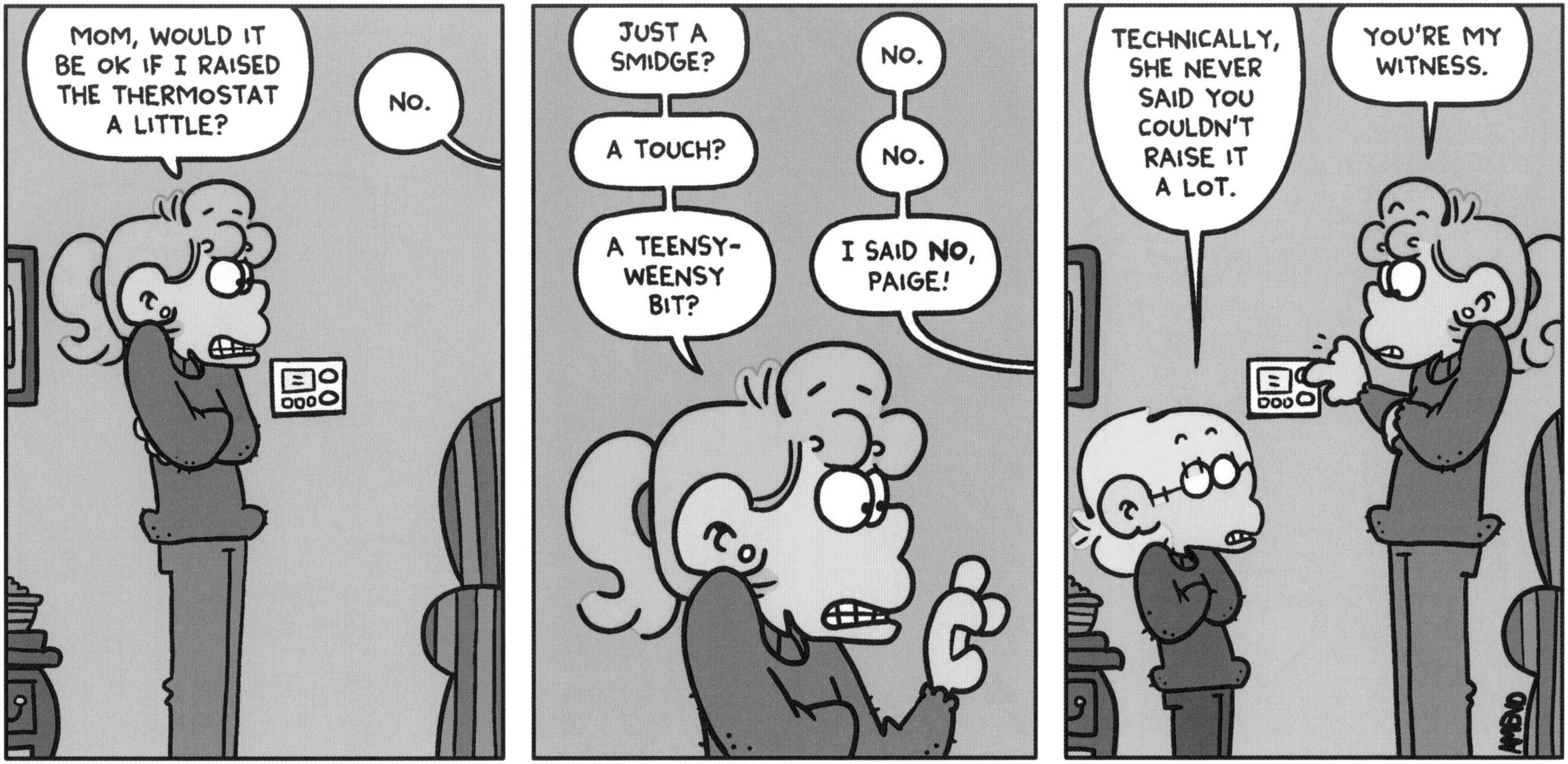
MOM, WOULD IT BE OK IF I RAISED THE THERMOSTAT A LITTLE?
NO.
JUST A SMIDGE?
NO.
A TOUCH?
NO.
A TEENSY-WEENSY BIT?
I SAID NO, PAIGE!
TECHNICALLY, SHE NEVER SAID YOU COULDN'T RAISE IT A LOT.
YOU'RE MY WITNESS.

Gingerbread Jedi

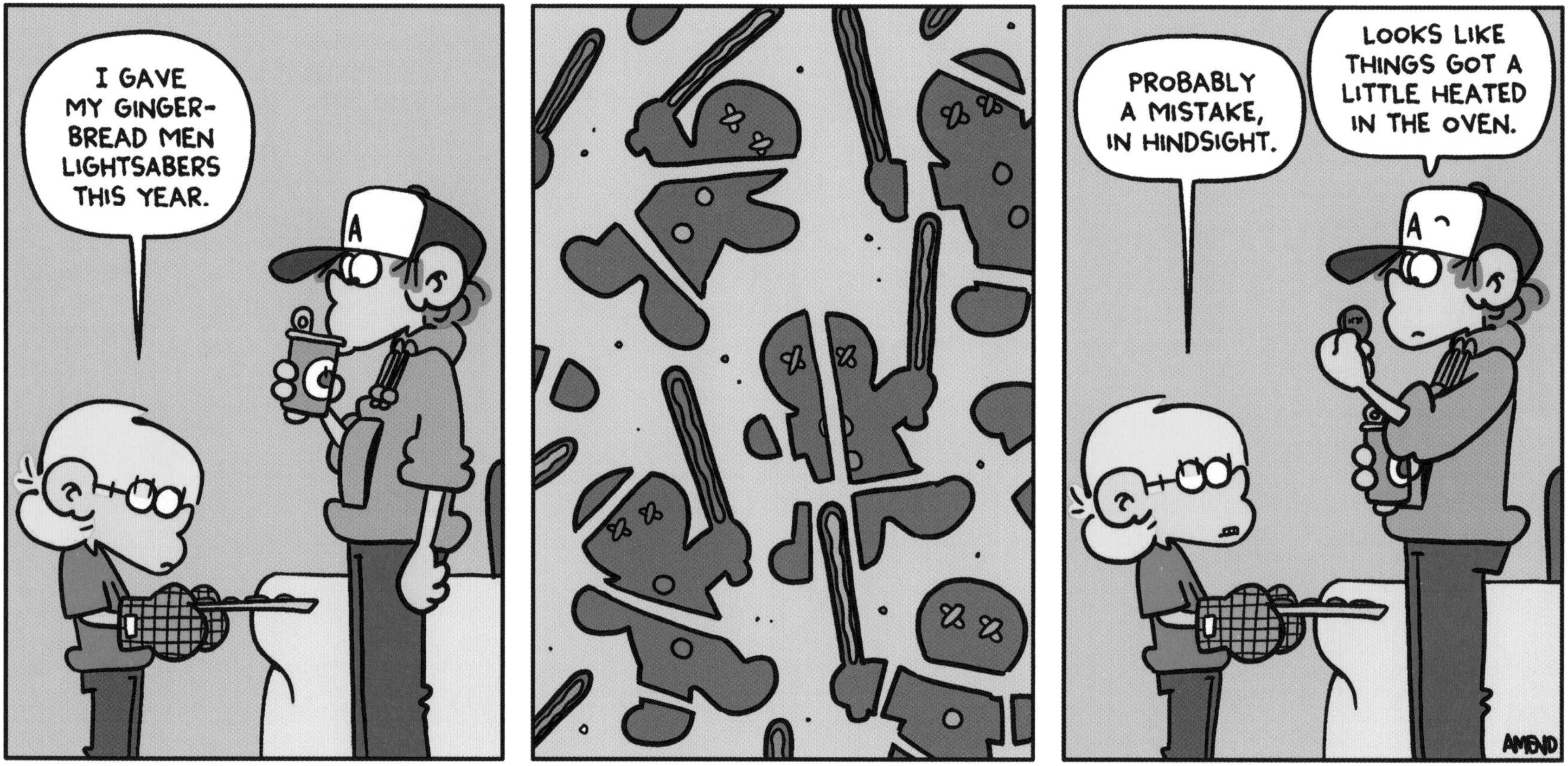
I GAVE MY GINGER-BREAD MEN LIGHTSABERS THIS YEAR.
LOOKS LIKE THINGS GOT A LITTLE HEATED IN THE OVEN.
PROBABLY A MISTAKE, IN HINDSIGHT.
AMEND

Uncanny Canes

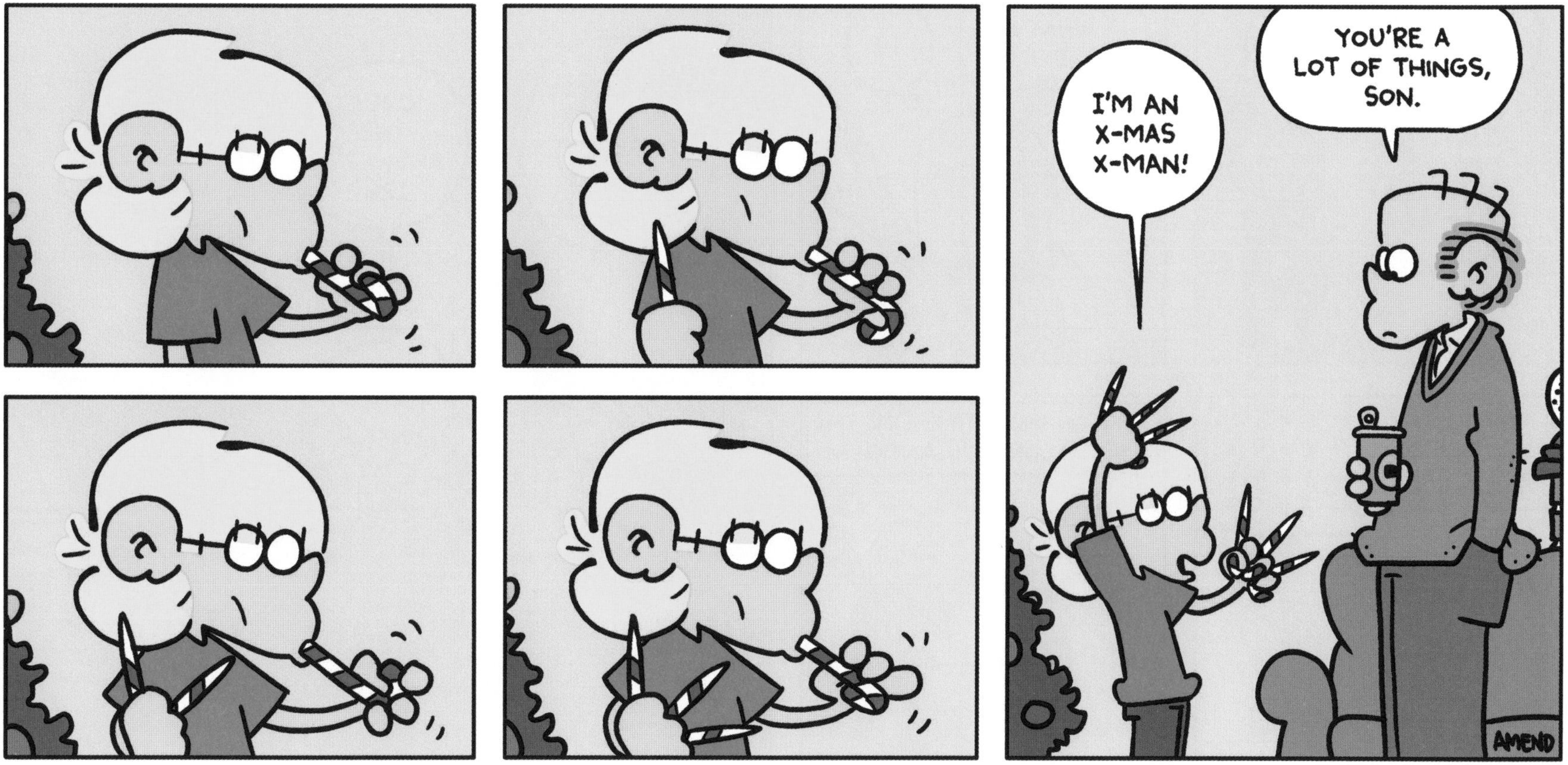
I'M AN X-MAS X-MAN!
YOU'RE A LOT OF THINGS, SON.
AMEND

Disney+

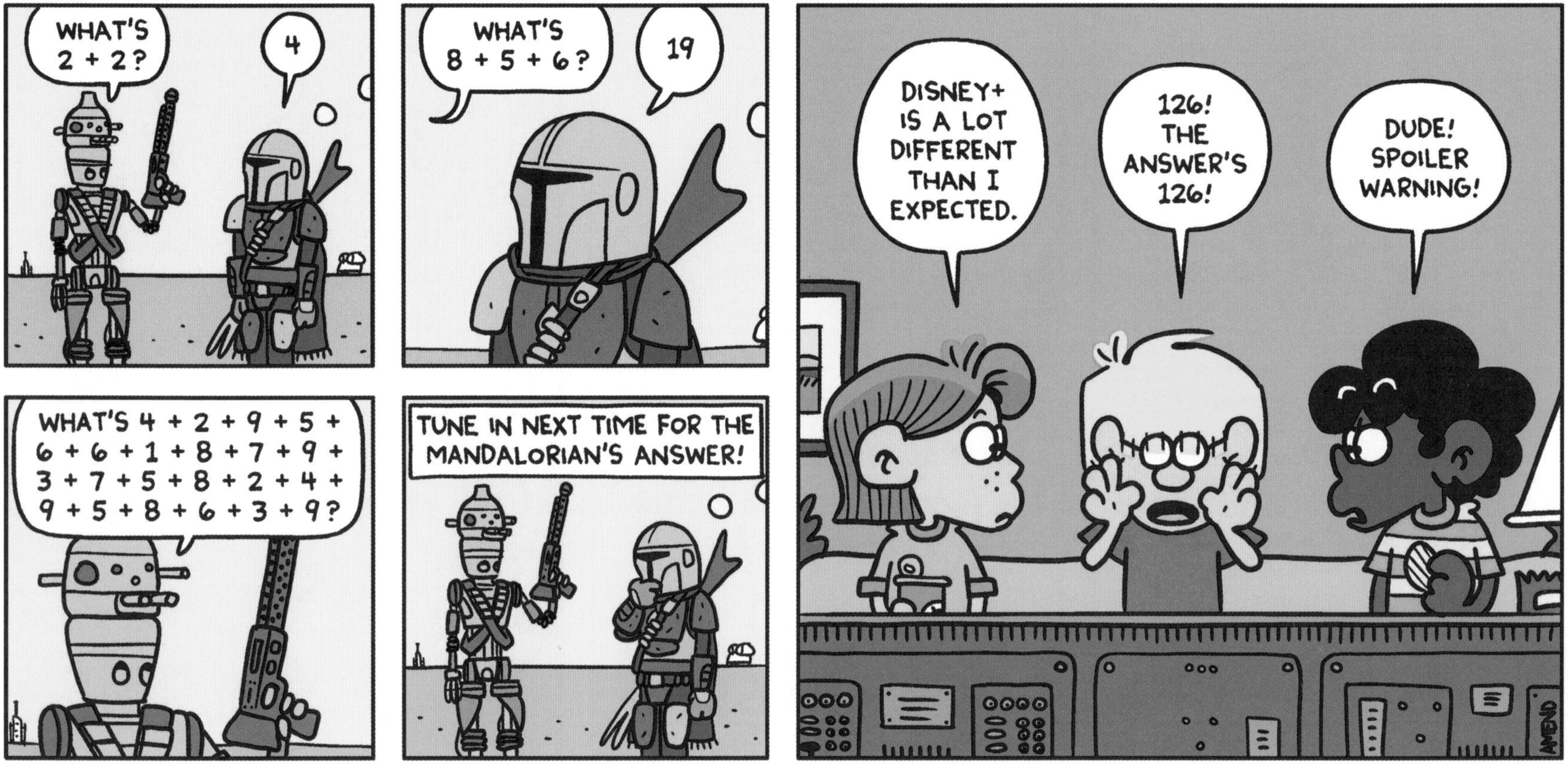

WHAT'S 2 + 2?
4
WHAT'S 8 + 5 + 6?
19
WHAT'S 4 + 2 + 9 + 5 + 6 + 6 + 1 + 8 + 7 + 9 + 3 + 7 + 5 + 8 + 2 + 4 + 9 + 5 + 8 + 6 + 3 + 9?
TUNE IN NEXT TIME FOR THE MANDALORIAN'S ANSWER!
DISNEY+ IS A LOT DIFFERENT THAN I EXPECTED.
126! THE ANSWER'S 126!
DUDE! SPOILER WARNING!
AMEND

Snow Blindness

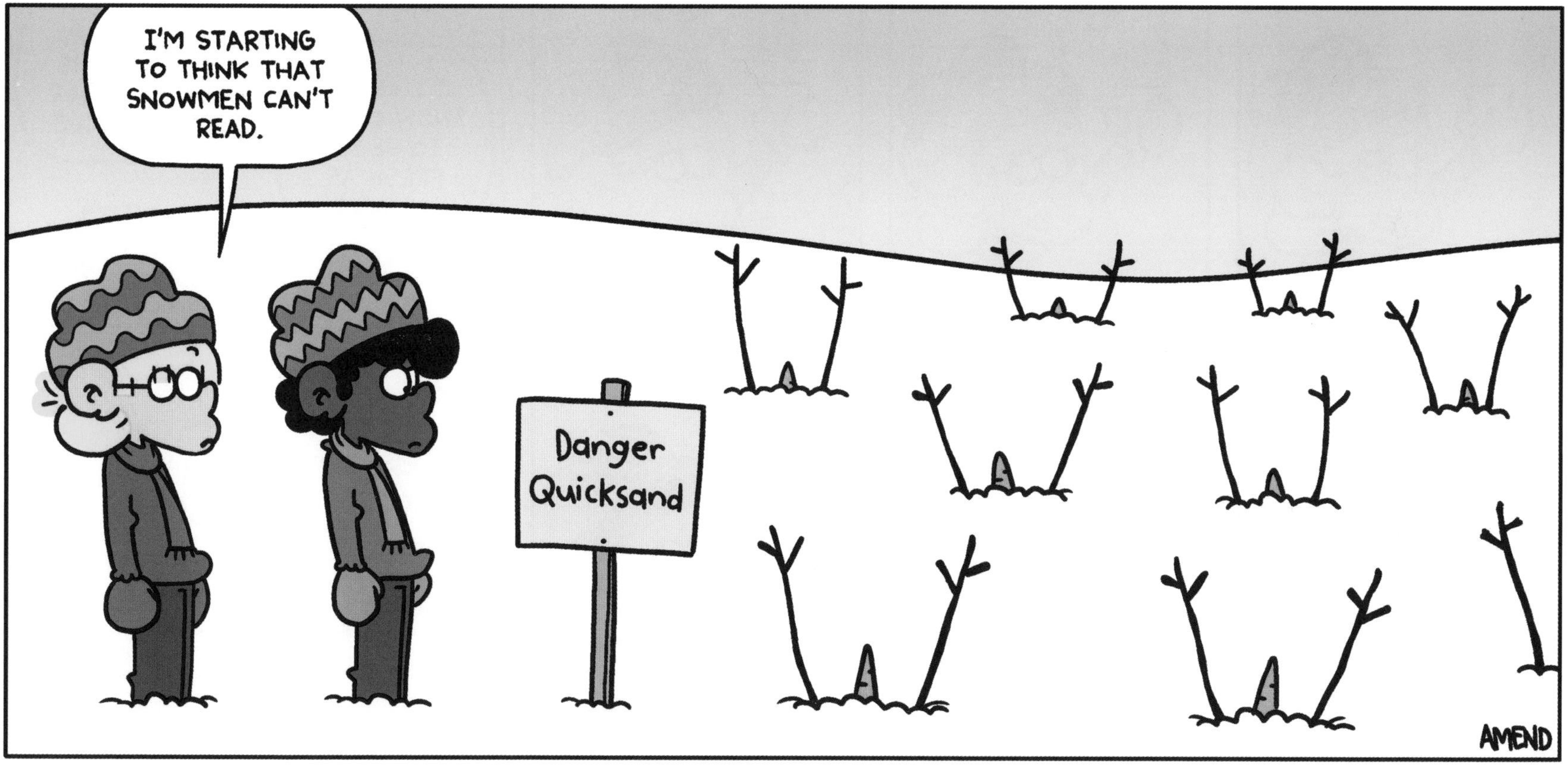
I'M STARTING TO THINK THAT SNOWMEN CAN'T READ.
Danger Quicksand
AMEND

Slow Cone

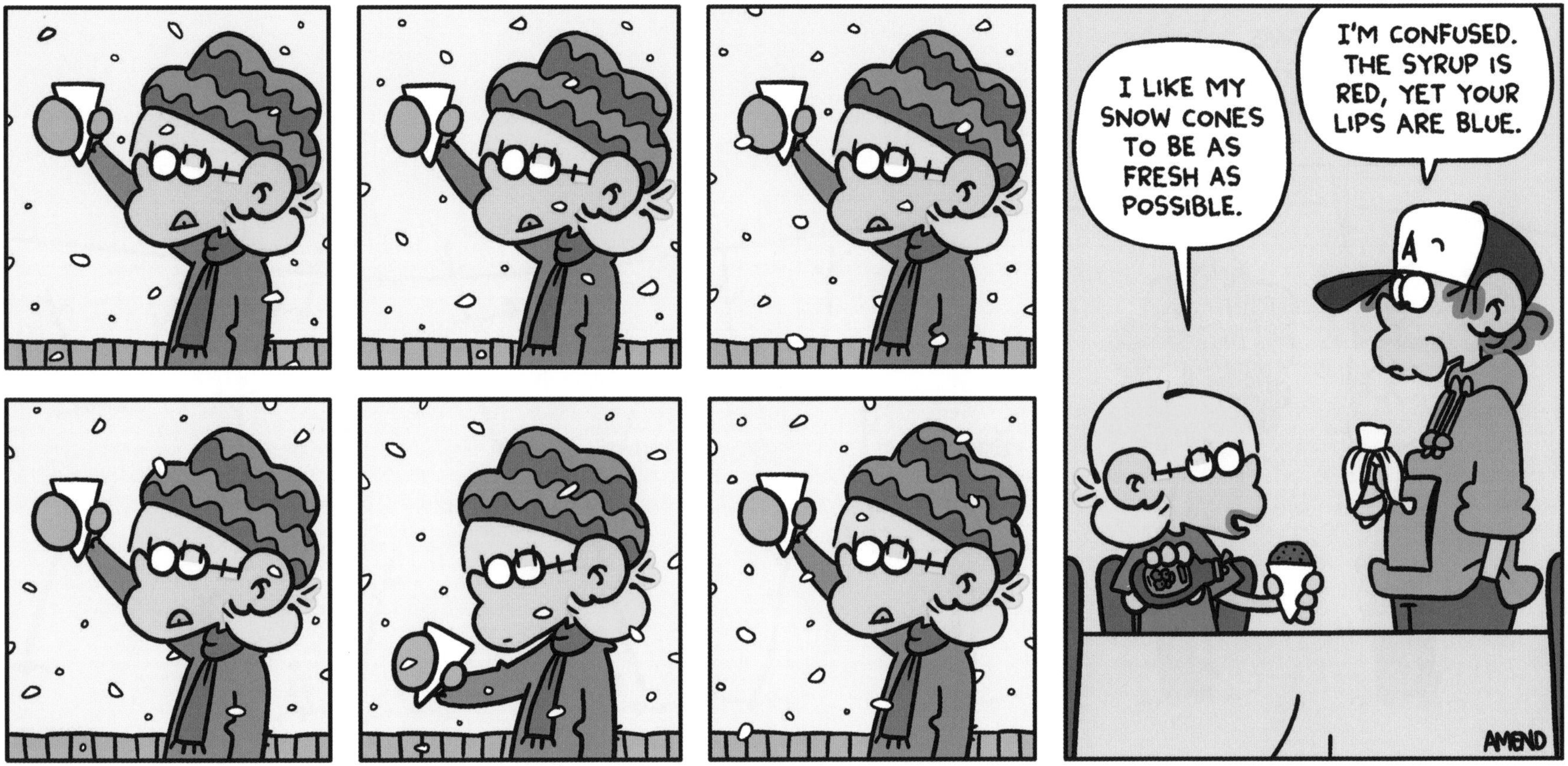
I LIKE MY SNOW CONES TO BE AS FRESH AS POSSIBLE.
I'M CONFUSED. THE SYRUP IS RED, YET YOUR LIPS ARE BLUE.
AMEND

Idiot Proof

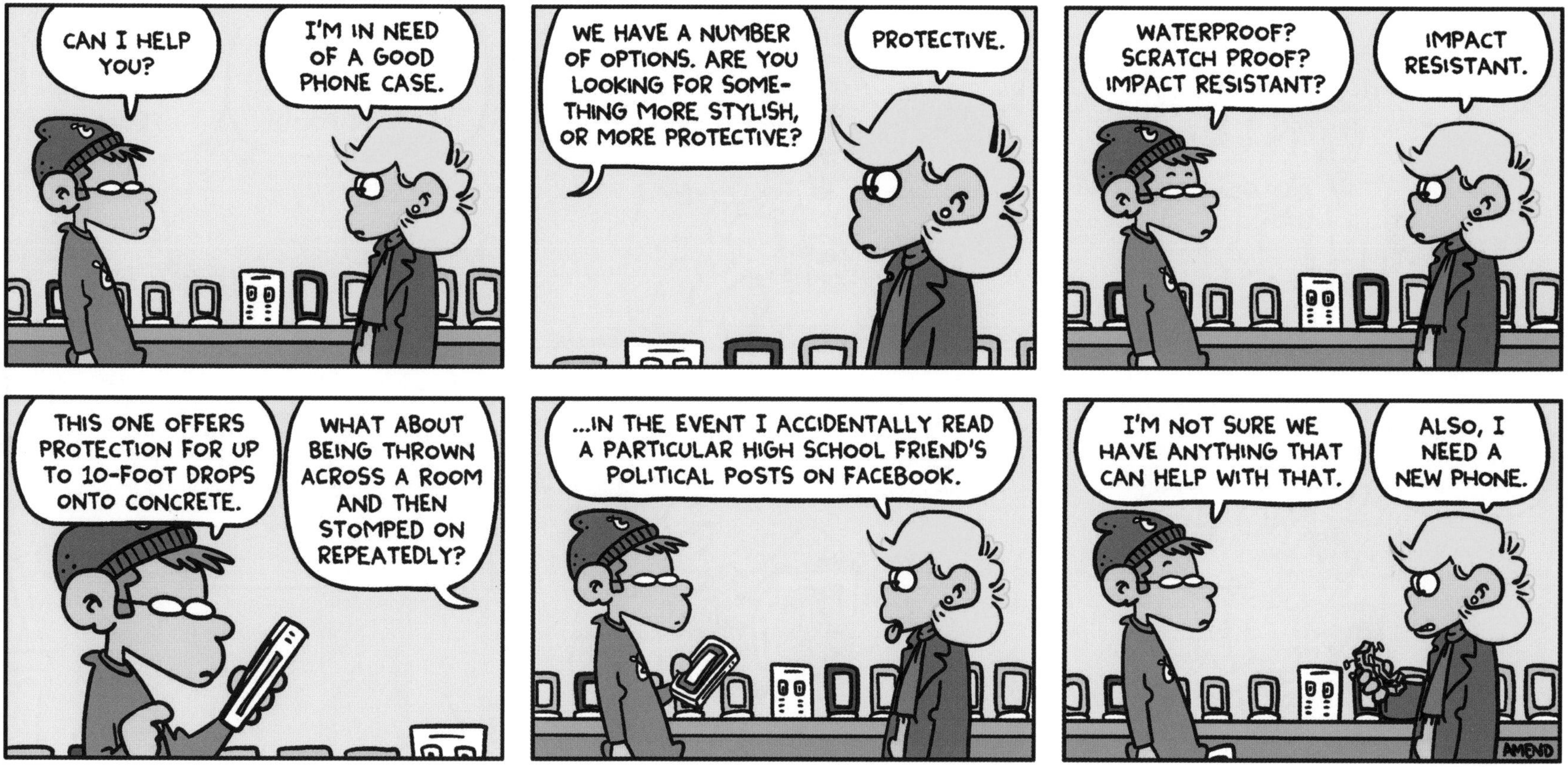
CAN I HELP YOU?
I'M IN NEED OF A GOOD PHONE CASE.
WE HAVE A NUMBER OF OPTIONS. ARE YOU LOOKING FOR SOMETHING MORE STYLISH, OR MORE PROTECTIVE?
PROTECTIVE.
WATERPROOF? SCRATCH PROOF? IMPACT RESISTANT?
IMPACT RESISTANT.
THIS ONE OFFERS PROTECTION FOR UP TO 10-FOOT DROPS ONTO CONCRETE.
WHAT ABOUT BEING THROWN ACROSS A ROOM AND THEN STOMPED ON REPEATEDLY?
...IN THE EVENT I ACCIDENTALLY READ A PARTICULAR HIGH SCHOOL FRIEND'S POLITICAL POSTS ON FACEBOOK.
I'M NOT SURE WE HAVE ANYTHING THAT CAN HELP WITH THAT.
ALSO, I NEED A NEW PHONE.
AMEND

Blendo Italiano

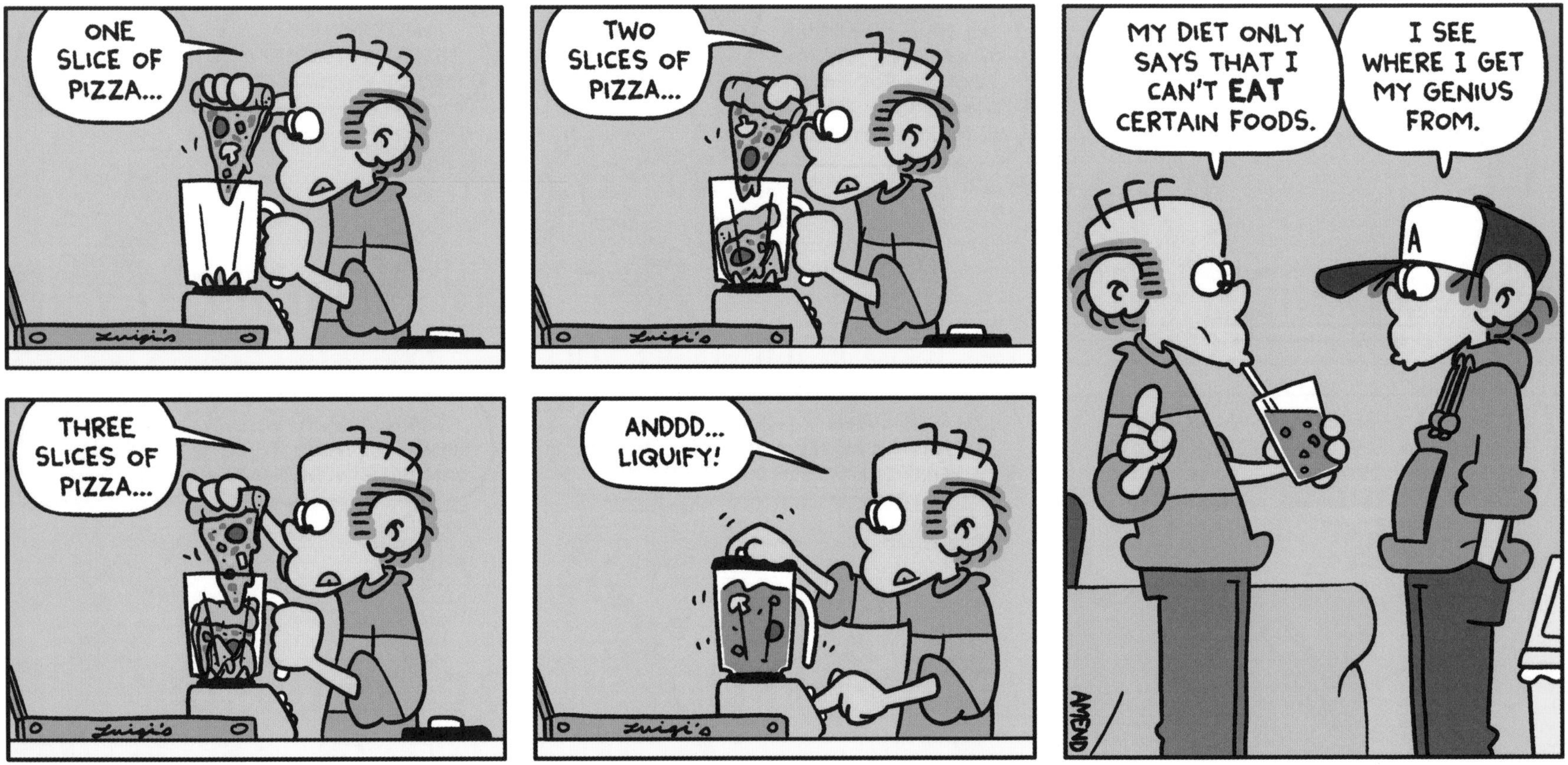

ONE SLICE OF PIZZA...
Luigi's
TWO SLICES OF PIZZA...
Luigi's
THREE SLICES OF PIZZA...
Luigi's
ANDDD... LIQUIFY!
Luigi's
MY DIET ONLY SAYS THAT I CAN'T **EAT** CERTAIN FOODS.
I SEE WHERE I GET MY GENIUS FROM.
A
AMEND

Quakertown Quince

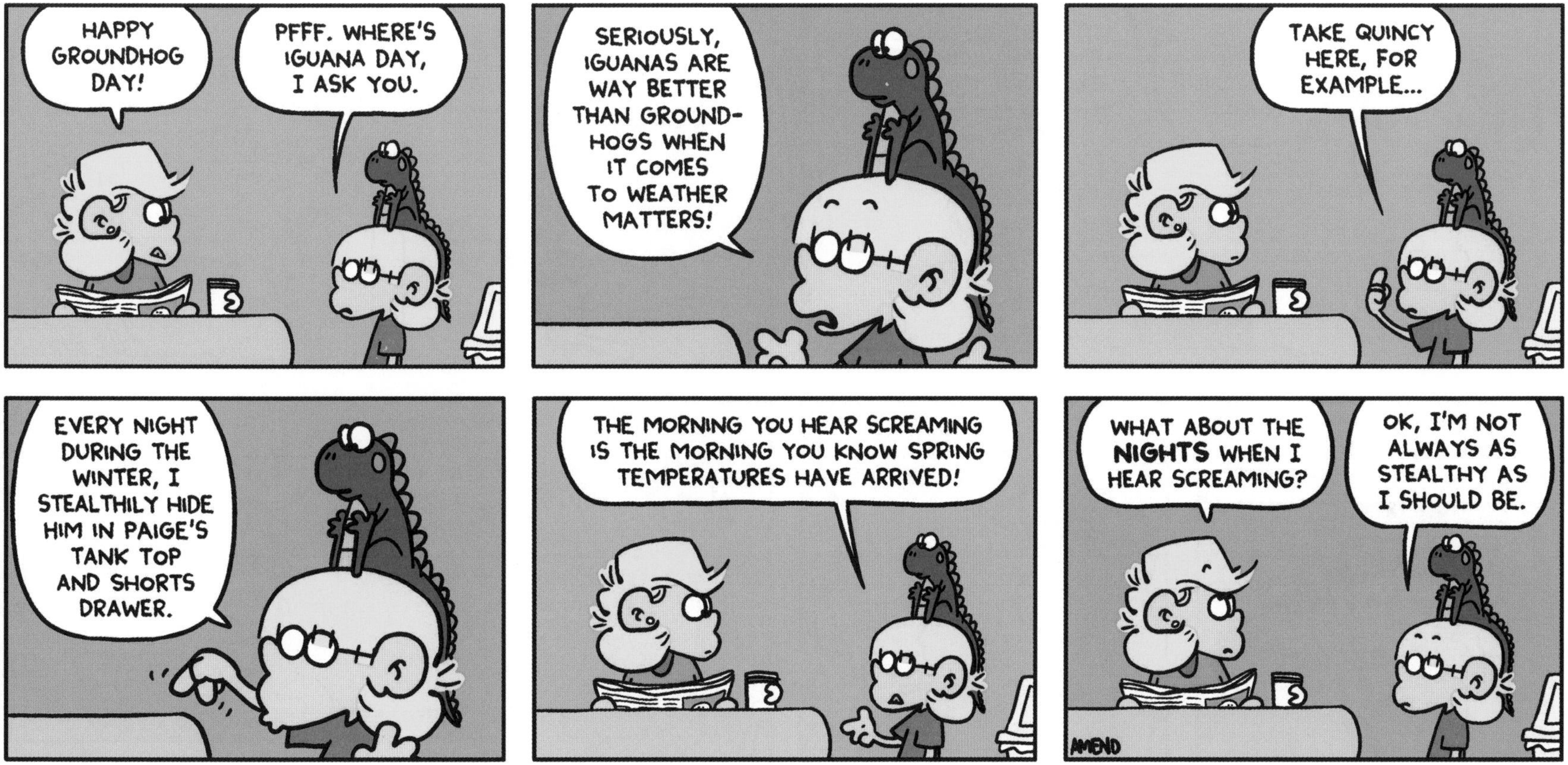
HAPPY GROUNDHOG DAY!
PFFF. WHERE'S IGUANA DAY, I ASK YOU.
SERIOUSLY, IGUANAS ARE WAY BETTER THAN GROUND-HOGS WHEN IT COMES TO WEATHER MATTERS!
TAKE QUINCY HERE, FOR EXAMPLE...
EVERY NIGHT DURING THE WINTER, I STEALTHILY HIDE HIM IN PAIGE'S TANK TOP AND SHORTS DRAWER.
THE MORNING YOU HEAR SCREAMING IS THE MORNING YOU KNOW SPRING TEMPERATURES HAVE ARRIVED!
WHAT ABOUT THE **NIGHTS** WHEN I HEAR SCREAMING?
OK, I'M NOT ALWAYS AS STEALTHY AS I SHOULD BE.
AMEND

Chocolate Sampler

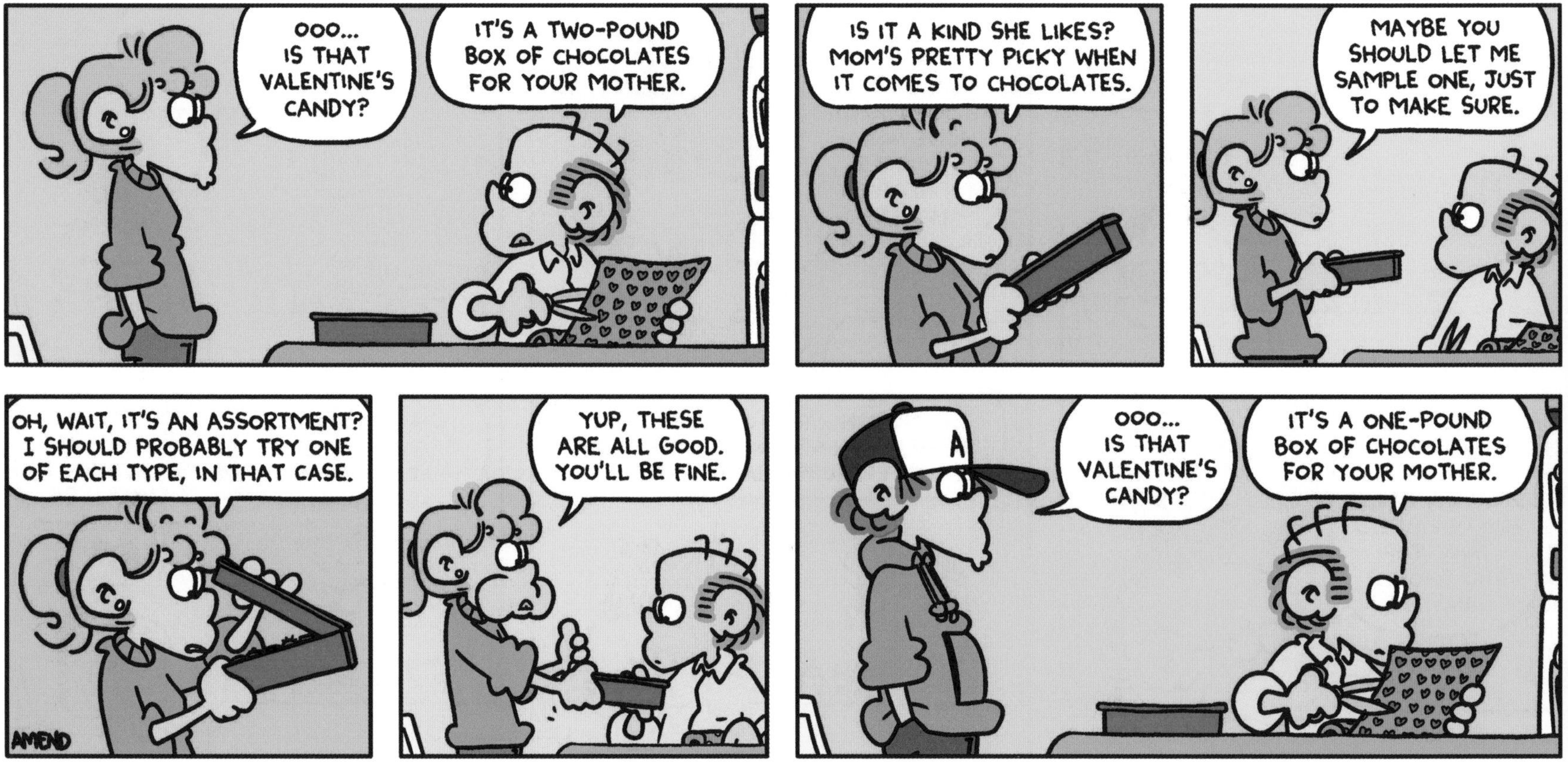
OOO... IS THAT VALENTINE'S CANDY?
IT'S A TWO-POUND BOX OF CHOCOLATES FOR YOUR MOTHER.
IS IT A KIND SHE LIKES? MOM'S PRETTY PICKY WHEN IT COMES TO CHOCOLATES.
MAYBE YOU SHOULD LET ME SAMPLE ONE, JUST TO MAKE SURE.
OH, WAIT, IT'S AN ASSORTMENT? I SHOULD PROBABLY TRY ONE OF EACH TYPE, IN THAT CASE.
AMEND
YUP, THESE ARE ALL GOOD. YOU'LL BE FINE.
A
OOO... IS THAT VALENTINE'S CANDY?
IT'S A ONE-POUND BOX OF CHOCOLATES FOR YOUR MOTHER.

Mega Combo

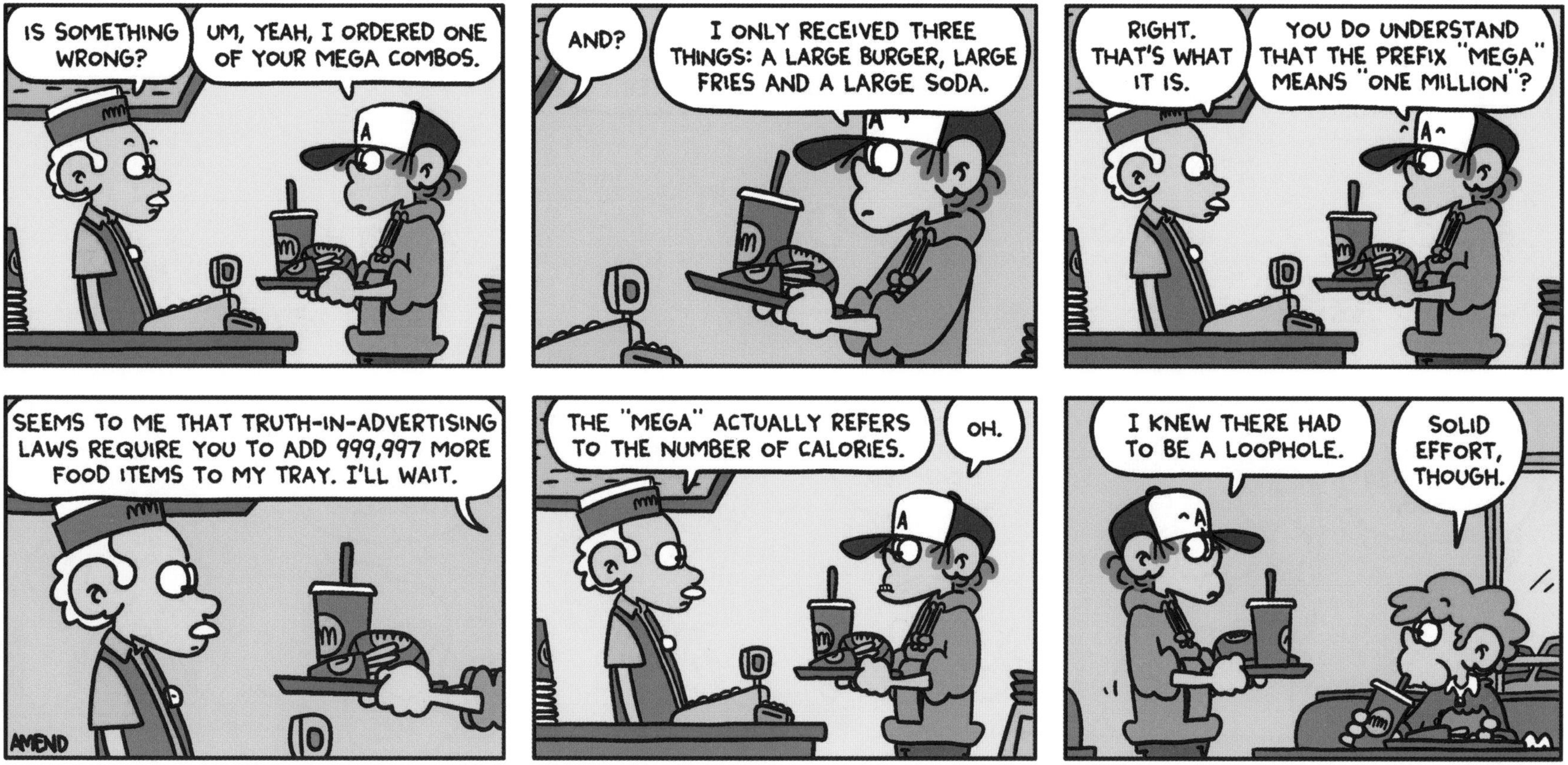
IS SOMETHING WRONG?
UM, YEAH, I ORDERED ONE OF YOUR MEGA COMBOS.
AND?
I ONLY RECEIVED THREE THINGS: A LARGE BURGER, LARGE FRIES AND A LARGE SODA.
RIGHT. THAT'S WHAT IT IS.
YOU DO UNDERSTAND THAT THE PREFIX "MEGA" MEANS "ONE MILLION"?
SEEMS TO ME THAT TRUTH-IN-ADVERTISING LAWS REQUIRE YOU TO ADD 999,997 MORE FOOD ITEMS TO MY TRAY. I'LL WAIT.
AMEND
THE "MEGA" ACTUALLY REFERS TO THE NUMBER OF CALORIES.
OH.
I KNEW THERE HAD TO BE A LOOPHOLE.
SOLID EFFORT, THOUGH.

Math Help

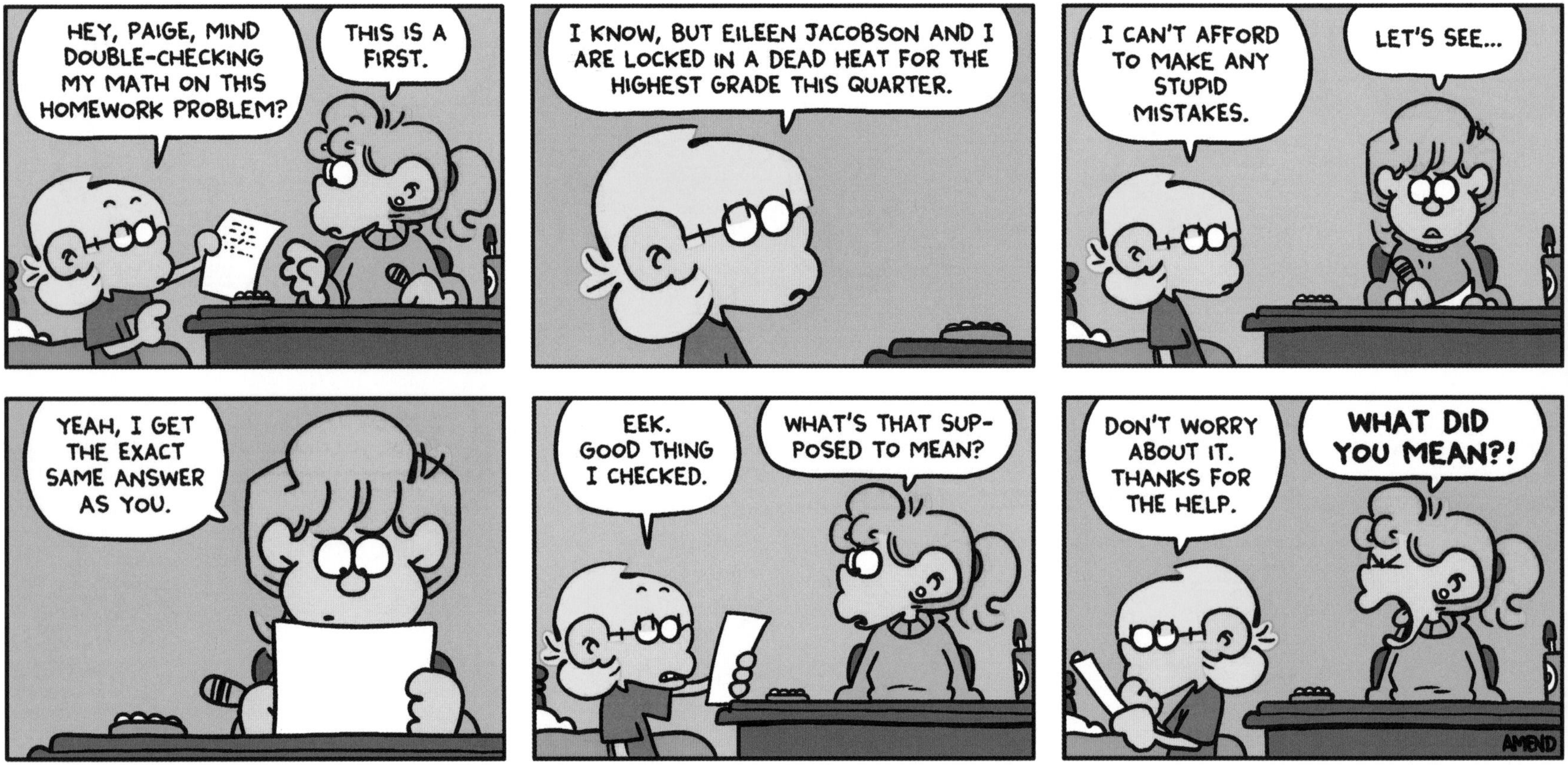
HEY, PAIGE, MIND DOUBLE-CHECKING MY MATH ON THIS HOMEWORK PROBLEM?
THIS IS A FIRST.
I KNOW, BUT EILEEN JACOBSON AND I ARE LOCKED IN A DEAD HEAT FOR THE HIGHEST GRADE THIS QUARTER.
I CAN'T AFFORD TO MAKE ANY STUPID MISTAKES.
LET'S SEE...
YEAH, I GET THE EXACT SAME ANSWER AS YOU.
EEK. GOOD THING I CHECKED.
WHAT'S THAT SUP-POSED TO MEAN?
DON'T WORRY ABOUT IT. THANKS FOR THE HELP.
WHAT DID YOU MEAN?!
AMEND

Cell Phony

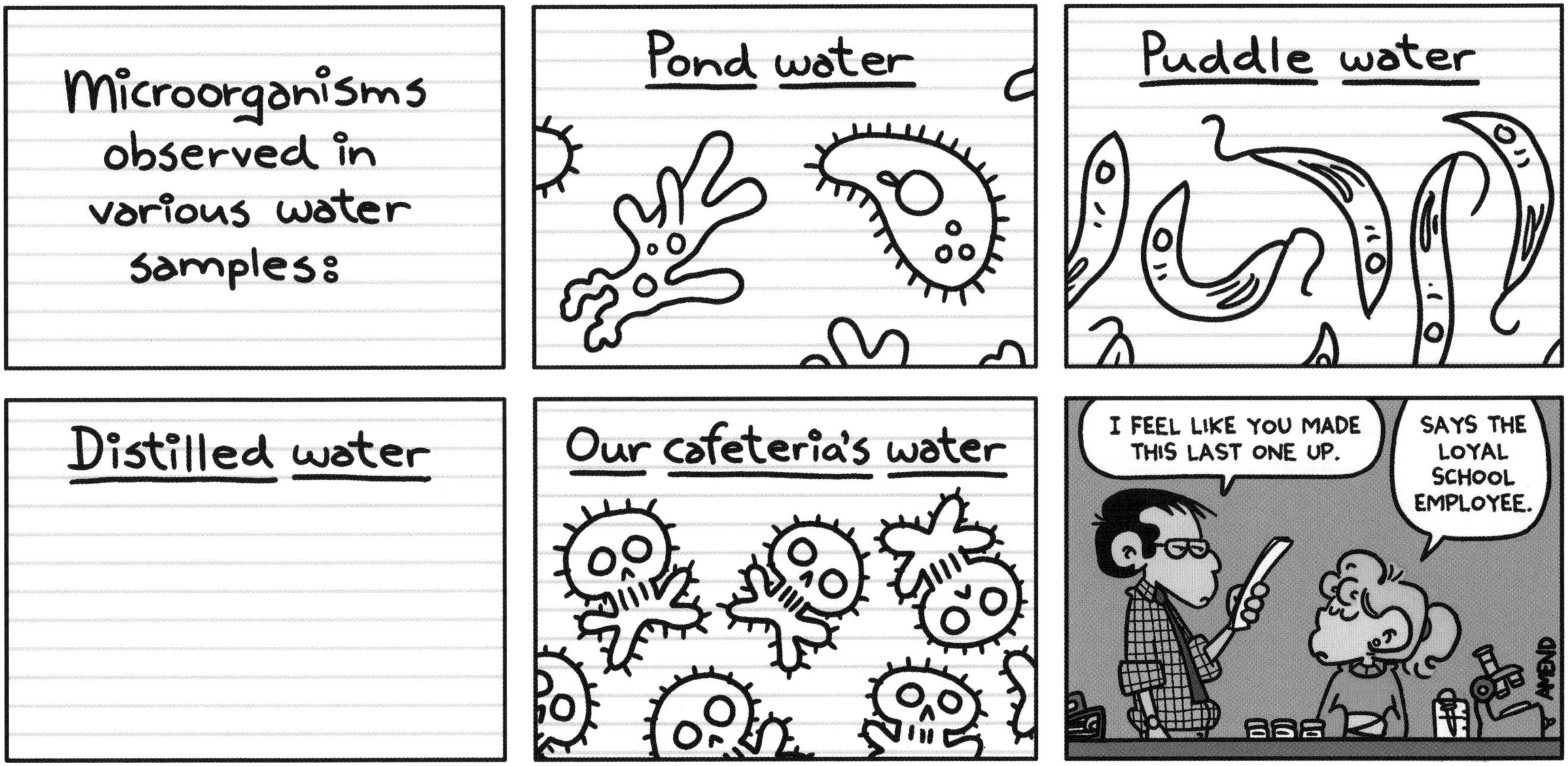

Microorganisms observed in various water samples:
Pond water
Puddle water
Distilled water
Our cafeteria's water
I FEEL LIKE YOU MADE THIS LAST ONE UP.
SAYS THE LOYAL SCHOOL EMPLOYEE.
AMEND

Witchering

WHAT'S WITH THE WIG?

I'VE DECIDED TO BECOME A WITCHER.

MOM WON'T LET ME READ THE BOOKS, PLAY THE GAMES, OR WATCH THE TV SERIES UNTIL I'M OLDER, WHICH TELLS ME THAT WITCHERS MUST BE REALLY, REALLY COOL.

FROM WHAT I CAN PIECE TOGETHER, IT SHOULDN'T BE TOO HARD.

I JUST NEED TO GET GOOD AT VANQUISHING HIDEOUS MONSTERS.

EN GARDE!

MAYBE I SHOULD WAIT UNTIL I'M A **LITTLE** OLDER.

WHAT'S WITH THE WIG AND BROKEN GLASSES?

AMEND

Productivity Boost

Panel 1:
AREN'T YOU SUPPOSED TO BE WORKING ON YOUR HISTORY PAPER?

I'M TAKING A BREAK.

Panel 2:
EVERY TIME I WRITE A CERTAIN NUMBER OF WORDS, I REWARD MYSELF WITH A 10-MINUTE SNACK BREAK. I FIND IT REALLY BOOSTS MY PRODUCTIVITY.

Panel 3:
WELP, BREAK TIME'S OVER... BACK TO WORK!

Panel 5:
ANYWAY, AS I WAS SAYING...

Panel 6:
WHAT ARE YOU DOING?! TAKING A BREAK AFTER EACH WORD?!

TRUST ME, IT'S STILL A PRODUCTIVITY BOOST.

AMEND

Pitch Count

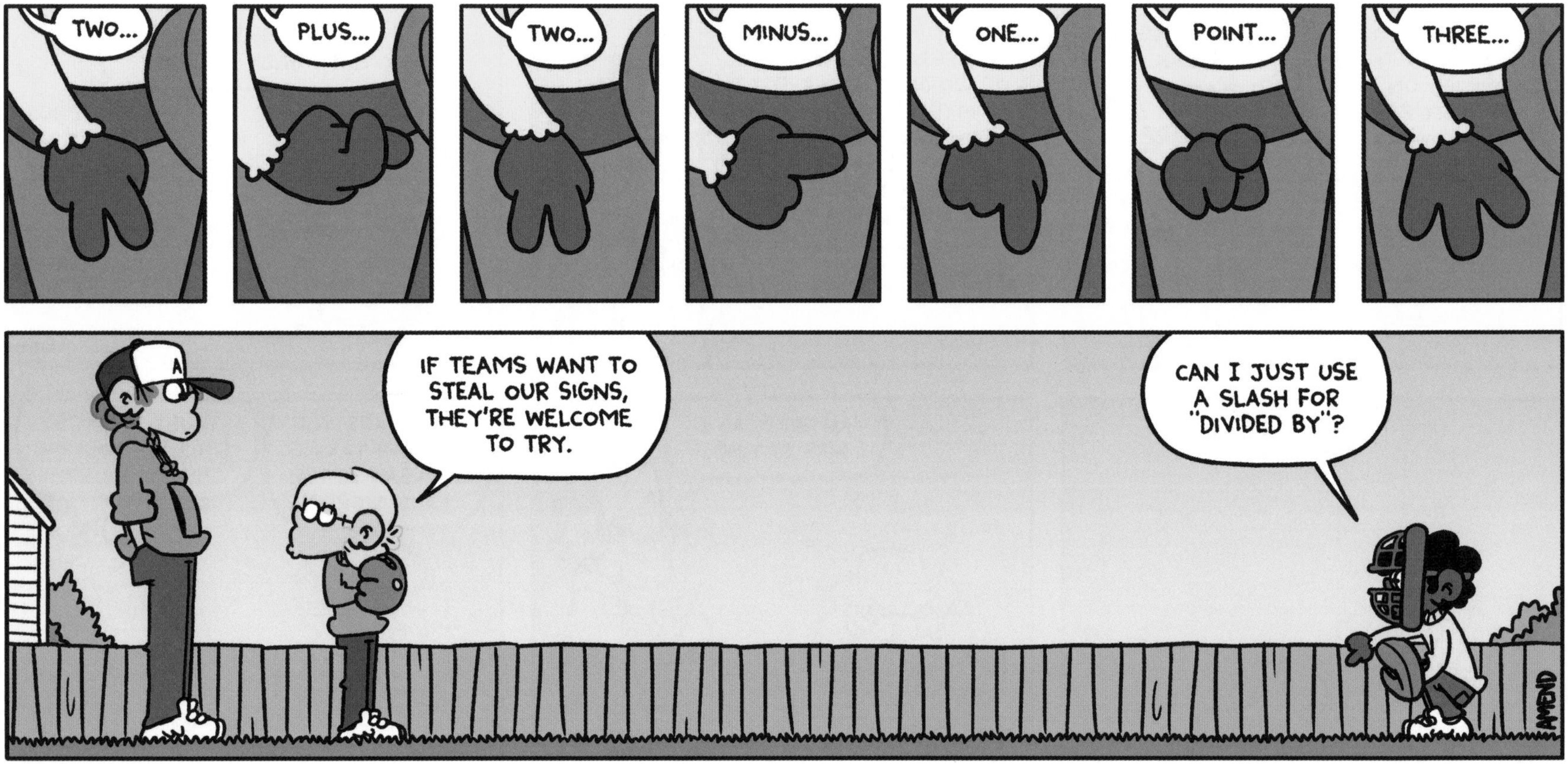

TWO...
PLUS...
TWO...
MINUS...
ONE...
POINT...
THREE...
IF TEAMS WANT TO STEAL OUR SIGNS, THEY'RE WELCOME TO TRY.
CAN I JUST USE A SLASH FOR "DIVIDED BY"?
AMEND

Glitched

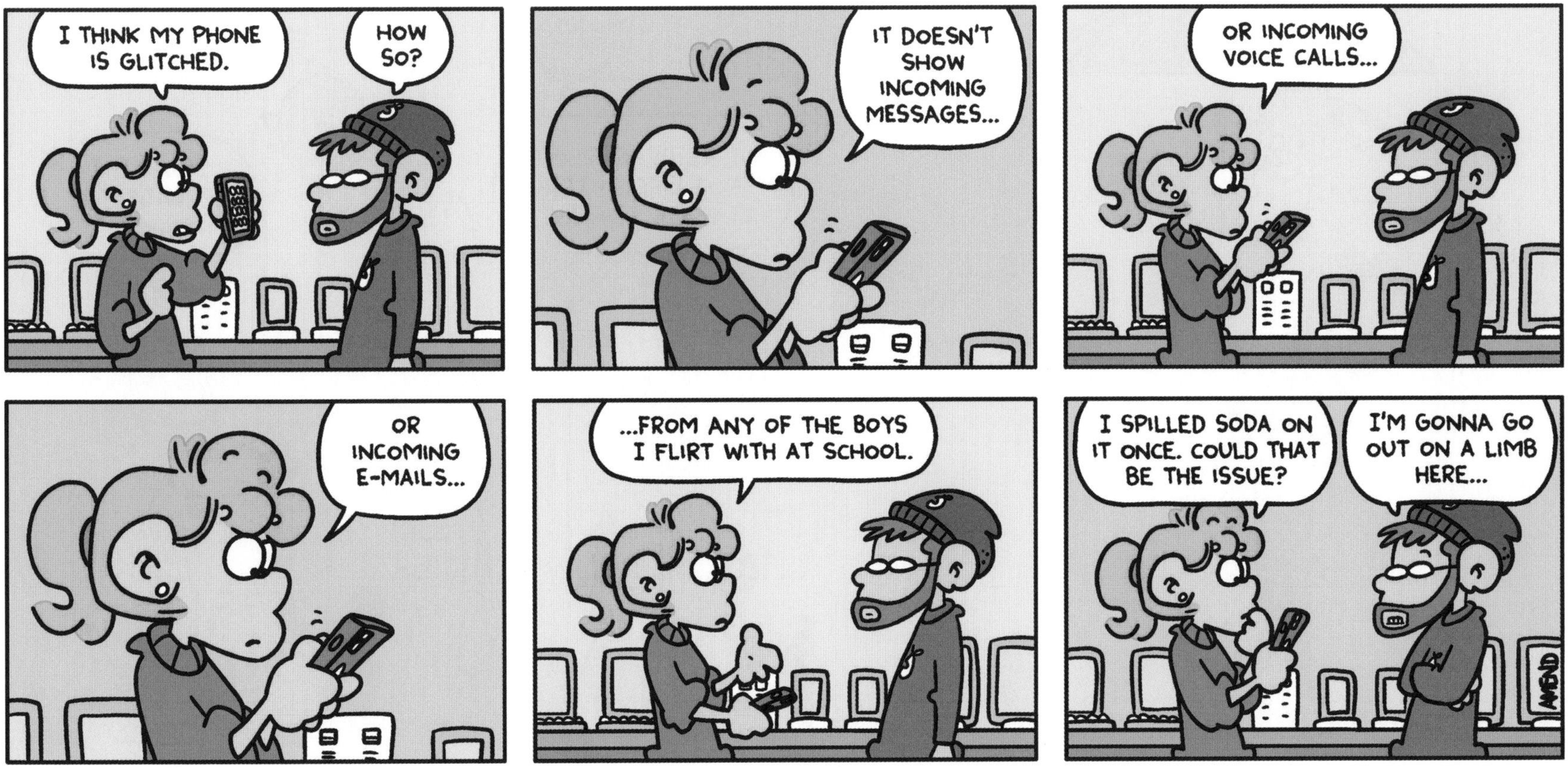
I THINK MY PHONE IS GLITCHED.
HOW SO?
IT DOESN'T SHOW INCOMING MESSAGES...
OR INCOMING VOICE CALLS...
OR INCOMING E-MAILS...
...FROM ANY OF THE BOYS I FLIRT WITH AT SCHOOL.
I SPILLED SODA ON IT ONCE. COULD THAT BE THE ISSUE?
I'M GONNA GO OUT ON A LIMB HERE...
AMEND

Kraken Up

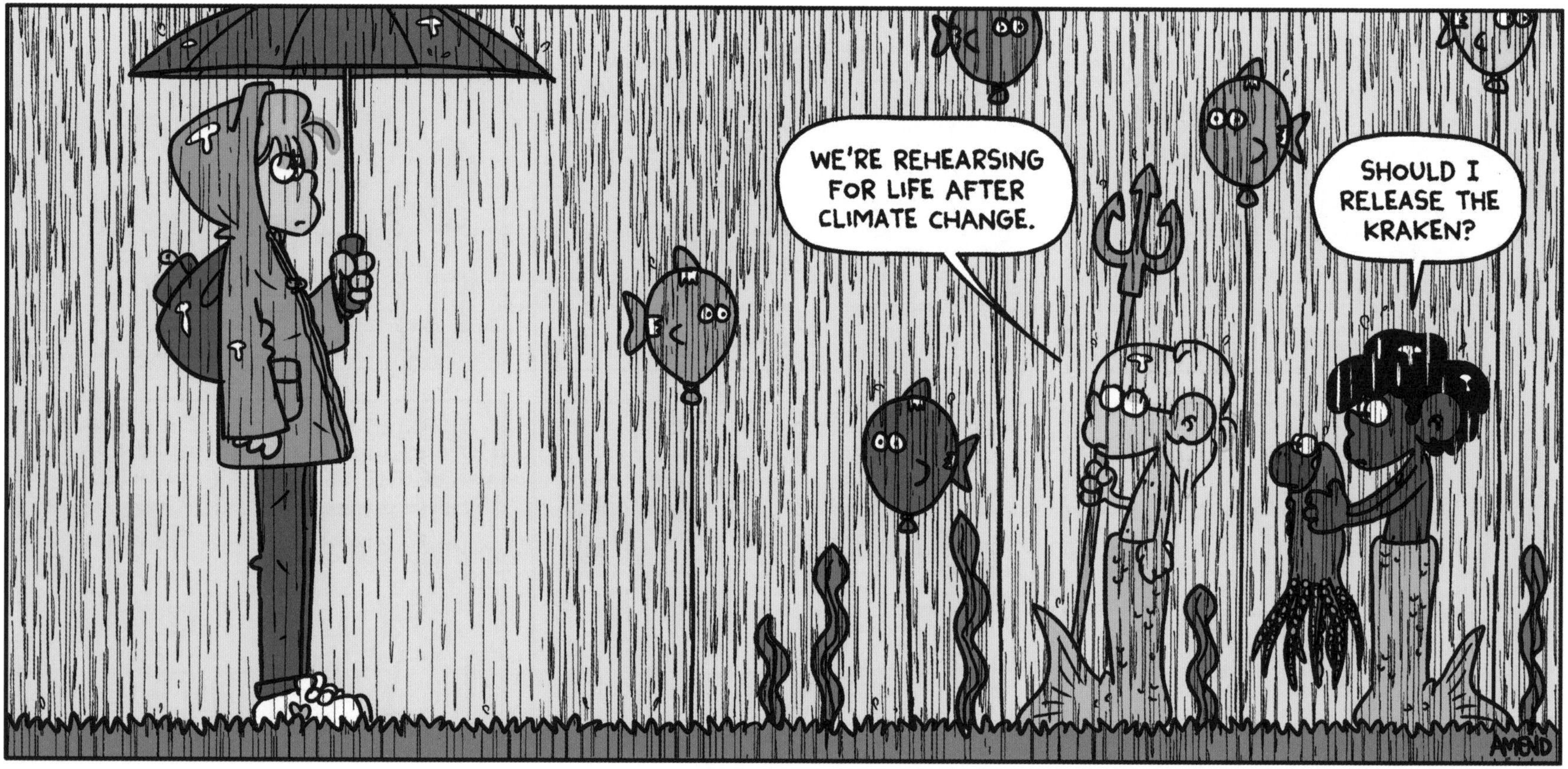
WE'RE REHEARSING FOR LIFE AFTER CLIMATE CHANGE.
SHOULD I RELEASE THE KRAKEN?
AMEND

Dominova

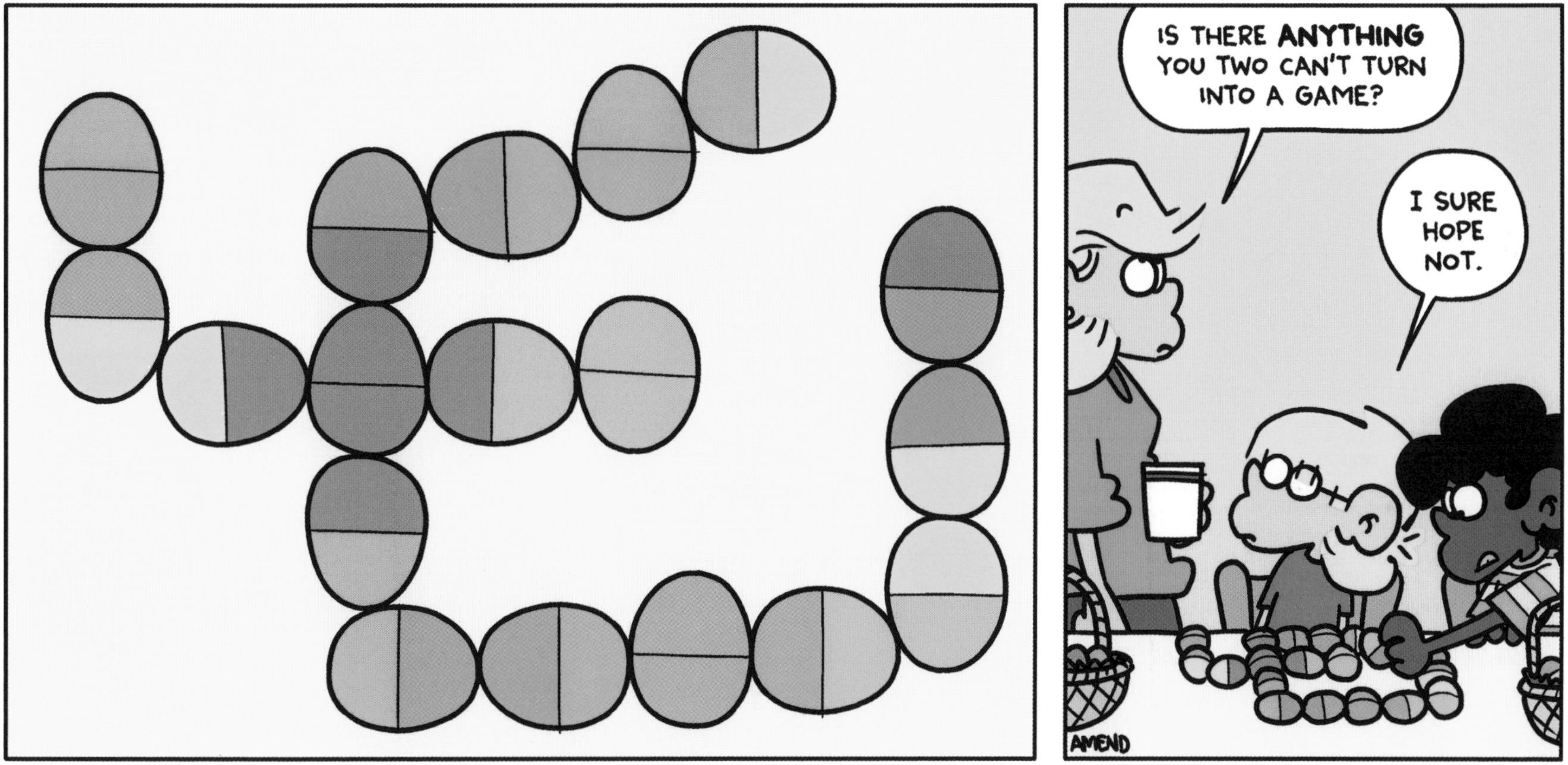
IS THERE ANYTHING YOU TWO CAN'T TURN INTO A GAME?
I SURE HOPE NOT.
AMEND

FoxTrot is distributed internationally by Andrews McMeel Syndication.

Deliciously FoxTrot © 2021 by Bill Amend. All rights reserved. Printed in China. No part of this book may be used or reproduced in any manner whatsoever without written permission except in the case of reprints in the context of reviews.

Andrews McMeel Publishing
a division of Andrews McMeel Universal
1130 Walnut Street, Kansas City, Missouri 64106

21 22 23 24 25 SDB 10 9 8 7 6 5 4 3 2 1

ISBN: 978-1-5248-6976-2

Library of Congress Control Number: 2021934838

www.andrewsmcmeel.com

www.foxtrot.com

ATTENTION: SCHOOLS AND BUSINESSES
Andrews McMeel books are available at quantity discounts with bulk purchase for educational, business, or sales promotional use. For information, please e-mail the Andrews McMeel Publishing Special Sales Department: specialsales@amuniversal.com.

The Way of the Chosen